Advanced Taekwondo

Advanced Taekwondo

SCOTT SHAW

Tuttle Publishing
Tokyo · Rutland, Vermont · Singapore

Please note that the publisher and author(s) of this instructional book are NOT RESPONSIBLE in any manner whatsoever for any injury that may result from practicing the techniques and/or following the instructions given within. Martial arts training can be dangerous—both to you and to others—if not practiced safely. If you're in doubt as to how to proceed or whether your practice is safe, consult with a trained martial arts teacher before beginning. Since the physical activities described herein may be too strenuous in nature for some readers, it is also essential that a physician be consulted prior to training.

First published in 2006 by Tuttle Publishing, an imprint of Periplus Editions (HK) Ltd., with editorial offices at 364 Innovation Drive, North Clarendon, VT 05759.

Library of Congress Cataloging-in-Publication Data

Shaw, Scott, 1958-
  Advanced taekwondo / Scott Shaw.— 1st ed.
     p. cm.
  Includes bibliographical references and index.
  ISBN 0-8048-3786-4 (pbk.)
  1. Tae kwon do. I. Title.
  GV1114.9.S52 2005
  796.815'3—dc22

                              2004025271

Distributed by

North America, Latin America
& Europe
Tuttle Publishing
364 Innovation Drive
North Clarendon, VT 05759-9436
Tel: (802) 773-8930
Fax: (802) 773-6993
info@tuttlepublishing.com
www.tuttlepublishing.com

Japan
Tuttle Publishing
Yaekari Building, 3rd Floor
5-4-12 Ōsaki
Shinagawa-ku
Tokyo 141 0032
Tel: (03) 5437-0171
Fax: (03) 5437-0755
tuttle-sales@gol.com

Asia Pacific
Berkeley Books Pte. Ltd.
130 Joo Seng Road
#06-01/03 Olivine Building
Singapore 368357
Tel: (65) 6280-1330
Fax: (65) 6280-6290
inquiries@periplus.com.sg
www.periplus.com

First edition
09 08 07 06   10 9 8 7 6 5 4 3 2 1
Cover photograph by Hae Won Shin
Printed in the United States of America

Contents

Introduction

The Korean martial art of taekwondo is the most commonly practiced form of self-defense in the world; with over fifty million practitioners worldwide.

The exacting kicks of taekwondo have come to be the defining factor for this advanced system of the martial arts—so much so that taekwondo has taken its advanced kicks, created an exciting sport, and entered the realms of Olympic competition. But, more than simply a style that places its predominate focus upon the development of the legs, taekwondo is an intricate system of self-defense. Taekwondo teaches its practitioners to become highly developed in all aspects of physical confrontation.

Taekwondo is defined as a hard-style system of the martial arts—with penetrating kicks and punches, and forceful linear attacks. However, taekwondo is much more than this. As one progresses through the ranks of this art, one comes to refine one's understanding of body mechanics to a level never embraced by the average individual. Hand in hand with physical mastery also comes a deep sense of personal understanding. The advancing taekwondo practitioner comes to a deep realization of self through the practice of this art.

With all of the refined techniques possessed by taekwondo, it is difficult to believe that the foundation of what is today known as taekwondo began just a little over a half a century ago in Korea. From these early beginnings, taekwondo has evolved into being one of the most exciting and advanced systems of self-defense and sport on the planet.

THE FOUNDATIONS OF TAEKWONDO

The foundation of taekwondo began near the end of World War II, when native Koreans, who had studied the Japanese martial arts, began to secretly teach these arts to other Koreans. The various systems of Japanese karate were taught secretly because the Japanese Imperial Army, which occupied the Korean peninsula from 1909 until 1945, forbid the practicing of any martial art except the sport of judo by Korean nationals. The majority of Koreans who were allowed to study other forms of the martial arts gained their knowledge while living in Japan or while in the service of the Japanese military.

When Korea was freed from Japanese occupation, the martial arts in Korea began a rapid resurgence. Swearing to never be overpowered by an occupying force again, many citizens were drawn to these systems of self-defense.

There were a number of *kwans* or "schools of self-defense" that appeared on the Korean peninsula soon after the end of World War II. Though many people wish to trace the foundations of these schools to the ancient Korean martial arts, historically this is not the case. All of the newly founded kwans were based on various systems of the Japanese martial arts, most notably Shotokan karate.

The first school to be established was Chung Moo Kwan, "The True Path School." This school opened its doors in 1944. Lee, Won Kuk, who studied Shotokan karate while living in Japan, founded Chung Do Kwan.

The second school to open was Chosun Yun Moo Kwan. This school eventually became known as Ji Do Kwan. The evolution of Ji Do Kwan began in 1931 when Lee, Kyung Suk, a Korean who taught judo, was allowed to establish the

Chosun Yun Moo Kwan school in Seoul. The story of this kwan is unique in that this school was open while Japanese occupation was still in place.

At the end of World War II, Lee, Kyung Suk asked Chun, Sang Sup to set up a course of kwon bop at his school. Kwon bop is one of the Korean terms used for Japanese karate. Chun, Sang Sup began his martial arts training in judo while in high school in Korea. He then relocated to Japan. It is during this period that he studied Shotokan karate.

Chun, Sang Sup enlisted the help of Yoon, Byung In to teach karate at Chosun Yun Moo Kwan. Yoon was a fourth degree black belt in Shudokan karate. Yoon, Byung In taught at the Chosun Yun Moo Kwan for approximately one year before breaking away and forming his own school, Chang Moo Kwan.

Chun continued on as an instructor until he was kidnapped and imprisoned by the North Korean military during the Korean War. He was never heard from again and was eventually believed to be dead.

Upon the loss of Chun, Sang Sup, teaching passed to the hands of Yoon, Kwe Byung, one of Chun's senior students. He renamed the school Ji Do Kwan, "Wisdom Way School."

The next kwan to be opened was Moo Duk Kwan, "The School of Military Virtue." There are two distinct divisions of Moo Duk Kwan, both of which evolved from a single source in modern Korea. The first is most commonly known as *tang soo do*. The Korean term "tang soo" literally translates as "knife hand." The Japanese character used to depict this term is the same one used for karate. The second division of Moo Duk Kwan is the Moo Duk Kwan division of taekwondo.

The founder of Tang Soo Do Moo Duk Kwan was Hwang, Kee, aka Kee, Chang Hang. Hwang, Kee was an expatriate of Korea during most of its Japanese occupation. Hwang, Kee immigrated to China, where he worked for the Southern Manchuria Railroad. In early interviews, Hwang, Kee states that he studied numerous systems of Chinese martial arts while living in China. Later, it was detailed that he also studied a system of Japanese karate while he was located in this region. The forms of tang soo do are almost exact duplicates of those practiced in Shotokan. It is believed that he studied Goju Ryu karate.

By 1965, the various kwans of the modern Korean martial arts were merging under the banner of taekwondo. Hwang, Kee resisted this trend, wishing to maintain control over his organization. Because of this, two of his advanced students, Im, Young Tek and Hong, Chong Soo, broke away from their teacher, formed their own branch of Moo Duk Kwan, and became a part of the Korea Taekwondo Association. From this act, two distinct systems of self-defense, bearing the title Moo Duk Kwan, emerged.

The next school to open was Chang Moo Kwan. As detailed, this school was founded by Yoon, Byung after his departure from the Chosun Yun Moon Kwan. He opened this school in Seoul in 1946. This same year Lee, Nam Suk was named the first official instructor of Chang Moo Kwan. When Yoon, Byung In went missing in action, during the Korean War, it was Lee, Nam Suk and Kim, Soon Bae, another advanced student of Yoon's, who reopened the school at the end of the war.

Kang Duk Won was the next school to open. It was actually the second incarnation of Chang Moo Kwan and came into existence in 1953, when Lee, Nam Suk and Kim, Soon Bae began to have conflicts with two other senior students of Chang Moo Kwan: Hong, Jung Pyo and Park, Chul Hee. These two men left and formed Kang Duk Won, "House of Teaching Generosity," in 1956.

Song Moo Kwan was founded in Kae Sung City, Kyung Ki Province, Korea by Ro, Byung Jick, on March 11, 1944. Ro's training in the martial arts began in 1936 in Japan. He studied Shotokan karate alongside Chung Do Kwan's founder, Lee, Won Kuk, under Shotokan karate's founder, Gichin Funakoshi. As was the case with Chung Do Kwan, this school was actually established prior to the end of Japanese occupation. The original classes of the kwan were taught at the Kwan Duk Jung School of Archery. Due to the repressive political conditions, the kwan was forced to close its doors a few months later. It was not until May 2, 1946 when Ro could reopen his school in Dong Hung Dong, Kae Sung City, Korea.

On June 25, 1950, Song Moo Kwan, which means "The Ever Youthful House Of Martial Arts Training," again closed its doors, due to the onset of the Korean war. On September 20, 1953 the school was reestablished in the Ah Hyung Dong, Mapo Gu district of Seoul.

Oh Do Kwan was founded by General Choi, Hong Hi and Major Nam, Tae Hi. Both of these men were advanced military officers in the newly formed army of liberated Korea. Their classes were originally taught at the Korean 3rd Army Base, in Yong Dae Ri, Korea.

Choi, Hong Hi relocated to Japan in his adolescence to further his education. While there, he studied Shotokan karate and earned a black belt. When World War II broke out, he was forced into the service of the Japanese military. After World War II, and the defeat of the Japanese occupying forces, he became a pivotal figure in the newly formed Korean military.

Nam, Tae Hi became a student of Chung Do Kwan immediately after Korean Independence. He quickly mastered the art and began teaching at the Korean Army Military Signal School in 1947. At this time, Nam, Tae Hi met Choi, Hong Hi. This laid the foundation for the birth of Oh Do Kwan. With these early kwans in place, Korea was set on a path of martial art development that changed the face of the martial arts forever.

The newly formed kwans established on the Korean peninsula remained separate entities until in the early 1950s. At this point, there was a drive to bring these various kwans together under one umbrella organization. Pushed forward by General Choi, Hong Hi, in the late 1950s this loose unification finally took shape, and the kwans came together under the banner of taekwondo. Though this process was and is an ongoing evolution—from this point forward, the history of taekwondo as a defined and unified art was set in motion.

EVOLUTION

The moment taekwondo became formalized as one unified art its evolution took on a whole new velocity. The advancement in taekwondo came at a much more rapid pace, and the art began to truly reflect its Korean heritage.

This evolution gave birth to the next generation of taekwondo practitioners. The central focus of the process was the advanced kicking techniques. It was the second generation of practitioners, those who were not trained by Japanese instructors, who truly began to give the art a new look. These practitioners guided the kicks of taekwondo, which veered away from the traditionally stiff Japanese kick and took on a whole new definition, velocity, and style. At this junction, the kicks of taekwondo become very stylized, very linear, and very fast.

THE ADVANCED PRACTITIONER

Through the evolution of taekwondo it has been the advanced practitioner who has guided the art. The advanced practitioner, having mastered the basic elements of the art, has taken his or her knowledge and pushed the boundaries of the art, making it an ever-expanding, advanced system of the martial arts.

The advanced practitioner defines the art by two primary principals: discipline and dedicated practice. From discipline, the practitioner drives himself to become the most competent practitioner of the art that he can be. With dedicated practice, the individual techniques of the art are driven forward to a new level of excellence. From these two principals, taekwondo has continued to evolve and be taught to an ever-increasing number of practitioners who bring to the art new understanding and new elements which cause the art to continue to evolve.

Part One

Advanced Concepts for Inner Development

Chapter 1

Taekwondo Philosophy for Today's Practitioner

Taekwondo, the way of the foot and the fist, is a highly refined system of the martial arts. Taekwondo is defined by its elaborate kicking arsenal. The practitioners of this art can propel themselves high into the air and deliver powerful kicking techniques with exacting precision. But, more than simply a system of martial arts which relies solely upon the legs, taekwondo is a highly defined system of physical and mental conditioning that provides the practitioner with a personal pathway to self-discovery.

Initially, when one begins to study taekwondo, one's focus is locked solely upon mastering the basic skills of the art: the stances, the blocks, the punches, and the kicks. As one progresses through the ranks, and develops the basic skills of this system of martial arts, the advanced practitioner's focus shifts to the more refined elements of taekwondo. At this level, the practitioner begins to refine his or her mental and physical understanding, true combative effectiveness, and overall mental preparedness by seeking out the deeper teachings of this art. Here, the advanced practitioner embraces the philosophic roots of taekwondo and the meditative aspects of the art in order to become a more complete practitioner.

Because taekwondo has become an Olympic sport, with much of its training now focused upon competitive effectiveness, many people question whether taekwondo possesses deep philosophic roots. The answer to this is yes.

Taekwondo was born in a nation that had undergone nearly five decades of brutal occupation. Hand in hand with this occupation came the attempted systematic destruction of Korean culture. Historic manuscripts were destroyed by the Japanese occupying forces, leaving the nation with virtually no remaining historic records detailing Korea's ancient heritage. The Korean populous was forced to speak and write the Japanese language. And, the practice of the indigenous Korean martial arts was forbidden.

Rising out of the ashes of this annexation, modern Korean civilization struggled to regain and redevelop its own unique cultural identity. With this came the determination to never be overpowered by an invading force again. From this ideology also came the birth of taekwondo.

Taekwondo is a style of martial art developed in the twentieth century. Though the physical aspects of this art are based in development that has taken place in this modern era, the philosophic roots of this system reach far back into ancient Korean culture.

All practitioners of taekwondo share the philosophic root origins of this system of the martial arts. At the advanced levels, the practitioner comes to embrace these teachings in order to become the most complete practitioner possible.

THE HISTORY AND PHILOSOPHY OF THE HWA RANG

The ancient Hwa Rang, "Flowering Youth," Warriors have played an essential role in the philosophic development of Korean culture and taekwondo. Though taekwondo itself is not founded upon the doctrines of these ancient warriors, those doctrines' influence on Korean culture has been prevalent in all military and martial arts developed on the Korean peninsula. Thus, each practitioner of taekwondo looks to his or her philosophy as a guiding light.

The Hwa Rang Warriors

The Hwa Rang came into existence during the sixth century A.D. The foundations that gave birth to this elite group of warriors can be traced to approximately 200 B.C., during the Chinese Qui Dynasty (221–206 B.C.). This is the point when formalized contact began between China and the Korean peninsula. This interaction was intensified with the placement of Chinese military colonies on the Northern Korean peninsula during the Han Dynasty (202–220 B.C.). From these contacts, the Korean peninsula began a period of rapid advancement in agriculture, health science, military strategy, and formalized governmental statesmanship. Taoism, Confucianism, and later Buddhism were all introduced into Korea from China.

During this period in history, three tribal kingdoms formed. The kingdom of Silla came into existence in 57 B.C., the kingdom of Koguryo was solidified in 37 B.C., and the kingdom of Paekche formed in 18 B.C. This was the beginning of what became known as the "three kingdom period" of Korean history.

Buddhism Enters Korea

Buddhism entered the Korean peninsula state of Koguryo in A.D. 372, when the Chinese monk Sun-do was sent from the Chinese state of Ch'in by King Fu Chein on an official mission to introduce Buddhism to the Korean kingdom. The East Indian monk Malananda arrived, via China, with a royal escort, in the Korean state of Paekche in A.D. 384.

By the point when Buddhism was introduced into the Korean states, Chinese religious culture and social customs had already been transmitted several centuries before. From this early transmission was born the formation of royal and aristocratic Korean society. Thus, when Buddhism came to Korea, via royal Chinese envoys, it was readily accepted in the Korean royal courts with little dissent. The Korean state of Silla, however, was the exception to this process. Silla did not readily accept the Buddhist doctrine. It held fast to the Confucian aristocratic ideology. In fact, attempts at introducing Buddhism were initially met with open hostility.

The Buddhist monk A-do, in the beginning of the fifth century A.D., had limited success with the introduction of Buddhist ideology into the Korean kingdom of Silla. Rural peoples in the outlying regions of the kingdom only marginally accepted it.

In 514, King Pop-hung of Silla finally accepted the Buddhist doctrine and attempted to secure the acceptance of the religion in his kingdom. His efforts, however, were met with great hostility from the aristocracy of his court, who enjoyed the privileges of the Confucian school of thought. Buddhism was not accepted by the royal court of Silla until it had been commonly practiced for a century by the other two Korean states, Koguryo and Paekche, and by the common inhabitants of the Silla kingdom for several decades.

The Birth of the Hwa Rang

During the sixth century the three kingdoms on the Korean peninsula continued to draw sharp cultural lines between themselves and the expansionistic Chinese T'ang Dynasty (A.D. 618–907). From this was born an extended period of war on the Korean peninsula, which gave birth to the Hwa Rang warriors.

The Hwa Rang warriors were first presented to the court of King Chin-hung in the Korean peninsula kingdom of Silla in A.D. 576. King Chin-hung, whose given name was Sammaek-chong, was the nephew of King Pop-hung, who was the first to accept the Buddhist doctrine in Silla.

The Original Flower

Won Hwa, "Original Flower," was the female leader of this group of Buddhist monk warriors. The Hwa Rang army was based in the Buddhist doctrine of no-self. They believed that their current human form was only a portal, whereby, through proper karmic action they could raise their consciousness onto their higher level of Buddha-self. Thus, these warriors did nothing for themselves but, instead, devoted their entire lives and all of their actions to their supreme spiritual teacher, Won Hwa, who led them down the path of Buddhist warrior knowledge.

It is essential to note that there was not one single Won Hwa, as was initially falsely believed. There were, in fact, many female matriarchs that guided the various platoons of this elite warrior group.

The Hwa Rang were the first organized group to take the understanding of ki, align it with Buddhist meditation, and perform what was considered supernatural feats. Due to their developed ability to channel ki energy at will throughout their body and their nonattachment for their physical being, they could propel their bodies into the fierce current of freezing Naklong River in the dead of winter and not be phased by the effect. Additionally, they could sit in deep meditation in the snows of the Taebaek Sanmaek mountains, where they were trained, clothed only by a loin cloth and emerge unscathed.

Induction of the Hwa Rang

Once the first group of Hwa Rang were revealed to King Chin-hung and their expertise revealed, he became certain that these warriors were the means by which he could defeat his attacking neighbors. Through years of war, King Chin-hung's soldiers had proven loyal to the kingdom but not exceptional in battle, because they were unable to defeat Silla's geographical neighbors: Koguryo, Paekche, and the invasive T'ang Chinese. Therefore, the court of King Chin-hung set about organizing a group of young talented noblemen, who were exceedingly loyal to the thrown and could be extensively trained in all forms of martial warfare—with the hope of them emerging victorious in battle and defeating their invasive neighbors.

Because wealth and aristocracy were prevalent throughout Silla's royal court, King Chin-hung's court found it difficult to find young willing participants to enter the strict order of the Hwa Rang. Thus, the court of King Chin-hung's initial method to lure young noblemen into the Hwa Rang induction program was to enlist the help of two beautiful court women to gather men around them. The names of these two girls were Nam-mo and Chun-jung. Several hundred young noblemen did, in fact, congregate in their presence.

Chun-jung became jealous of Nam-mo, however. She poisoned her wine and threw her into the river, killing her. The Silla royal court subsequently put Chun-jung to death, and the group of men surrounding the women disbanded.

The next method used to induct young men into the Hwa Rang was to choose handsome male youths of noble birth. The age of these boys was as young as twelve years old. These men were then dressed in the finest clothing, and their faces were attractively painted with elaborate makeup. They were extensively instructed in Buddhism, medical science according to the *Yellow Emperor's Classic of Internal Medicine (the Nei Ching)*, poetry, and song. It was believed those who fared well in these activities had the grace to become advanced warriors. Thus, a certain number of them were recommended to the Court of the Hwa Rang.

The Training of the Hwa Rang

The second generation of Hwa Rang was trained in all forms of known martial warfare. These warriors were taught the advanced practices of meditation, making each of their physical movements a service to their leader and an action ultimately in the service of the Buddha.

It was the belief of the Hwa Rang that meditation not only took place in the traditional fashion, in a sitting posture, but also when one focused one's personal spirit and then entered into battle with a highly refined purpose and vision of a victorious outcome. Thus, the battles the Hwa Rang fought became a spiritual exercise in enlightenment.

To the Hwa Rang, the necessary killing of an opponent was beneficial to the ultimate karmic good of their society. From the necessary mortal action they took, the Hwa Rang believed that they would gain good karma and be raised to a higher level of incarnation in their next birth.

It must be understood that during this period in Asian history, there were numerous societies of Buddhist monks who retreated from the world and chose to kill no form of living life either as a food source or as a means of self-defense. This is what set the Hwa Rang apart from other formalized groups of Buddhist monks. Their tradition taught them that the kingdom of Silla was the land of the Maiterya (the unborn Buddha), and as such, killing for their society was, in fact, a holy act. Therefore, the Hwa Rang believed that each life they took, in necessary combat, was a movement of meditation and would lead them on to Buddhahood.

Once a Hwa Rang was fully trained, he was put in command of a military troupe composed of several hundred common soldiers. From the battles won by the Hwa Rang came the unification of Korea. History would not be served if it were not stated that this unification was achieved by very bloody means, which resulted in the death of a large percentage of the population of the Korean peninsula.

The Martial Arts of the Hwa Rang

The Hwa Rang were expert swordsmen, archers, and masters of hand-to-hand combat. The Korean martial art system of su bak was, in fact, the fighting system designed and developed by the Hwa Rang, though Korean legend dates its inception to the mythological Korean ruler, King Tan-gun (c. 2333 B.C.).

Su Bak

Su bak, a fierce method of hand-to-hand combat, is the first documented martial art style to exist on the Korean peninsula. Because martial warfare during the time of the Hwa Rang served only one purpose, to kill the adversary, su bak was a deadly art form designed to kill an opponent with one powerful strike.

Not only did the Hwa Rang use weapons and hand-to-hand combat to defeat their enemies, but they were also the first group of formalized warriors to develop the ability to strike to disabling vital pressure points in order to disrupt the ki flow of their opponents. Thus, they were also the first formalized warriors to use an understanding of ki as a method of warfare.

Yu Sul

During the late three kingdom period, su bak became fragmented, and differing schools of the art came into existence. During this period of fragmentation, a new system of Korean martial arts was formed. It was named yu sul. Yu sul was a softer grappling system of defense, utilizing ki energy as opposed to simple brute force. With cultural transmission between the island nation of Japan and the three Korean kingdoms taking place during this time period, it is understood that yu sul was the predecessor to Japanese kenjutsu, the forefather of jujitsu.

With the birth of yu sul, there became two very different schools of martial thought on the Korean peninsula. They were the hard-style attacking methods of su bak, which possess predominantly striking techniques, and the softer, manipulative defenses of yu sul.

During this time, su bak became known as tae kyon. Tae kyon was written in the Chinese characters for "push shoulder." The Hwa Rang warriors obviously embraced this martial art form and, as mentioned, created their own addition to it, known as su bak gi or "foot fighting."

Tae Kyon

The Korean martial art of tae kyon was born at a time when martial arts, on the whole, went into a rapid decline on the now unified Korean peninsula, under the control of the Silla Dynasty. Tae kyon, as the immediate predecessor to su bak, was a very aggressive hard-style martial art system. As peace came to the Korean peninsula, there was little use for its practice among commoners.

The martial art system of yu sul declined and vanished from the Korean peninsula almost as fast as it had developed. By the end of the seventh century, no sign of it existed. Tae kyon, therefore, survived as the only fighting system with a link to the ancient su bak.

The Korean martial art system of tae kyon continued to be practiced by the Korean military from the time of the Hwa Rang forward. In the Korean military text *Moo Yea Do Bok Tong Ki*, written in the fifteenth century, the prescribed practices of the advanced warrior are detailed, based on the knowledge developed by the Hwa Rang. This text, in a association with the continually refining techniques of warfare, defined the Korean warrior until the modern era.

The Decline of the Hwa Rang

After the unification of Korea and the defeat of the invasive Chinese T'ang Dynasty, the mind of the Korean people rapidly began to shift from confrontations to more philosophic thoughts. The Hwa Rang, as warriors, fell into decline. For a time, due to their refined knowledge of ki and healing abilities, they became known as a group specializing in Buddhist philosophy, healing, music, and poetry.

Hyang-ga, "native song," was the gentle rhythmic poetic songs sung by the Hwa Rang. These songs, written by Hwa Rang or Buddhist monks, were believed to be vehicles for healing and creating divine intervention in human situations. The early Buddhism of Korea held tightly onto its reverence for divine intervention through the ever-present spirit world; thus, the music the Hwa Rang sang had as a purpose worldly and karmic healing. The Hwa Rang survived until the end of the seventh century when there is no longer any evidence of their existence.

Code of the Hwa Rang

Because the Hwa Rang were a refined group of spiritually based warriors, their actions were founded upon an exacting code of ethics. The eminent Buddhist monk, Wong-wang, is the man who formalized and laid down the Hwa Rang code of ethics. From this formalized code, the Hwa Rang were guided down a path that not only taught them to serve their king and kingdom, but also assured them of being fierce warriors in battle.

Code of the Hwa Rang has five parts:

1. Serve the king with loyalty.
2. Be obedient to your superiors.
3. Be honorable to all mankind.
4. Never retreat in battle.
5. Kill justly.

In the modern era many advanced practitioners of taekwondo look to the code of the Hwa Rang for guidance in their training. By embracing this philosophic ideology, the modern student of taekwondo can raise himself or herself to new levels of martial understanding and pay homage to the cultural root of this system of self-defense.

The First Rule of the Hwa Rang

Rule One of the Code of Hwa Rang teaches one to serve the king with loyalty. Loyalty is one of the primary elements of taekwondo training. While training, one must possess loyalty to one's dojang, teacher, fellow students, and system of martial arts, taekwondo.

Whenever one begins training with an instructor, one must immediately embrace a sense of loyalty toward the instructor. For it is the instructor who leads the practitioner of taekwondo down the road of mental and physical development. Without an instructor, there can be no training in taekwondo. Therefore, a sense of utmost loyalty must be extended to one's instructor if one hopes to learn the advanced level of knowledge this individual possesses.

A sense of loyalty is an ideology that has been left behind by many people in modern society. This is in no small part due to the fact that most people are only concerned about themselves. They do not care what effects their actions are having on other people. In martial arts, this is one of the primary factors that causes people to leave taekwondo training before they begin to master the more refined elements of this system of the martial arts.

Many trainees learn a few blocks and kicks and then believe that they have mastered the art. This is not the case. Training in taekwondo is a lifelong process. At each level of expertise, and as one progresses in age, taekwondo training changes and evolves. It is only through ongoing training that one comes to understand this subtle fact.

What you did and how you performed at twenty in taekwondo is going to be far different from what you do and how you do it at forty. For this reason, loyalty to the art is essential to ongoing mastery.

It is only with time that one is led to the advanced levels of taekwondo. Without single-pointed loyalty, defined by ongoing involvement and training, the advanced level of taekwondo can never be understood.

The Second Rule of the Hwa Rang

The second rule of the Hwa Rang dictates one to be obedient to one's superiors. This is an essential premise of not only Asian culture but also of taekwondo culture. This rule goes hand-in-hand with the first rule of loyalty.

When you walk into the taekwondo dojang for the first time, you have decided to begin training in taekwondo, and you are turning yourself over to the training expertise of the instructor. At this point, you are guided down the path to taekwondo mastery. Until you reach that point, however, there is always the necessity for an individual who guides you to the refinement of your techniques.

The image of the instructor, or the coach in terms of taekwondo competition, is based in a humility of understanding. Each instructor of taekwondo has developed a certain knowledge that you do not possess. This knowledge may be an understanding of the complete system of taekwondo that the master teaches to an untold number of students. Or, it may be something as simple as his or her noticing that if you change one of your techniques, just slightly, it will become much more effective.

Taekwondo is based upon a system of hierarchy. From the beginning student upward through the black belt, to the instructor, to the master, to the founder of the kwan, onto the leader of the organization. At each acceding level, the proponent of taekwondo possesses a new and unique knowledge. As each student who progresses through the ranks readily comes to understand, new knowledge and new understanding about the art of taekwondo is revealed at each new step. With this understanding, the advancing taekwondo practitioner always remains humble and pays respect to those who have walked the path of taekwondo before him or her.

The Third Rule of the Hwa Rang

The third rule of the Hwa Rang details one to be honorable to all mankind. This is perhaps the single most important rule in the philosophy of the Hwa Rang.

Much of the modern martial arts is based around a philosophy of, "my style is better than your style," "my school is better than your school," "my teacher is better than your teacher," "I know more and am better than you." If we look at this ideology, however, we can easily see that it is based on a very low level of human consciousness. Its root is based in insecurity, envy, and rivalry. All of these do nothing to improve the physical or mental practices of the advancing practitioner of taekwondo.

Being humble, as one advances through the ranks of taekwondo, is the most sought-after accomplishment. More than simply earning the coveted black belt, earning it and then wearing it with humility is the sought-after prize. If one is constantly putting himself at odds with the world around him, he can never come to know the inner peace which mastery of taekwondo can bring. Thus, he is separating himself from the true philosophic root of the art.

To be honorable to mankind means that you accept and respect all other people. This does not mean that you put yourself at odds with them. In fact, just the opposite. To be honorable means that if you are accosted by someone declaiming the previous statements, you simply accept it, do not become confrontational, and allow them to hold their own beliefs. Being honorable means being accepting and respectful of all.

The Fourth Rule of the Hwa Rang

The fourth rule of the Hwa Rang teaches that one should never retreat in battle. There are many ways that this rule can be interpreted and adapted into modern society. Certainly not the least of which is that one must stay focused on one's training in taekwondo and not fall away due to complacency.

Each person who trains in the art of taekwondo reaches a point where he or she begins to question the appropriateness of ongoing training. This can come about for an untold number of reasons: school, a job, family relationships, and even boredom. Though all of these reasons can be understood to be logical reasons for withdrawing from taekwondo training, it is those practitioners who hold fast to their commitment to the art and continue to train who reap the most benefits.

As time has progressed in modern society, the sedentary nature of many people's lives has caused them to develop ill health. Medical science has proven that it is essential that we all find a means of cardioaerobic conditioning to keep our bodies fit and healthy. This is true for all ages. If undertaken for no other reason, the ongoing training in taekwondo is an ideal method to keep one physically fit. In no other form of fitness training is one allowed to provide cardioaerobic conditioning to one's body, while refining one's understanding of self-defense, as in martial arts.

The Fifth Rule of the Hwa Rang

The final rule of the Hwa Rang is to kill justly. Certainly, it is hoped that no one will ever have to defend himself or herself at this level. Nonetheless, as a means of self-defense, taekwondo does provide the advanced practitioner with the ability to defend oneself appropriately in any type of physical encounter.

From a more metaphysical perspective, due to the fact that the advanced taekwondo practitioner is so highly trained in the refined art of combat he or she no longer possesses the need or desire to physically overpower an attacking opponent to this ultimate end. Instead, through years of practice practitioners have developed the ability to defend themselves in the most minimal and energy-conserving manner possible—thereby possessing the ability to emerge victorious from a confrontation without the need to resort to this ultimate level of self-defense.

From this refined level of self-defense mastery comes a new understanding of combat effectiveness that allows advancing practitioners to move beyond the need to exhibit their physical proficiency in the art of combat and, instead, they shift their training focus to the more mentally reflective aspects of taekwondo. Advancing practitioners thereby begin to use this rule as a means to destroy or "kill" personal ignorance. Ignorance may be defined as jealousy, egotism, envy, arrogance, or any thought or actions that set the practitioners into a state of mental or physical disharmony with the world around them.

With this as a mindset, advancing taekwondo practitioners can consciously focus themselves not only on making themselves the most proficient proponents of the art possible, but also, on becoming a positive influence, on others—helping to guide those they encounter to a more refined sense of consciousness.

DEVELOPING A TRAINING PHILOSOPHY

As each practitioner of taekwondo walks through the doors of the taekwondo dojang, the first sight is the intense physical training that takes place hand in hand with taekwondo. The physical training of taekwondo is made up of exercises, training drills, and combative techniques designed to school the student in all aspects of physical development and discipline.

The individual's level of physical and mental development in taekwondo is delineated by the color of the belt he or she wears. Novice students begin with the white belt, progress through the yellow, blue, red, and finally, if they train long and hard enough, earn the black belt.

The training of the taekwondo student is more than simply a pathway from white belt to the coveted black belt, however. Each step along the way provides the practitioner with new insight into both the physical and the mental aspects of combat and human development.

You cannot enter a taekwondo class and train by yourself. Taekwondo training, by its very nature, is designed to make the individual work with other students of the art. With each new interaction, from the basic to the most advanced levels of the art, the taekwondo practitioner, as a result of this interaction, comes to understand new things about not only himself or herself, but about human nature and human ability as well.

At the heart of the physical development of the taekwondo practitioner is the development of the skills of physical combat. The advanced practitioner comes to understand that mastering the various techniques in physical combat is not solely accomplished simply because one can beat up another person either in the ring or in street combat. The advanced practitioner comes to understand that mastery of the various levels of defense and offense presented in taekwondo allows him or her the ability to be physically assured in all circumstances. Because of this, one possesses the ability to walk away from confrontations instead of being dragged into them simply to prove who is the better combatant.

Developing a Philosophy for Competition

Much of the focus of modern taekwondo has shifted from a self-defense orientation to that of competition. To the outsider, competition is dominated by who wins the match, the championship, or the gold medal.

This limited perspective of competition does not dominate the truly advanced taekwondo practitioner. Instead, advanced practitioners train their body so that it becomes as precisely developed as possible, in all aspects of the physical training of taekwondo, in order to compete to learn more about themselves—not simply to defeat an opponent.

When two highly trained proponents of the art enter the ring, they are pitting their best abilities against each other. From this, the advanced taekwondo practitioner is allowed to witness what areas of his or her training need to be improved upon. Thus, competition is not so much simply a contest of who can defeat whom, it is an arena where one can study oneself and emerge knowing what levels of one's training need to be improved upon.

TRAINING THE MIND

Training the mind is a fundamental element of taekwondo. This is particularly the case as one advances through the ranks of this art.

It is commonly understood that meditation is an essential element in martial arts training. Formal seated meditation is a necessary practice to calm and focus your mind. But in many ways, simply by training in taekwondo the practitioner is led down the path of meditation. For example, when you first began training in taekwondo, no doubt an advanced class member showed you a new technique. Most probably, you possessed no understanding of how to actually perform this technique. Yet, you observed the basic structure of the technique, and you practiced and practiced, until it was finally mastered. Though you had no intention of meditating on this technique, that is exactly what you achieved.

Meditation witnesses you focusing your consciousness upon a single object. You must maintain your concentration upon this object for a period of time. By training in taekwondo, often you will find that you have performed a meditative action by focusing precisely upon the betterment of your technique, and you have meditated without even knowing it.

Advanced taekwondo practitioners naturally take this process to the next level. They begin by acknowledging that they are going to focus on one specific technique and practice it in order to not only come to a new mastery of the technique but also to arrive at a deeper understanding of their own body mechanics.

Physical Meditation versus Seated Meditation

Training your body and mind in seated meditation takes a more focused effort, on your part, than does simply being lured into meditation by the physical techniques of taekwondo. Certainly, most traditional taekwondo classes either begin or end by the instructor calling the class together and calling out the word *munyum*. This is the Korean word for meditation. At best, these meditation sessions are only a few moments for you to watch your breathing and to possibly take note of how your body and your mind are feeling. But due to the adrenilized nature of a taekwondo class, this is hardly true meditation. For the advanced taekwondo practitioner to truly develop the ability to not only calm but also to acutely focus his or her mind, formalized meditation is necessary.

The practice of meditation has been handed down for centuries. Many people, particularly those of Western descent, view meditation as some metaphysical mind game practiced only by monks living in a monastery. Meditation is not some abstract science that can only be practiced by holy men. Meditation is an easy and very rewarding process.

How to Meditate

Meditation is most effectively practiced, especially in its early stages, in a quiet serene environment. This is not an absolute requirement for the practice of meditation, but periodic noise tends to distract and draw the attention of your mind. So, quiet environments are best.

In meditation, your body must be kept in a firm upright position. To begin, sit on the floor in a cross-legged posture and close your eyes. Your spine must be kept erect so that your internal energy will continue to flow in a constant and unhindered motion. Allow your body a few moments to settle into the seated posture.

Once you feel firmly seated and comfortable, begin to observe your breath. Do not attempt to control it, simply let it enter and exit naturally through your nose. Once your mind has grown accustomed to this process, begin to attach the number one to each in-breath and the number two to each out-breath. Mentally repeat, "one," "two," "one," "two."

Your mind will tend to wander when you first begin to practice meditation; this counting will help to bring back your concentration to the life-giving force of breath.

The purpose of meditation is to still your mind. Therefore, you do not want to think, visualize, or fantasize when you are practicing meditation.

When you first begin the practice, thoughts will naturally come to your mind. Just like the physical techniques of taekwondo, meditation takes practice. For most of your life, you have allowed your mind to rapidly move from one thought to the next. Thus, your mind has been trained to think. It has not been trained not to think.

If you find yourself thinking during meditation, do not become upset with yourself. Simply refocus your consciousness on your One, Two breathing exercise and again embrace thoughtlessness.

When you begin to meditate you should practice for ten minutes, twice a day. As you become more comfortable with the process, you can increase this process to twenty minutes twice a day.

Chapter 2
The Development and Usage of Ki in Taekwondo

When one hears of the usage of ki in association with the martial arts, taekwondo is not the first art that comes to mind. Other systems of self-defense, such as aikido or hapkido, are generally the arts that are associated with training their practitioners in the usage of ki. Though this is the common belief, it is not necessarily the truth. Simply listen to a taekwondo practitioner unleashing an offensive technique and the martial art yell, or *"Ki hap!,"* is heard. What this martial art yell means is that the practitioner is pulling ki from his or her center point, or *tan jun,* and is unleashing it with the onslaught of the technique.

PHYSICAL STRENGTH VERSUS KI

Physical strength is not a universal strength. Thus, it should not be unnecessarily feared.

Physical strength, such as heightened muscle development, is a process of body enhancement that is easily achieved by prescribed physically orientated weightlifting exercises. This type of strength development is, however, quickly lost when the exercises are discontinued. Muscle development is, therefore, a temporary form of strength.

Individuals who develop internal strength through the use of ki, on the other hand, never lose their understanding of how to effectively access ki. Thus, this form of internal strength and energy is always available to them.

THE FOUNDATIONS OF KI IN TAEKWONDO

In modern taekwondo, the science of ki is commonly only taught to advanced practitioners. This is so because it is believed that for a taekwondo student to truly comprehend the workings of the advanced science of ki, he or she must first possess a mastery of the physical aspects of the human body. Therefore, discussion of the existence of ki within this art is commonly limited to those practitioners who have been involved with taekwondo for many years.

Though this situation commonly exists in the dissemination of the science of ki in the modern school, it was not always the case. In the early stages of the evolution of taekwondo, in early post–World War II Korea, the essentials of ki development were commonly taught to novice students, as well. As time has progressed, however, and the focus of taekwondo has shifted from a complete system of martial arts to simply an advanced form of self-defense and competition, many advanced practitioners have shifted away not only from teaching but also from ever learning the process of ki development and usage. With this, an essential element of the original art of taekwondo has been lost.

For this reason, it is essential that the advanced taekwondo practitioner realign himself or herself with the original essence of this art, in order to become not only a more complete martial artist but also a more ideal representative of taekwondo.

THE HISTORY OF KI

Ki, or internal energy, was first written about in the ancient Chinese document *Huang Ti Nei Ching Su Wen*, or *The Yellow Emperor's Classic of Internal Medicine*. This text is commonly referred to as the *Nei Ching*.

The *Nei Ching* is written on the subject of healing in the form of a dialogue between the Huang-ti, the Yellow Emperor, and his minister Chi-po. Huang-ti was a mythological ruler of China, who, according to legend, lived from 2697 to 2599 B.C. He is said to have invented most aspects of Chinese culture. Though Chinese folklore claims that the *Nei Ching* was written during the life of Huang-ti, the text is historically dated at approximately 300 B.C.—during the Warring States Period of Chinese history.

In the *Nei Ching*, ki is described as the universal energy that nourishes and sustains all life. It flows through the universe and, thus, through each individual. An abundant, unrestricted flow of ki in the body allows one to remain healthy; while a diminished or impeded flow of ki in the body leads one to illness.

The *Nei Ching* describes how ki circulation is directed by invisible channels in the human body, similar to veins. These channels are known in English as meridians. In the Korean language, they are known as *pu dan ui kyung*.

The Transmission of the Knowledge of Ki

Formalized Chinese contact with the Korean peninsula began in approximately 200 B.C., during the Chinese Qui Dynasty (221–206 B.C.). From these contacts, the Korean peninsula was led into a period of rapid advancement in agriculture, health science (which included the doctrine of the Nei Ching), and formalized governmental statesmanship. Confucianism, Taoism, and later Buddhism were all introduced to Korea from China. From Korea, Chinese philosophic ideals were first transmitted to the island nation of Japan at the bequest of King Kunch-ogo (A.D. 346–375). Two Korean scholars, A-Chikki and Wang-In, were sent to Japan to instruct the Japanese crown prince in the Confucian doctrines. They brought with them copies of the *Analects of Confucius, Chien Cha Wen*, the *Thousand-Character Classic*. This first transmission of Confucian thought became one of the most culturally influential events in ancient Japanese history.

Korea began to embrace Buddhism as the early centuries of the Common Era unfolded. Korean Buddhist monks were sent to Japan in the fifth century A.D., introducing Buddhism to the island nation. The Buddhist monk Kwall-uk crossed the Sea of Japan in A.D. 602, bringing with him a large number of Buddhist sutras, historical books, medical books, and works on astronomy, geography, and the occult arts. Kwall-uk was instrumental in the founding of the Sanron School of Buddhism in Japan.

Because there was no evidence of Chinese medical practices in Japan until this period, it is believed that this is when the knowledge of ki, detailed in the *Nei Ching*, was first transmitted from Korea to Japan. Though Chinese and Korean medicine rapidly expanded throughout Japan and was practiced by monks and priests from this time period forward, the use of ki, for other than medical purposes, did not evolve in Japan until the twelfth century with the dawn of the samurai. From the continued contact between Korea, China, and Japan, ki was assimilated into Japanese culture, where its practice has taken a firm hold.

The science of ki was passed down through history predominately via Buddhist monks. The science of ki as a source of martial art warfare was, however, predominately formalized and refined in Korea and Japan by various schools of martial arts. The evolution of ki continued until it ultimately reached the point that it has ascended to in the modern era, when it is propagated not only as a science of health but also as a method of self-defense.

With both the direct and indirect contact which has occurred throughout the centuries, the science of ki has come to be an essential part of both Japanese and Korean culture. The continued evolution of its understanding, particularly in association with the martial arts, must be attributed to both of these cultures.

UNDERSTANDING KI ENERGY IN THE HUMAN BODY

As described, ki flows through the human body along invisible circulation channels known as meridians. There are a total of twelve primary or "constant" meridians in the human body. The reason these twelve meridians are referred to as constant is because ki energy circulates through them in a constant and continual delineated path. Ten of these meridians are defined by and govern specific organs of the human body. These meridians are: the gall bladder meridian, the liver meridian, the lungs meridian, the large intestine meridian, the stomach meridian, the spleen/pancreas meridian, the heart meridian, the small intestine meridian, the bladder meridian, and the kidney meridian. The final two constant meridians—the heart constrictor meridian and the triple warmer meridian—are related to the control of bodily functions. The heart constrictor meridian dominates the continual flow of blood throughout the body, and the triple warmer meridian controls the energy of respiration. (See the Meridian Pathways illustration on page 203.)

Each of the constant meridians possesses a location on both the right side and the left side of the body. Ki flow along the meridians is, therefore, exactly directed to specific regions of the body the meridian effects. Furthermore, when an individual is experiencing a blockage of ki flow along any of the constant meridians, exacting stimulation can be applied to reinstate proper ki circulation.

There are two other meridians that also aid in the control and circulation of ki throughout the human body; they are the conceptual meridian, and the governing vessel meridian. Because they do not possess a direct relationship to a specific body organ and are not an integral element of the body's primary ki circulatory system, they are referred to as secondary meridians, *puch ajok kyung*. These secondary meridians influence highly specific ki channels and bodily activities.

Ki flow, through each of the body's meridians, progresses in a constant and unchanging direction of either "ascending" or "descending." Either *um* (*yin*) or *yang* dominates each of the meridians.

Ki and the Human Breath

Breath is what links your body to ki. This is established by the fact that you can live a few days without water, several without food, but without life-giving oxygen, you immediately cease to exist.

Ki is consciously brought into your body through ancient breath control techniques known in Korean as *ki gong*. These ancient techniques are not hard to practice. In fact, you can immediately prove their validity by simply taking in a few deep breaths right now—right where you are, and immediately enhance the ki flowing through your body.

TAN JUN

To consciously utilize ki in life and in self-defense, one must possess an abundance of ki and know how to focus its energy precisely. The first step in obtaining the ability to consciously focus your ki energy for external use is initially accomplished by concentration on your center point, or tan jun. This location is more commonly known by the Japanese term *hara*.

Tan jun is the center point of the human body. This location is highly revered in Asian culture, because it is the point of ki congregation in the human body. The tan jun is located approximately four inches below the navel. This bodily location is the source point of all usable ki in the human form. The martial arts practitioner who desires to utilize ki energy efficiently must first define this location. This can be accomplished by performing a tan jun defining exercise.

Once the location of your tan jun is firmly delineated, all ki-orientated strikes and self-defense applications are accomplished by initially focusing on this center point. The Korean phrase "ki hap," the yell associated with all punching, kicking, and throwing techniques, signals the fact that the practitioner is pulling ki up from this location and then releasing it as part of any offensive or defensive technique he or she is unleashing.

Pressure Points

Pressure points, or *hyel* in Korean, are precise access sites along a meridian. These hyel, when properly stimulated by acupuncture, *chim sul*, or acupressure, *ki hap sul*, enhance the flow of ki along a specified meridian. Applying exacting pressure to these locations aids the body in recovering from ki blockage or ki deficiency.

Ki stimulation of a specific meridian is commonly understood to aid in adding ki flow to a specific meridian of the body; additionally, if an impact is applied to these hyel in a precise and specific manner, they can also be accessed to hamper the flow of ki in an individual. This is where taekwondo begins its understanding of ki self-defense.

Ki Interruption

As has been explained, there are numerous locations on the human body that will directly access ki meridian pathways. These hyel can be employed to interrupt the flow of ki in an attacking opponent. In the most elemental form of ki-orientated self-defense, taekwondo teaches its students to strike precisely to a hyel. With this defensive application of the science of ki, you can effectively stop the flow of ki in your opponent along the specific meridian pathway you are impacting. Thereby, the flow of ki to the element of the body that specific meridian affects is halted, and your opponent will be hindered in his offensive abilities.

Understanding Pressure Point Strikes

Striking to a hyel does not necessarily immediately knock a person out or cause a body part to become instantly numb, as has been propagated by many martial arts charlatans and in many Hong Kong Kung Fu films. What this type of self-defense does achieve, however, is the interruption of the overall ki force in an attacker. This type of self-defense may be understood by the analogy of a body part that has fallen asleep, when proper circulation has been cut off from it.

When applying forced pressure to specific hyel, your goal is not to magically render your opponent lifeless. What you are planning to achieve is both short term and long term interruption of your attacker's ki energy.

A focused pressure point strike is initially accomplished by focusing your energy in your tan jun. Then, as your strike travels toward its final hyel impact point, you expel your focused ki, with a "ki hap!" and strike your opponent on one of these precise locations. As a result, his ki will be interrupted, and you can continue on with additional self-defense as necessary. (See the Pressure Point Locations on page 199.)

Nonforceful Ki Interruption

When a martial artist uses ki interruption techniques, in the midst of self-defense, he or she does not possess the time to exactly locate a specific hyel, as does an acupressurist when applying healing touch therapy. Equally, he or she does not generally have the time to hold a pressure point for more than a few seconds. It is for this reason that the advanced taekwondo stylist must not only possess an exact understanding of meridian pressure points, to make ki self-defense effective, but also must possess the ability to strike or apply debilitating pressure to them rapidly and precisely.

The hyel that is most appropriate to apply pressure to, in the midst of self-defense, is the one that is most easily accessible from your current position. In other words, you should never attempt to excessively relocate your body when moving forward with ki self-defense. If you attempt to awkwardly rearrange your positioning, you allow your opponent the ability to launch a secondary attack at you. Therefore, the hyel you utilize in any ki self-defense must be readily accessible.

Striking to an Obvious Hyel

In the midst of self-defense you will want to be able to end any confrontation as soon as possible. Therefore while using ki-orientated targeting at the early stages of your ki-strike development, you would want to target a location that can be powerfully hit with one offensive technique, with the intention of ending the confrontation as quickly as possible.

Following are ideal first-strike points to successfully interrupt the flow of ki in your opponent.

1. **Top of the skull, *tugol.*** This is a hyel of the gall bladder, liver, bladder, and governing vessel meridians. Striking it disorientes the opponent by interrupting ki circulation to the brain.
2. **Central forehead, *apima.*** This is a hyel of the gall bladder, bladder,

triple warmer, and governing vessel meridians. By striking it, you will substantially disorient your opponent. This disorientation will last for several minutes, in which time you can leave the scene of the attack or continue with additional self-defense as necessary.

3. **Behind the ear, *kwi hori*.** If you place your finger behind the back of your ear, you will feel a slight protrusion of the bone. This is a hyel for the gall bladder and triple warmer meridians. This pressure point also affects the functioning of the inner ear. Because the inner ear directly affects balance, striking this location will cause your opponent to lose his balance and become disoriented.

4. **Jaw bone, *tok*.** The hyel to access on the jaw bone is located at the point where the jaw arches exactly at the point where the jaw bone curves and extends out toward the chin. This pressure point also affects the function of the inner ear, and thus, the balance of the opponent. It is also a hyel for the stomach, the small intestine, and the triple warmer meridians. Striking it disorientes your adversary and affects his balance.

5. **Central, upper, chest, *kasum chungsim*.** This hyel is located on the sternum. (The long flat chest bone, proceeding vertically, joining the ribs.) Its exact location is approximately 1 inch above the solar plexus. It is a hyel of the kidney and conceptual meridians. Due to its close proximity to the heart and the lungs, striking it sets the opponent's breathing off-balance. This sporadic breathing will remain constant for approximately two minutes, or longer, depending on the power of the strike.

6. **Ribs, *kal pitdal*.** Take the tips of your fingers and follow your ribs from the central portion of your body to the side, while applying slight pressure. You will immediately feel a pressure point when you come to the lower side of your ribs. This is the hyel you desire to locate when in combat. This is a hyel of the gall bladder, liver, stomach, and spleen meridians. All of these meridians, in one form or another, affect the flow of blood throughout the human body. A strike to this location significantly interrupts the individual's blood flow.

7. **Top of the hand, *son*.** Located at the exact center of the top of the hand, in between the hand bones leading to the middle and third fingers. This is a hyel of the triple warmer meridian. When you strike this pressure point, your adversary's hand is numbed and its proper function is disrupted.

In more forceful situations you may simply want to rapidly strike your opponent in order to disrupt his intake of breath, which will then, immediately, interrupt the flow of ki into his body. The primary breath-interrupting pressure points are the groin, the tan jun, the abdomen, the kidneys, the side of the ribs, the solar plexus, and the throat. By delivering a powerful strike to any of these locations, you will instantly disrupt the flow of ki into his body and induce a state of disorientation in him, allowing you to unleash additional self-defense techniques as necessary.

The Straight Punch Ki Interception

At times, in the midst of combat, you may not possess the ability to rapidly strike your opponent on one of his obvious pressure points. For this reason, it is important to develop the understanding of how to hit more obscure targets.

If we view the case of ki self-defense in regards to the straight punch, what we see is that once the opponent's straight punch has been blocked, his arm is fully exposed. This allows you two primary locations in which to apply appropriate ki-interrupting pressure to an accessible hyel. These locations are the inside of his elbow and his wrist.

The inside of the elbow possesses a hyel for the heart meridian, *su so um shim kyung* in Korean. To interrupt ki flow along this meridian, you can reach in with your free hand and take a firm grip of your attacker's elbow. With your middle finger, place substantial pressure on this hyel.

When you block the ki flow along the heart meridian, the proper beating of your opponent's heart is interrupted. Thus, blood flow to all areas of his body is hampered. Because all bodily functions are highly reliant on proper blood flow, this causes an interruption of your opponent's overall aggressive energy. Thus, controlling his attack becomes much easier.

Is Ki Interruption Enough?

As discussed, ki blockage is not enough to guarantee victory in any confrontation. Therefore, once you have interrupted your opponent's ki flow along his heart meridian, you must follow through with additional self-defense moves.

In the case of the blocked straight punch, because you now possess control over your opponent's elbow, allow your pressure point finger to remain in place, while using your other hand to shove the upper part of his punching arm back into his body. By doing this, you will have created a flux point from which you can continue forward with your own directed pattern of energy and send him backward, over an extended leg, onto the ground.

The second hyel, easily accessible to the blocked straight punch, is your opponent's wrist. On the wrist there is a hyel—on the bottom portion, approximately 1 inch from the wrist bone—that accesses the heart meridian and the lung meridian, *su tae um pay kyung* in Korean. Through this hyel, you have the potential to disrupt not only your opponent's heart beat, but also his breathing patterns.

When defending yourself with the anticipation of accessing this hyel, you will first deflect your opponent's straight punch. Once it has missed its intended target point on your body, you will reach your hand in and take a hold of this pressure point, encountering it with your middle finger. You perform this grabbing technique at the same time that you place your other hand on your opponent's outer elbow. From this position, you will maintain control over his entire arm movements and, thus, he will not be able to easily launch another punching attack at you.

Once you have accessed his wrist hyel and his elbow is in check, you can easily force him, face first, toward the ground. This is accomplished by applying appropriate pressure to the back of his elbow, while maintaining your locking control on his wrist hyel.

Ki and the Frontal Chokehold

If you find yourself in a face-to-face confrontation and an attacker has rapidly taken you into a frontal chokehold, there are two accessible pressure points to perform initial ki self-defense upon. Both are located on the neck.

The first frontal chokehold–orientated hyel is one located at the forward base of the neck It is known as *mok hyel* in Korean.

To locate this hyel, take your middle finger and follow the front of your neck downward until it meets your clavicle or collar bone. Just before this bone ends, at the central region of your neck, apply pressure downward, as if you were pushing inside, behind this bone. This hyel is equally located on both sides of the forward neck. Hold pressure to this hyel for a few moments and your breath will begin to be interrupted. Hold the pressure for longer periods of time, and the breath and the ki are substantially disrupted.

The next appropriate hyel, for frontal chokehold defense, is located on the side of the neck. This hyel can be accessed at the base of the jaw bone, just at the point where the jaw bone arches and moves downward toward the chin. This hyel accesses the triple warmer, *su soo yang sum cho kyung* in Korean, the gall bladder, *juk so yang dam kyung*, and the small intestine meridians, *su tae yang so jung kyung*. By applying appropriate pressure to this hyel, you will substantially disrupt the flow of ki to two organs of your opponent's body, as well as his respiration patterns, which are dominated by the triple warmer meridian.

Pressure Point Self-Defense

There are numerous hyels throughout the human body. The pressure point you access in ki self-defense is only dominated by your precise knowledge of their location and your ability to effectively reach them.

Ki-orientated self-defense is based in the understanding of bringing the nonphysical world into the realms of the physical. Just as the sound waves of music being broadcast from a speaker cannot be seen, they are, nonetheless, experienced. Ki is similar. Though ki cannot be physically touched, the essence of its energy has been documented for centuries.

KI GONG EXERCISES

Ki gong exercises are formalized techniques that were developed in ancient times, designed to bring the practitioner into conscious interaction with ki. Ki gong exercises incorporate breath control and bodily movement. From the practice of these exercises, taekwondo practitioners will begin to experience how to bring excess amounts of ki into their body, thereby making themselves more refined and focused practitioners of the art.

Ki Gong One—Begin to Breathe Consciously

Breathe deeply in through your nose. Feel the air as it enters your lungs and expands your stomach muscles. Hold it in place for a few seconds—experience the fullness you feel. Now, exhale the breath completely through your mouth. Before you take in your next breath, experience the emptiness your lungs are experiencing.

Do this exercise for three complete breath cycles. Upon completion you will feel invigorated.

Ki Gong Two—The Four-Phase Breath

Sit in a cross-legged position. Take a few moments and settle into your position. When you feel that you are ready, silently inhale deeply in a continuous flow though your nose.

It is important to remember in ki gong that you never force the intake of breath because this only causes resistance, thus creating an imbalance in the flow of your ki.

Visualize the breath entering your body, expanding to every part of your torso. Allow the breath to fill your lungs. As the intake of breath is in progress, consciously allow your stomach to naturally expand with the breath's presence. See the breath reaching to your tan jun and illuminating this region.

Once your intake of air has been naturally completed, feel its presence remain throughout your body. See your tan jun pulsating with its essence.

Do not allow breath to leave your body in a broken flow. This disrupts ki. Therefore, allow your breath to exit in a natural consciously continuous motion.

As your breath exits your body, visualize any impurities your body may possess, leaving you with the exhalation of your breath. All which remains is positive ki energy. Continue this exhalation process until your lungs are completely empty.

Once you have completely exhaled, do not attempt to immediately refill your lungs. This may take a bit of practice, for many people panic from the initial feeling of lack of oxygen. Instead of immediately breathing, feel how light your body has become from the absence of air. Observe the emptiness and the purity it possesses.

When it becomes time to breathe, do so. Allow the consciousness of ki to again enter your body.

The Four-Phase Breath can be used to enhance ki visualization and circulation in your body. When you first begin to use this ki breath control method, allow each phase to last approximately five seconds, or whatever amount of time feels natural to you. At the outset, do not attempt to hold any phase longer than you feel comfortable. This can disrupt the natural flow of ki in and out of your body and may even cause you to pass out. As you continue with your further development of ki gong, you will find, due to the increased amount of ki circulating throughout your body, that the time of each phase of this breath control will naturally increase until each phase may last as long as one minute.

Ki Gong Three—The Tan Jun–Defining Exercise

Stand with your legs separated, approximately even with your shoulders. Allow your knees to be slightly bent. Your feet should be pointing forward in a natural pattern. Bend your elbows slightly. Extend the fingers of your hand until they are naturally straight. Do not tighten the muscles of your hand, but allow your fingers to be semirelaxed and naturally separated. Bring your two hands in front of your tan jun. Separate your thumbs from your forefingers, allowing them to form an inverted triangle with approximately one inch of separation between both your thumbs and forefingers.

Once you have achieved this stance, close your eyes and breathe slowly, yet deeply. Allow your breaths to go deep into your abdomen. Once you achieve a relative state of calm, after approximately ten natural breaths, begin to visualize the location of your tan jun.

Now, pivot your wrists, until your open palms face upward. Bring your fingers together and allow them to point toward one another. Breathe deeply in through your nose as you visualize your breath entering your body in a golden flow through your tan jun. As you perform this exercise, bring your hands slowly up your body, accompanying your breath, until they reach your chest level.

Once you have taken in a full breath, hold it in naturally for a moment. Then, as you release it, pivot

TAN JUN–DEFINING EXERCISE 1   TAN JUN–DEFINING EXERCISE 2

TAN JUN-DEFINING EXERCISE 3   TAN JUN-DEFINING EXERCISE 4   TAN JUN-DEFINING EXERCISE 5

KI HAND

your palms over to a downward-facing position, and allow the breath to naturally leave your body as your hands travel downward to their beginning position. As your breath leaves your body, visualize it exiting through your tan jun in a golden flow.

From this exercise, the exact individual location of your tan jun will clearly come into focus, and you will develop the ability to easily direct ki throughout your body, from it. You should perform this tan jun breathing technique at least ten times, anytime you need to refocus your body, mind, or ki energy.

Ki Gong Four—Tan Jun Breathing

Begin by standing with your feet apart, slightly wider than your shoulders. Rest your elbows to your side at a 45-degree angle. Allow your fingers to extend in a relaxed fashion. Hold them loosely separated. Give yourself a moment to become comfortable in this position as you begin to visualize ki-filled breath entering your body through your nose and extending downward toward your tan jun.

At the point your mind is consciously focused on ki, breathe in a deep breath and consciously direct it to your tan jun. As this breath comes into your body, in a slow natural fashion, step forward in a informal front stance. Feel ki energy enter your body as your knees lightly bend.

In association with your in-breath and knee bending, allow your forefingers to extend as the other fingers of your hand bend at the first knuckle level. This forefinger extension is known as the "ki-hand" because certain power-orientated meridians culminate in this finger.

Now, consciously exhale. As you do, guide your arms to extend forward, with your muscles slightly tightened. See the ki energy traveling from your tan jun, extending down your arms, and emanating from your hands.

Stretch your arms out slowly, from shoulder level to the point where your elbows maintain a slight natural bend. The out-breath and the body movement associated with this ki gong exercise should take place simultaneously.

Once you have reached the completion of your out-breath, maintain a light muscle tension. Feel the ki energy emanating from your hand.

This exercise is not only a tan jun–focusing technique, but it also allows ki energy to be directed to your hands and arms. It is ideal to perform this technique when you know that you will need extra upper body strength or when you will be using your hands to heal someone through acupressure or massage.

KI EXTENSION AND THE USE OF KI IN SELF-DEFENSE

To use ki energy in association with self-defense, you must initially master how to effectively extend your ki. By extending your ki, in a directed fashion, you will add enormous power to any self-defense technique you employ.

Dynamic tension is a method of consciously tightening the muscles and tendons of a specific bodily region. From this practice: your breath, body, and mind are brought into clear association with ki, and defined meridian pathways are stimulated. Thus, ki energy is focused to specific regions of your body from where it can be extended.

Ki Gong Five—The Boulder Push Exercise

Begin in a standing position, with your hands loosely at your sides. Focus your attention and begin to breath very consciously, watching your breath enter your body and extend downwards from your nose to your tan jun. Once you feel calm and possess a good sense of your center point, take in a new breath through your nose and move your left leg forward into front stance. Remember to maintain conscious focus on your breath entering your nose and proceeding to your tan jun. As you step, bend both of your elbows slightly and turn your wrists until your open palms are facing upward at approximately your waist level.

Once your intake of breath is complete, allow the breath to remain locked in your tan jun. Feel the ki energy radiate in your body as you bring your upward-facing palms, along the side of your body, to your chest level. Once at chest level, allow your open palms to turn outward and face in front of you.

As you exhale your ki breath, tighten all of the muscles of your shoulders, back, arms, and hands. Powerfully push forward with your open palms, visualizing the ki energy exiting your palms into a large boulder in front of you. The boulder moves with the power of your push. As your arms extend, allow your left arm to remain slightly in front, with your right arm slightly behind, pushing forward.

Once your breath is completely exhaled, observe the emptiness for a moment, as your arms remain extended. Feel the ki radiating from them.

When it becomes time to take a new breath, breathe in a new ki breath and return to your original standing position with your hands loosely at your sides. When the breath is complete, feel how full of ki your arms and hands have become. Allow the breath to exit naturally, feeling the ki remaining.

As it becomes time to take your next breath, step forward with your right leg this time, and perform the same exercise on your right side.

The Boulder Push Exercise is ideal for focalizing ki into your arms, shoulders, and hands, when you are anticipating the need to perform strenuous physical

BOULDER PUSH EXERCISE 1   BOULDER PUSH EXERCISE 2

movements with them. This is so because this exercise stimulates the meridians of these limbs, thus providing additional ki power to them.

As you practice these two extension exercises, witness how first your upper arm, then your lower arm, and finally your hands and fingers begin to feel more and more strength with each out-breath—which travels from your hara out to your fingers. Experience the strength your hands feel as ki energy permeates from your fingers.

Once you begin to feel the power and energy that you have consciously directed from your hand, with these two ki extension exercises, you can begin to focus and then extend this same ki energy from any part of your body. Simply focus your mind, concentrate on your tan jun and breathe your ki energy to extend from any location of your body you desire.

The Straight Punch Ki Exercise Six— Extending Ki through the Straight Punch

As all martial artists understand, at times when self-defense is necessary, it may be necessary to aggressively strike out at an attacking opponent. If you simply allow the wild emotion of the moment and the force of adrenaline to guide your defense, you cannot consciously take control of the altercation. For this reason, the advanced practitioner of taekwondo learns to consciously extend ki, while striking out in times of battle.

The first form of a forward offensive strike, which most novice martial artists are taught, is how to deliver the straight punch. The straight punch is a refined punching technique. This is because it follows a very linear path to its target. Because of this, not only is it a very rapid striking technique, but also successfully blocking this style of punch is much more complicated, as well.

To take the straight punch to the level of a ki technique, it must be performed in conscious association with your breath. Therefore, settle into a front stance and take a few deep breaths, watching the ki enter your nose and proceed to your tan jun. Once you are focused, begin the punching technique. Unleash your straight punch in a very slow and controlled manner. Punch as if you were performing a dynamic tension exercise by tightening all of the muscles of your body. Slowly perform this punch as you exhale through your nose the ki energy that you have stored in your tan jun. Visualize this ki energy extending from your tan jun, up your body, and along your arm. As your punch reaches its climax, mentally witness the ki energy forcefully extending from your fist into an imaginary target in front of you.

This type of ki extension practice is not limited to the straight punch. According to your own martial art abilities, you can associate it with any punching or kicking technique you desire. The ultimate goal of this type of ki extension training is to allow you to become very conscious of the fact that ki can emanate from your body. In the case of self-defense, you can, therefore, focus and utilize your ki by consciously directing it to an exact location on your opponent's body.

Just Breathe

Ki is the inexhaustible energy of this universe. It is everywhere. As you now understand, tapping into this universal energy is accomplished by performing breathing exercises. At its most elemental level, however, tapping into ki energy is as easy as breathing in. And, to unleash ki energy all you have to do is breathe out. Therefore, to begin to unleash ki energy with each of your taekwondo techniques all you need to do is exhale.

All taekwondo practitioners are taught to unleash a "ki hap!" with each offensive technique. For many, this becomes an unconscious action, with no concentration on the tan jun or ki. With this, the ki hap comes to possess no meaning.

Instead of simply releasing a "ki hap!" when you perform a technique, consciously breathe out as you release the maneuver. The moment you do this you will instantly realize that you have increased the power of your technique.

Begin to practice this exhalation with every style of technique you deliver. After you have begun to do this very consciously, you can again add the "ki hap!" if you desire. From this, you will begin to use enhanced ki energy with every technique with the simple ease of consciously exhaling.

Part Two
Advanced Techniques— Refining the Fundamentals

Chapter 3
The Stance

At the heart of taekwondo techniques is the stance. The stance is the position you take before any technique is unleashed. In the early development of taekwondo, the formalized stance was one of the key elements of the art. No offensive or defensive technique was unleashed unless the practitioner had first settled into the stance that was ideally developed for this technique. The front stance, the back stance, and the horse stance were the stances commonly employed by the novice and the advanced practitioner alike.

The stance is also at the root of the taekwondo forms. The stance is one of the primary elements judges who view taekwondo promotion look to, in order to determine if the practitioner has developed the mastery to move on to the next level of the art. The stance is also one of the primary components of judging the taekwondo practitioner when he enters into forms competitions at taekwondo tournaments.

The reason that the stance is such an essential element of taekwondo is that the practitioner must possess an acute sense of balance to properly execute any technique. If you are not stationary upon your feet, you may fall to the ground when unleashing a kick. If you are blocking, without the proper stance, the offensive opponent will easily overpower the block. For these reasons, the stance is understood to be the foundational element of taekwondo.

THE CENTER OF GRAVITY

To enter into a proper stance, one must not only know how to set one's legs and the body into proper placemen but must also understand how to find the body's center of gravity. This center of bodily gravity is defined by the tan jun.

As mentioned, the tan jun is located approximately 4 inches below the navel. The reason that this has come to be such a highly revered location on the body of the martial artist is that it is known to be the body's natural center of balance. It is the location from which all techniques must be unleashed if they are to possess grace and balance. This bodily location is also understood to be the point where ki or internal energy congregates in the human body.

Precise methods to define this location in your body are presented in Chapter 2.

UNDERSTANDING THE FORMAL STANCE

Many practitioners of modern, eclectic styles of the martial arts believe that there is no need for the formalized stances of taekwondo. There is, however, a deeper understanding of the mastery of stance employed in taekwondo.

By mastering the stances of taekwondo, the practitioner comes to a new and deeper understanding of his or her body and how that body can best be anchored to the ground when unleashing the various offensive and defensive techniques possessed. As one progresses through the ranks of taekwondo, this understanding continues to develop and becomes more refined. From this, the advanced practitioner is allowed to move forward from the formal stances and embrace a new understanding, where a less formal stance may be employed. It is essential to note that all of the less formal stances possess the foundational characteristics presented in the formal stances, they are simply less regimented.

THE FIGHTING STANCE

As taekwondo has continued to evolve, it has continued to become one of the most advanced systems of self-defense in the world. Hand in hand with this development, it has also come to be known as one of the most expansive systems of martial arts competition. This is easily illustrated by taekwondo's becoming an Olympic sport.

As sport competition has come to be one of the primary defining elements of taekwondo, the taekwondo stance has evolved to embrace this competitive methodology.

In the early development of taekwondo, if one were to witness a sparring match, one would have seen the participants entering into a deep formal stance prior to unleashing their offensive and defensive techniques. As taekwondo quickly began to evolve after World War II, and the extensive kicking arsenal it now possesses began to be integrated into the art, these deep formalized competitive stances began to be replaced by more efficient, combat-orientated stances. Today, the fighting stances have come to be one of the essential elements of taekwondo training.

Understanding the Fighting Stance

The traditional taekwondo fighting stance has you standing with your legs naturally apart, maintaining a generalized balance. Your elbows are bent at a 45-degree angle and are suspended at mid-torso level—a few inches away from your body. Your hands are formed into fists. One arm, referred to as the lead arm, is generally higher and out in front of your other arm. Your rear arm maintains a rear protective positioning.

The fighting stance is used in training when the taekwondo practitioner is practicing the various punches and kicks. It is also used in sparring, as a means of readiness to protect against any oncoming attack or to unleash an offensive assault.

The Combative Side Fighting Stance

Taekwondo is a scientific system of self-defense. As such, each component of its offensive and defensive arsenal is precisely studied in order to refine each element to the degree where it is most effective in all forms of combat. This is also the case with the fighting stance.

Virtually all systems of self-defense dictate that when you enter into a fighting stance, you do so by facing your opponent with your lead side forward and

FIGHTING STANCE

| SIDE FIGHTING STANCE | LOW FIGHTING STANCE |

your body at a 45-degree angle. This common formula is not the case, however, with Taekwondo's combative side-fighting stance.

When combat is eminent, whether it be in the dojang or on the street, the advanced taekwondo stylist is taught to turn his or her body to the degree that only his or her side is exposed. From this, there is much less target area for the opponent to strike. In addition, ease in retreating from an attack or rapidly moving forward is amplified due to the fact that one's body is in a position where it can quickly slide back or slide in, as necessary.

Low Fighting Stance

To perform the low fighting stance, you begin by entering into combative side fighting stance. You then lower yourself down, by bending your knees approximately 30 percent more than in the normal fighting stance.

The low fighting stance is a combative technique in the advanced taekwondo practitioner's arsenal. It is ideally used when you are observing your opponent's movements and you wish to rapidly strike out at him with an offensive flurry. Because you are in low position, you can rapidly spring forward, propelling yourself with your retracted legs in toward your opponent.

THE ADVANCING STANCE

At each level of training, the taekwondo practitioner develops and then redevelops his understanding of the taekwondo stance. As one advances through the art, the fighting stances become more and more streamlined, while the traditional ones are performed in a more exacting manner. In each case, the advancing practitioner of taekwondo understands that the stance is the root of all taekwondo techniques. Therefore, the ongoing development of this most essential element of taekwondo is never overlooked.

Chapter 4
The Block

Throughout all levels of taekwondo, the practitioner is taught how to block the onslaught of an oncoming punch, kick, or weapons assault. The advancing taekwondo practitioner must understand that a block is not just about stopping an oncoming attack. It is about stopping and redirecting this attack in a direction that will open your opponent to the degree that your counterattack can be launched.

Though this appears to be a logical understanding of the blocking system, all practitioners do not practice it. Many simply block for the sake of blocking and do not immediately follow through with counterattacking measures.

BLOCKING INJURY

One of the first things that novice taekwondo practitioners will encounter when attempting to block an oncoming attack is that they will meet force with force, bone to bone, and they will substantially bruise, injure, and perhaps break the blocking component of their own body. Usually, this will be the forearm, because this is the primary component of blocking used in taekwondo.

In the early stages of the development of taekwondo, the forceful block came out of its heritage from the traditional Japanese martial arts. As taekwondo has continued to evolve, this forceful blocking technique continues to be used to train the novice student in the fundamentals of taekwondo. However, advanced practitioners move away from the use of these techniques as they come to master new and more efficient levels of blocking.

BLOCKING WITH THE HANDS

As one progresses through the ranks of taekwondo, the practitioner moves forward and begins to understand some of the subtle elements of this art. The style of blocking used by advancing practitioners also begins to evolve.

Advancing taekwondo practitioners quickly come to understand that the traditional taekwondo forceful blocks not only have the ability to injure the blocking element of their body but are also very slow to perform. For this reason, advancing practitioners begin to add new elements to their blocking vocabulary.

One of the first techniques commonly employed by the advancing taekwondo practitioner, in the realms of sparring, is the use of blocking with the open hands. In this case, the hands are not formed into precise blocking tools, such as a knife hand, as is demonstrated in the forms of taekwondo. Instead, blocking with an open hand becomes a common tool for the defense of an oncoming kick.

Though the open hand block becomes very common as one advances through the ranks of taekwondo, a very big problem occurs when using this method to intercept a kick.

A taekwondo kick is a very powerful offensive weapon. By attempting to block it with an open hand, you have the potential to snap your fingers back and break them.

If you encounter your opponent's oncoming kick with the palm of your hand, there is less chance of injury. But, as anyone who has stepped into the sparring ring can attest to, there is no way to truly know or anticipate what your opponent will unleash while in the midst of combat. Furthermore, even though you may see a kick traveling in your direction, and you may even know what style of kicking technique it is, your opponent may slightly alter the path of this technique as it is traveling toward you. As a result, the kick may encounter your fingers instead of your palm, snapping them back, and spraining or breaking them.

THE ART OF DEFLECTION

There is another method employed by the advanced practitioner of taekwondo that keeps the body free from injury. That method is known as deflection.

By using deflection as a primary tool of defense against offensive techniques, you not only lessen the chances of your being injured but also gain substantial control over your opponent's physical movements. This is accomplished by allowing your opponent to make his initial aggressive actions. Then, once his technique has been instigated, you simply guide his fighting techniques away from your body, utilizing his own expended energy and gained momentum.

In taekwondo's advanced art of deflection, you never forcefully encounter or block the assaults of an aggressor. Instead, you simply intercept the energy of his attacks and redirect it to your own benefit. This forces your opponent to uncontrollably continue forward in the direction of whatever offensive technique he has launched. By defending yourself in this fashion, you use little of your own energy; instead, you take advantage of the already expended energy of your opponent, thus, placing him in a less than favorable position for further counterattacks.

The simplest application of effective opponent deflection has you do nothing at all to intercept or even touch your adversary once he has launched an aggressive attack at you. In its most rudimentary method, taekwondo's art of deflection has you simply move out of the path of any oncoming strike. For example, your opponent launches a kick at you. By simply sidestepping this attack, your opponent's technique will have missed you, and you, in turn, can then powerfully counterstrike at him with an offensive technique of your own. Because his kick has missed, he will be open to receiving a counterattack. This is so because it takes a moment to regroup once an offensive attack has failed. In this moment of indecision is when the advanced practitioner of taekwondo takes advantage of the situation and powerfully strikes his or her opponent. This style of defense is ideally illustrated in Olympic taekwondo events.

MULTIPLE METHODS

There is no one method for how to block each style of attack. Advanced practitioners master all of the basic blocking techniques in taekwondo. They then streamline these techniques to make them as rapid and as useful as possible. Advanced practitioners integrate deflection into their blocking arsenal. With this knowledge, they may simply move out of the path of an attack, hold the opponent in place for a moment with an outstretched hand, and then deliver a powerful counterstrike.

Throughout the pages of this book, as each style of advanced offensive technique is discussed, advanced methods of counteracting these attacks will also be detailed. From this, the advancing practitioner in taekwondo may gain new insight into the most effective way to encounter and block all of the techniques in taekwondo.

THE TRADITIONAL TAEKWONDO BLOCK

As one advances through the ranks of taekwondo, the various forms of the traditional blocking come to possess a very different meaning than in the early stages of training. In the early stages, the formal block trains the novice student in how to move and encounter the various forms of controlled attacks. As the taekwondo student moves through the ranks, the traditional block becomes more of a means of finding a perfection of movement in association with the forms. Just as the ballet dancer must perfect every movement in ballet to the best of his or her ability, so too must the taekwondo practitioner come to master all of the formal techniques of taekwondo.

As the taekwondo practitioner advances through the ranks, the traditional moves are used less and less in sparring and in reality-based self-defense practice. This is a natural evolution and is experienced by every practitioner. This is not to say that the traditional block does not have a place in advanced taekwondo. It does. It becomes a training method to launch your body into exactingly performed techniques. From this, you become a more complete practitioner of the art of taekwondo.

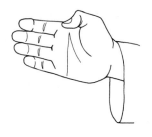

Chapter 5
The Hand and Arm Strike

Taekwondo is defined by its advanced kicking arsenal. It is also the kicks of taekwondo that have come to dominate the rules of Olympic sport taekwondo.

In Olympic taekwondo, though the hands may be used to strike a competitive opponent in his or her central body region, these points are rarely recorded. This fact has caused may sports-orientated taekwondo instructors to leave behind the roots of this art, where both the hands and the feet were developed as equal weapons of self-defense.

Though the feet have come to dominate the modern art of taekwondo, simply by looking at the forms of this system, it is easy to see that taekwondo possesses a plethora of hand and arm striking techniques. The fist, the knuckles, the knife hand, the circle hand, and the elbows are all part of this vast system of self-defense. To this end, advanced practitioners of taekwondo never leave behind all of the tools of this art. Though they may train extensively in the rules that make up Olympic sport competition, they also train their body and mind to be prepared to unleash the most devastating hand and arm strikes if the situation ever presents itself.

Whereas the novice practitioner of taekwondo learns and practices all of the basic strikes of this art, the advanced practitioner refined these techniques, making the most effective weapons possible. To this end, we can view taekwondo's arsenal of hand and arm techniques and come to understand how they are employed by the advanced practitioner.

At the root of all advanced taekwondo hand and arm strikes is rapid penetration of an opponent's defenses. With this understanding, advanced practitioners develop their hand and arm strikes so that they are rapid, penetrating, and powerful tools of offense.

THE STRAIGHT PUNCH
The straight punch uses the front fist. The punch is generally the first line of defense that one naturally turns to for self-defense applications. Though there are numerous punching techniques one can use in a physical confrontation, taekwondo has isolated the most useful of these and teaches how to best utilize them as both an offensive and a defensive tool.

Taekwondo's primary punching technique is the straight punch. By its very design, the straight punch allows the practitioner to make contact with the intended target in the most expedient and powerful fashion possible.

THE LINEAR HAND STRIKES OF TAEKWONDO

Front Fist (*chung kwon*). Your knuckles are the striking tools.

Knuckle Fist (*jin joo mok*). The striking tool is the outside tip of the extended knuckles.

Circle Hand (*won yuk soo do*). The striking point is located between your thumb and your forefinger, once they have been widely opened.

Palm Hand (*chang kwon*). A powerful striking weapon located at the base of your palm.

THE NONLINEAR HAND AND ARM STRIKES OF TAEKWONDO

Back Fist (*ye kwon*). Your fist is held in vertical fashion. The striking weapon is your knuckles and, to a lesser degree, the back of your hand.

Bottom Fist (*yoo kwon*). The striking point of this weapon is between your wrist and your last knuckle.

Knife Hand (*soo do*). The striking tool is located between the base of your little finger and your wrist.

Inside Knife Hand (*yuk soo do*). The striking point of this technique is located between where your thumb recedes and the middle knuckle of your first finger.

Elbow (*keum chi*). The striking weapon is where your elbow bone protrudes once it has been bent.

The taekwondo straight punch is driven forward, directly toward your target, in a linear fashion. Your shoulder muscles and triceps propel it. Your fist can make contact with your opponent in either a vertical or horizontal positioning.

The taekwondo straight punch is ideally delivered when the elbow of your punching arm remains slightly bent upon making target impact. This is accomplished by accurately judging the distance and making contact with your opponent before your arm reaches the point where it must stretch or extend unnaturally to reach its desired strike point. By allowing your elbow to remain slightly bent, whenever you use a straight punching technique, you not only maintain maximum body balance, but you also keep your elbow safe from possible hypertension as the momentum of the punch drives it forward.

The key element that gives the taekwondo straight punch its power is the fact that you make contact with your target before you have extended your punching arm fully. The reason for this is that your straight punch reaches its target as close to its point of inception as physically possible. This allows you to continue forward with the force and power of the punch—extending it deeply into your opponent. If, on the other hand, you have to reach to make contact with your opponent, you will have utilized and wasted a large portion of the power of your punch before it ever impacts its intended strike point.

FRONT FIST

The Taekwondo Straight Punch Versus the Roundhouse Punch

The advanced practitioner of taekwondo utilizes the straight punch as the preferred punching technique because it has several advantages over the more common roundhouse punch. When the roundhouse punch is delivered, the punching arm initially swings outward and then swings in toward its target. Because of this,

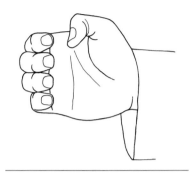

KNUCKLE FIST

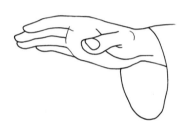

CIRCLE HAND

PALM HAND

BACK FIST

the roundhouse punch is not only much slower than the straight punch, but it is also much more obvious and easily defended against.

OTHER LINEAR HAND STRIKE TECHNIQUES

Through the design and application of the straight punch, the advanced practitioner of taekwondo learns to deliver other linear techniques in the same very direct manner. With application, these techniques not only become very fast and powerful but also become very hard to block, because of the extreme linear nature of their delivery.

The Knuckle Fist

The knuckle fist is formed by making your hand into a fist. You then extend your knuckles forward. Offensive delivery is made with this weapon by projecting your bent elbow from mid-body level. The forward motion of this punch is driven forward with your shoulder and arm muscles. As the knuckle fist is refined into a highly specific striking tool, its impact is ideally delivered to the solar plexus or central throat of an opponent.

The Circle Hand

The circle hand is formed by separating your thumb from your forefinger, tightening the muscles and tendons of your hand, and striking, in a linear fashion, to the frontal region of an attacker's neck. The circle hand, which strikes an opponent's throat, is also immediately delivered in a very linear style of attack. From this, the opponent is struck and debilitated before he has the opportunity to block this offensive technique.

The Palm Strike

The palm strike, like the straight punch, is delivered in a very linear fashion. In the palm strike, you bend your fingers at your second knuckle, which exposes the base of your palm. By bending your fingers in this fashion, the muscle that extends from your thumb across the base of your hand is tightened, thus providing a powerful striking weapon. Your palm is then brought back to your shoulder level. It is unleashed by snapping the strike toward its target with your shoulder muscles.

The palm strike is most effectively used to target locations on your opponent's head, such as, underneath the base of his nose (which can prove deadly), across the bridge of his nose, his temples, or the side of his jaw.

The Back Fist

The use of the back fist in modern taekwondo has virtually been abandoned. This offensive technique was, however, an integral part of the original teachings of the art.

The back fist is an extremely rapid offensive weapon. To unleash the back fist, your elbow is bent and your fist is brought back to your chest at shoulder level in a vertical position. The back fist is then unleashed at its target by first snapping your elbow out and then extending the distance of the back fist's attack from your shoulder. The back fist is generally aimed at your opponent's head.

The back fist is extremely difficult to defend against. This is so because it is a very rapid striking weapon, and once impact is made, your fist is in rapid recoils. The back fist can, therefore, be used multiple times when additional striking measures are necessary.

The Bottom Fist

The bottom fist is formed in a traditional fist fashion. The striking element of this weapon is the base of your hand, between your wrist and the base of your little finger. The bottom fist is delivered in a downward striking motion. It is ideally targeted at the top of the head, or the bridge of the nose of your opponent when you are both in a vertical position. In other instances, this strike can be used to strike downward to any location on your opponent's body you find open for immediate attack.

BOTTOM FIST

The Knife Hand

To form the knife hand, extend the fingers muscles and tendons in the hand and tighten your wrist. The initial mistake that many novice taekwondo practitioners make when attempting to use the knife hand as a weapon is to relax the tension in their hand, either just before or when the knife hand strikes. This should never be done, for you can easily break bones in your hand.

The basic strike weapon of the knife hand is along the base of the hand. This extends from where the wrist ends to where the little finger begins. This is along its arched side and is the location where the knife hand develops the most strength by the aforementioned tightening techniques.

The extension of the arm and then the snapping of the elbow propel the knife hand strike. The momentum developed by the snapping out of the elbow should never be allowed to entirely control your knife hand assault. The elbow should remain slightly bent when the knife hand technique is delivered, thus allowing you to maintain control over your movement.

The knife hand is not a randomly effective weapon such as the fist—which can be allowed to strike virtually anywhere on an opponent's body. Instead, the knife hand is ideally suited to strike very specific locations on an opponent's body: the front of his neck, across his nose, to his temples, and the side of his ribs.

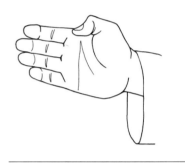

KNIFE HAND

The Inside Knife Hand

The inside knife hand is formed in much the same way as the traditional knife hand. Initially, the muscles of the fingers and hand are tensed. The difference between this offensive technique and that of the traditional knife hand is that impact in made with the inside ridge of your hand. To this end, the thumb of the striking hand is pulled tightly into the palm, thereby exposing the inner ridge of the hand.

Due to the fact that it is very easy to damage the hand and thumb if the technique is unleashed improperly, this advanced taekwondo hand striking technique is only used by the most advanced practitioners, who truly understand this hand technique's proper usage. The ideal opponent striking points for the inside knife hand are the side of an opponent's neck, the front of his neck, and across the bridge of his nose. Because this technique does not possess a lot of power, it is not an ideal technique to be used on other, more firm, bodily locations.

INSIDE KNIFE HAND

The Forward Elbow Strike

As can be seen in a number of the forms of taekwondo, the forward and the rear elbow strikes are commonly employed tools of offense and defense in the arsenal of taekwondo hand and arm strikes. To the advanced practitioner, the elbows become exacting weapons in numerous self-defense applications.

ELBOW STRIKE

The forward elbow strike witnesses you bending your elbow, exposing the protruding elbow bone at the base of your forearm. This bone is your striking tool. This forward elbow strike is ideally targeted at a vital strike point on your opponent's head.

To perform the forward elbow strike, bring your elbow up to shoulder level and pivot your body at waist level. By stepping in with your lead foot, you make extremely powerful impact to your target.

The forward elbow strike is an ideal weapon to be used in close contact fighting. It is an ideal weapon on your opponent when your opponent is moving in on you or has taken a powerful forward hold on your body. The ideal strike points for this type of defense are your opponent's temples or anyplace on his face.

The Rear Elbow Strike

The rear elbow strike is an ideal weapon to use if an attacker has grabbed ahold of your body from behind. If you have been grabbed from behind, the rear elbow strike witnesses you pivoting backward, unleashing your bent elbow from shoulder level, and making impact to virtually any part of your attacker's body.

If you have not yet been grabbed from behind but your attacker is close, you can add the additional momentum-driven movement of your body into the strike by pivoting at your waist level as you release your rear elbow strike.

Chapter 6
The Kick

Taekwondo is defined by its extensive arsenal of advanced kicking techniques. No other system of self-defense in the world has such an elaborate and exacting array of foot and leg techniques.

In the early development of taekwondo, its kicking arsenal was defined by the standard kicking techniques used by the various schools of Japanese karate. As the first generation of taekwondo instructors studied the Japanese martial arts, they taught what they had learned. Thus, the kicking techniques were used in a very limited fashion compared to what is commonly practiced in the art today.

The taekwondo kick began its evolution at the hands of the first generation students of the art—the students of the original teachers. It was this generation that expanded the range, application, and utilization of the taekwondo kick until it reached the point where it is today.

This evolution, which began in the 1950s, was not limited to that stage of development in the art. When taekwondo became the national sport of Korea, the taekwondo kick witnessed a new wave of evolution. At this point, due to the competitive nature of the art, the taekwondo kick began to become more stream-lined. This process saw some of the momentum-driven power of the kick being left behind in exchange for rapid development.

The advanced practitioner who has mastered the basic techniques of this seminal element of taekwondo, not only masters new and unique methods of delivery but also uses the taekwondo kick as a defensive tool. The advanced practitioner possesses a unique and ever-expanding understanding of the taekwondo kick that has caused this system of martial arts to continue to develop and evolve.

The debate has long continued about the combat effectiveness of the taekwondo kick. It has been stated by some people, the predominance of whom are non-taekwondo stylists, that the taekwondo kick is much too elaborate to have any effectiveness in a street combat situation. The majority of these critics, however, do not comprehend the actual application of the various taekwondo kicks or how they were designed to be used effectively.

FIGHTING FEET

Taekwondo's origin, dating back many decades, and its modern redevelopment in the mid-twentieth century, places ultimate importance on the use of the legs as an appropriate and effective weapon. With this in mind, we can view the individual elements that make up some of the most combat effective kicking techniques in the taekwondo arsenal and come to our own conclusion and understanding about the true effectiveness of the taekwondo kick.

Many individuals initially compare the taekwondo kick to the use of the hands as a combative weapon. This concept of comparison, in itself, is erroneous, because the hands and the legs are completely different in both their structure and use. The hands, in reference to offensive strategy, may be used in various ways: as a knife hand, a fist, a back fist, and so on. Though these techniques allow one to be very focused when attacking, none of these weapons possesses the force or power of the developed kicking techniques that define taekwondo.

One may then ask, why does one use the hands as offensive weapons at all, if they do not have as much strength as the legs? The answer to that is equally obvious. The hands and the developed legs are two completely different elements of the body and each must be consciously developed in accordance with the other to gain ultimate victory in a confrontation. You must use the effective elements the hands possess as well as consciously developing the use of your legs, which takes much more effort and training, and then link them into one cohesive unit to be a truly effective warrior.

To begin the study of the advanced taekwondo kick, the most important thing to remember is to not anchor your base leg so firmly to the ground that you cannot easily redirect your kicking energies and either retreat, when necessary, or rapidly change your kicking technique to another form of offense. By assuming that the kick you initially have launched is sufficient to defeat your opponent, you greatly limit yourself in any combative situation. If, for example, your initial kick is blocked, deflected, or simply misses, you must be able to quickly reform your kicking strategy and launch a secondary attack. Therefore, one of the key elements of advanced taekwondo kicking is to remain light on your feet.

The second problem, which occurs if you anchor your base leg firmly on the ground, arises from the momentum-driven speed and power of the advanced taekwondo kick. If you anchor your base leg firmly on the ground, you can quite easily injure your knee when the power of your kick causes your kicking leg to travel in, toward your opponent. This is especially the case with the circular kicks of taekwondo, such as the roundhouse or the spinning heel kick.

This light-on-your-feet kicking strategy is developed by the advanced taekwondo practitioner through continual practice and eventual mastery of the various kicking techniques that are applicable to street combat. Once you have achieved this ability, you can quickly redirect or revamp any kicking technique you are engaged in performing and thus have an even greater ability to win any confrontation.

ADVANCING THE BASIC KICK

Elevating the basic kicks of taekwondo to an advanced level is accomplished quite simply by slightly redefining the way in which they are unleashed. From this, the most basic kick becomes a weapon of awesome power when unleashed by the advanced practitioner of taekwondo.

To begin to define the process of redesigning the basic taekwondo kick and elevating it to the advanced level, we can view the most elemental, and debatably perhaps the most universally effective when performed properly, kick used in the taekwondo arsenal, the front kick.

The Front Kick

The front kick by its very design is fast, penetrating, and effective. There are, however, limitations to the effectiveness of the front kick when it is performed improperly.

There are two main problems with the traditional taekwondo front kick that the advanced practitioner overcomes to make it a truly effective weapon of offense and defense. The first problem is that the front kick is generally launched exclusively from the rear leg, and its energy is expended rapidly upward. This gives the traditional front kick very little range. By launching the front kick in this manner, it becomes completely ineffective unless your opponent chooses to remain stationary, directly in front of you. Simply by leaning back, he moves out of the front kick's range; the kick easily will miss him. Thus, when the kick is applied in this manner, the front kick is not a universally effective weapon of offense or defense.

The second flaw with the traditional front kick is that it can be easily countered by the trained opponent who quickly rushes in on it—leaving you off-balance and prone to a counterattack. The ideal example of this occurs when you are about to unleash a front kick and your opponent moves in, right on top of it. Your kick has been jammed, and you cannot release it. Most probably, your opponent has rushed in on you to deliver a powerful strike, such as a straight punch to your face. Thus, not only has your kick been negated, but also you have received a powerful first strike.

Redefining the Front Kick

To develop the ability to make the front kick a truly effective weapon in the advanced taekwondo arsenal, it must be refocused at a target that will not be easily missed.

To come to understand how to do this, begin by taking a fighting stance. Prepare to launch a basic front kick from your rear leg. Instead of focusing the power of this kick upward, focus it deeply in toward the solar plexus level of an imaginary opponent in front of you. Now, launch your front kick toward your imaginary target.

Simply by extending your front kick in this fashion, you have easily covered the distance between yourself and an opponent. With this approach, you will have made contact. From this simple refocusing technique, you have made the basic front kick much more effective.

The Leaning Back Front Kick

The leaning back front kick is the next traditional front kick modification that the advancing taekwondo practitioner employs in regards to the basic front kick. With sparring as a central focus of taekwondo training, the leaning back front kick is an ideal weapon to be used during sparring matches.

To perform the leaning back front kick, simply unleash a front kick in the traditional manner, focusing in toward your opponent. As you do so, simultaneously lean your body back at waist level.

What this does is extend the distance between your opponent's body and your own. This allows him less chance to strike you in your upper body or face—the two areas of sanctioned contact in taekwondo sparring matches. Thus, though

Leaning Back Front Kick 1   Leaning Back Front Kick 2

you may well have gained a point, your opponent will have not been provided with the same opportunity.

The Momentum-Driven Front Kick

You now understand the factors that help you to transform a traditional front kick into an advanced front kick. By slightly altering this kick again, you can take it to the next level—making it a truly effective offensive and defensive weapon.

To achieve this, you must initially understand that the front kick is not limited to the range of how far your striking leg can extend from its current positioning. There is no reason in any confrontational situation that you should remain firmly planted and locked into any location. This is the first lesson that the advancing taekwondo practitioner masters in extending the range of the front kick.

Partner training is an ideal method to develop the ability to launch this advanced front-kicking technique. In partner training you are provided with actual human targeting experience. As such, face off with a partner who is several feet in front of you. You are both in fighting stances, with your fists raised. The common tactic is to cautiously move in more closely toward your opponent and then begin the sparring match. Though this type of encounter is common, it is no doubt the quickest way to lose a fight.

Instead of graciously facing off and moving slowly in toward your opponent, why not take advantage of his stationary positioning and use it to your own

The front kick, by its very nature, is a very direct linear kick. It has the ability to readily penetrate your opponent's defenses quickly and easily. It can powerfully shoot in, under your opponent's clinched fists, and deliver a powerful blow to his midsection before he even knows what hit him. This can set the stage for your victory in the confrontation.

advantage? One of the most effective ways of achieving this is by utilizing the momentum-driven front kick.

Though the traditional front kick has little distance or range capability, this same kicking technique can be slightly altered so that you have the ability to gain substantial distance and readily attack your opponent. To achieve this, begin by taking a fighting stance. Ready yourself to perform a front kick. Now, instead of performing this front kick as a stationary technique, as you have done in the past, visualize a target several feet in front of yourself. As you snap your front kick outward, allow the momentum-driven power of this kick to pull your body forward. Do not attempt to control or overbalance yourself during this experience. Simply allow the momentum that your striking leg unleashes to pull you forward, sliding your base foot along the ground. Do not attempt to hinder this forward motion. Let it move you closer in toward your target.

As you practice this momentum-driven front kick, you will come to realize that you can effortlessly travel several feet in toward your opponent without ever losing your balance. This type of front kicking technique not only gives you additional range, but it also gives you additional power. This is so because the force of your body weight is moving in toward your target. Thus, next time you and an opponent face off, immediately drive forward with a momentum-driven front kick, deliver it under his guard, and you will powerfully strike the first blow in the competition.

The Inside Front Kick

A little-known and rarely used technique in the taekwondo front-kicking arsenal is the inside front kick. This kick is performed by bringing your kicking leg slightly in across your body, as you rapidly bring it up into its final target, which is generally the head or under the arm of your opponent. This kick is snapped up at knee level, similarly to the front kick, but instead of moving straight up, as the front kick does, a right leg kick is ideally suited to powerfully impacting the right side of your opponent's head, thus crossing your body.

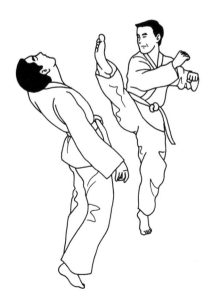

INSIDE FRONT KICK

ROUNDHOUSE KICK

As an offensive tool, the inside front kick is ideally suited to follow a defensive block. For example, once your opponent's oncoming punch has been deflected, you can easily strike him with this kick. The effectiveness of the inverted roundhouse kick comes from the close proximity to your opponent you may find yourself in. At this distance, once his punch has been blocked, you can easily grab his arm or a piece of clothing and lock him into place long enough for the kick to be effectively performed.

The Axe Kick

The axe kick is another very effective offensive weapon in the advanced taekwondo arsenal. This kick is extremely effective in close-quarters infighting. The axe kick is performed by rapidly raising your rear up, in a linear fashion, and then powerfully bringing your heel down onto the shoulder of your opponent. The impact of this kick releases a devastating blow—often to your adversary's shoulder.

The primary method the advanced taekwondo practitioner utilizes to unleash this kick in close quarters infighting is to grab the opponent by his clothing. This will halt his movement for an instant. Then, by immediately lifting your leg and forcefully slamming it into his shoulder, you rapidly disable your opponent.

As a defensive technique, the axe kick is very effective once your opponent has launched a punch. First of all, you must deflect this punch with an in-to-out block. Then by immediately bringing the axe kick up and striking to your opponent's shoulder, you can disable your opponent.

AXE KICK

OUTSIDE AXE KICK

The Stepping Axe Kick

The axe kick is not only very effective in close quarters but becomes equally effective as a rapid and penetrating lead-in technique when it is used in stepping fashion. To perform the kick in this fashion, your base leg rapidly steps behind your kicking leg as you quickly move in toward your opponent. The kicking leg is simultaneously brought up, in vertical fashion, until you achieve appropriate kicking distance, and then you unleash the power of this kick onto your opponent's shoulder.

Not only is the stepping axe kick one of the most powerful kicks in the advanced taekwondo arsenal, but it is also very difficult to defend against, due to the speed in which it is performed. Your opponent only has one option to keep from being attacked by this kick and that is to get out of its way.

The Side Kick

The traditional taekwondo side kick can move from the realms of a relatively ineffective kick to that of an advanced strategic weapon when its execution is slightly altered. As was illustrated in the case of the traditional front kick, simply by allowing your base leg to free itself up, rather than being firmly anchored to the ground, you allow your base leg the ability to slide forward across the floor. From this, the momentum developed by the power of the rear-leg-launched traditional side kick not only adds enormous range to the kick but also increases its power. This is so because the force of your entire body is behind it. Furthermore, by allowing your base leg to be less rigid, you add an enormous amount of speed to this basic kick.

The side kick launched from the front leg is not only a very rapid form of self-defense, but it also will hold the oncoming opponent in his tracks quite effectively.

To illustrate this fact, have a training partner rush in toward you. As a result of side kicking him from your forward leg, and aiming at his rib region, the kick will penetrate underneath his offensive technique. With this, you will initially hold him at bay so that you can continue through with additional counterattacking techniques to achieve victory in the confrontation.

As taekwondo has evolved over the decades traditional kicking techniques such as the side kick and the roundhouse kick have become more linear in their deployment. This is especially the case with the use of these kicks by the advanced practitioner.

The side kick is no longer launched from solely a rear leg position in a slow and deliberate fashion. The newly developed advanced taekwondo side kick witnesses the practitioner bringing his kicking leg up in a very linear front kick fashion. The kick is then unleashed by pivoting the body and bringing the kicking leg in toward its target. Though some of the traditional side power is diminished by delivering the side kick in this fashion, it has become an extremely rapid technique.

SIDE KICK INTERCEPTION

The Stepping Side Kick

One of the most powerful and effective kicks in the advanced taekwondo kicking arsenal is the stepping side kick. This kick is performed by allowing your base leg to rapidly move behind the kicking leg, thus giving you added distance. Your kicking leg is extended in side kick fashion to impact your opponent.

The stepping side is not only rapid and powerful, but defense against it is quite difficult to actualize due to its speed. The only option your opponent may have is to rapidly retreat from it; in which case, you simply continue through with

> The stepping side kick rapidly penetrates your opponent's zone of defense, and by its very design, this kick has the potential to injure anyplace it impacts. Not only is it very effective in tournament fighting, but on the streets the stepping side kick can instantly end the confrontation brought about by a street assailant.

an additional rapid step behind your kicking leg giving you more distance, and then unleash the power of the kick.

The second option for defense against the stepping side kick is equally counterable. In this defense, your opponent may move to one side of the kick. If this occurs, you can effectively link the use of your hands with the taekwondo kick and instantly launch a back fist or straight punch technique, depending on which side of your body your opponent has sidestepped to.

The Back Kick

A similar technique to the side kick, structurally speaking, is the back kick. The back kick is generally highly misunderstood. It is one of the most effective kicks in the taekwondo arsenal—as has been demonstrated in numerous tournaments. The back kick is executed by pivoting your body behind itself on the ball of the foot of your base leg and using your kicking leg, in a turning-around side kick fashion. This kick not only leaves very few vulnerable strike points exposed to your opponent but can also be used in a continual sequence from one back kick, on to the next, and the next, if desired.

The misconception that many practitioners have about the back kick is based on the fact that they are performing it incorrectly. First of all, your head must always pivot first, before the kick is executed, to locate your target before the kick is ever launched. In this way, if your opponent rapidly moves, you can simply alter your kicking technique into a different offensive technique. Second, the back kick is not simply limited to the range that your kicking leg can achieve from its current base positioning. The back kick should be launched deeply into your opponent. This is accomplished by allowing the momentum of the kick itself to extend the entire weight of your body deeply into your target, in a way not dissimilar from the distance-adding technique for the front and side kick, which was previously discussed.

The defense against the back kick is to step to the side or step back. If your opponent steps to the side, the motion of the back kick can continue through to that of a spinning heel kick, which is of course much more elaborate, yet nonetheless can be very effective in this situation. If your opponent continues to retreat backward, the rapid execution of one extended back kick followed by another will eventually target him. Furthermore, the impact of the first back kick may send your opponent reeling back. Continuing through with additional back kicks will no doubt ensure your victory in the confrontation.

The Jumping Front Kick

The jumping front kick is generally the first offensive jumping kick that a taekwondo student is taught. The jumping front kick is traditionally launched by beginning in a fighting stance and then snapping the rear leg forward and up in

The jumping front kick, when delivered in a traditional fashion, is not only a very obvious kicking technique, but it is also a very slow one. The reason the traditional jumping front kick is so obvious and slow is that the rear, nonkicking, leg is launched first and directs the kick upward and forward. This makes this kick very easy to defend against by the competent opponent.

order to gain enough momentum so that one's body is lifted from the ground, allowing the other leg to snap forward in front kick fashion in the air. Though this is the accepted method of delivering this jumping kick, there are many offensive problems with performing the jumping front kick in this fashion.

The traditional jumping front kick is designed to ideally target upward strike locations such as under an opponent's jaw. Because this upward path is the course this kick follows, it possesses an extremely limited range of distance and limited targetability.

Once the traditional jumping front kick has been launched, it is very difficult to redirect its path or implementation. When a traditional jumping front kick is unleashed, a trained opponent possesses the ability to easily see the approach of this oncoming kick. He, thus, will only need to sidestep its path of assault, and the kick will miss. He can then easily deliver a counterstriking measure. The more advanced practitioner can quickly sidestep the onslaught of the traditional jumping front kick and intercept the kicking leg and throw the practitioner to the ground.

Refining the Jumping Front Kick

As you have previously learned, the basic front kick is a very simple, linear technique. It possesses no excess movement and has very direct targeting application. This is the reason it is so fast and so effective in physical combat. If you take the simple approach of the basic front kick and apply its structure to a jumping kick, you will then be able to develop a jumping front kick that is not only very fast but difficult to defend against.

JUMPING FRONT KICK DEFENSE 1

JUMPING FRONT KICK DEFENSE 2

JUMPING FRONT KICK DEFENSE 3

Begin to redevelop your jumping front kick into an advanced taekwondo weapon by taking a fighting stance. Visualize an imaginary target in front of you or position yourself in front of a hanging bag. Launch a basic front kick from your rear leg. Feel how simple and easily this kicking technique is achieved. Now, stand back a little farther from your target and perform the momentum-driven front kick. As previously detailed in this chapter, allow the power of your rear leg to move your base leg along the floor. Again, mentally observe how easily this kicking technique was unleashed.

To take the front kick to the level of a very effective jumping technique, you only need to allow this same power and momentum to drive you upward. To achieve this, locate yourself in front of your target. Ready yourself in a fighting stance. Just as you are about to launch this front kick, allow the knee of your base leg to bend very slightly. Now, kick your rear leg powerfully forward in front kick fashion. Do this, as you simultaneously allow your slightly bent base leg to launch you upward, off the ground. Allow the momentum of this technique to drive you deeply in, forward, toward your target.

What you have achieved is a jumping front kick that does not rely on both legs to give you the momentum to raise your body up off of the ground. With this approach, not only have you simplified the jumping front kick technique, but you have also made it substantially faster and much harder to defend against.

As previously detailed with other taekwondo kicks, whenever you perform a jumping front kick it is very important to remember that you never completely snap out the lower section of your striking leg until you are assured of making powerful contact with your target. This is so because if you snap your kick out before your target is in range, you will expend the power of the kick too early, before you are assured of achieving powerful contact with your opponent.

This style of jumping front kick makes it quite easy to drive in deeply toward an opponent and strike to either his midsection or his face. When you perform the redefined jumping front kick, your opponent's ability to rapidly retreat is greatly lessened, because you are on top of him rapidly, before he has the ability to read your oncoming offensive moves. If, in fact, he does successfully move backward or sidestep your attack, you can land so that you are balanced and enter into a secondary fighting technique very easily. Thus, you will not be unnecessarily bound to only one offensive maneuver.

JUMPING FRONT KICK 1   JUMPING FRONT KICK 2   JUMPING FRONT KICK 3

The advanced jumping front kick is an ideal first-strike weapon against an opponent in competition. This is so because you can rapidly move in on him. It is additionally a very powerful self-defense weapon. For example, your opponent unleashes a roundhouse kick or spinning heel kick toward you. You quickly lean back out of its path so that the kick will miss. The moment the kick has missed is the ideal opportunity to launch a powerful jumping front kick. By doing this, you will immediately make striking contact with your opponent and take control over the competition.

As you now understand, once the nuances of the taekwondo kicks are truly understood, not only can they become much more effective in tournament competition but also they may be put to use victoriously in street combat. Those who criticize their usage either do not have the desire or do not have the ability to practice these effective combat techniques and put them into proper use.

KICKING STRATEGY FOR COMPETITION

At the heart of taekwondo training is the kick. As the kick defines taekwondo, this weapon has come to also define taekwondo competition.

As taekwondo has evolved over the decades, competition has become one of the primary elements of this art. In competition, the advancing taekwondo practitioner is allowed to test his or her skills in the ring against practitioners. With kicking as the center point of taekwondo, it is the competition-orientated kick that must be studied and mastered if one wishes to emerge victorious in taekwondo competition. For this reason, the advancing practitioner continually refines his or her offensive and defensive kicking techniques in order to make them the most efficient weapons possible.

MASTERING THE TAEKWONDO KICK AS A DEFENSIVE WEAPON

To begin to understand how to use the taekwondo kick as a competitive defensive weapon, you must first understand that if you are continually in an offensive posture—hoping to outkick or overpower your opponent, then you will not be able to use your kicks as defensive tools. This overemphasized offensive mindset is prevalent among many modern Olympic-style taekwondo practitioners. They are commonly taught that by kicking and kicking some more, sooner or later they will win the match by points. Though this may be partially true, this competitive ideology also may lead to your being defeated by someone who practices the same competitive strategy and delivers his or her kicks more effectively in any given match. Understanding this, the modern advancing taekwondo stylist can begin to redevelop his or her expansive kicking arsenal and use kicks not only as powerful weapons of offense but also as precise defensive weapons.

Defining the Defensive Kick

When you begin to use the taekwondo kick as a defensive weapon, there are three primary rules that must be observed in order to make your feet effective weapons of defense:

1. The defensive kick must be easy to unleash.
2. The defensive kick must be very fast.
3. The defensive kick must travel to its target in the most expedient manner possible.

THE OFFENSE OF DEFENSE

When a taekwondo kick is used as a defensive weapon, it must be understood that if you possess the opportunity to launch a preemptive kick, such as a front kick to an attacker's solar plexus or a front kick under his chin, then this is your opportunity to land the first strike. From this, you may possibly set the stage for winning the competition. If this option presents itself, you should take advantage of this opening.

This style of defensive offense is not always applicable in sanctioned matches, however. Thus, the science of the defensive taekwondo kick must be studied further to see how it can be used most effectively in all types of competition.

Rule One

The primary rule of the taekwondo defensive kick is that it must be easy to unleash. This is important, for if a kick is complicated or elaborate, it will be too complex to actualize, and your opponent will no doubt deliver his attack to your body before you can intercept it.

Rule Two

The second rule goes hand in hand with the first. Your kick must be very fast. The problem with some of the kicks used in demonstration-oriented taekwondo is that these kicks are very flamboyant and pretty to watch. Their application, however, is very slow. To this end, these kicks must be left behind in competition if you wish to emerge victorious.

Rule Three

The third and final rule of the defensive taekwondo kick is that it must proceed to its target in the most efficient manner possible.

As taekwondo has evolved over the past five decades, its methods of delivering powerful kicking techniques have become more and more refined. Taekwondo has left behind many of the exaggerated kicking movements common to the Japanese martial arts, which influenced taekwondo's early development. What has emerged is fluid, very rapid, linear kicking techniques seen only in this Korean-based martial art. With this evolution, the defensive applications of the taekwondo kick have increased manyfold as the kicks have become much easier to unleash, and due to their linear design, much harder to defend against.

The Taekwondo Forward Side Kick

To come to a better understanding of how the taekwondo kick has evolved, making it much easier to unleash in offensive and defensive applications, we can view the advanced modern taekwondo side kick.

The advanced modern taekwondo side kick is brought straight up, as if a front kick were being launched. Once your leg has reached approximately waist height, your leg is then pivoted at hip level, and the kick is snapped out in side kick fashion. This style of forward side kick can be launched from either your rear or forward leg.

The reason it is important to develop the ability to perform a side kick in this fashion is that it is extremely fast and can be launched from virtually any standing positioning. It does not require that you bring your rear leg up to the side and then pivot your entire body, alerting your opponent to your intentions before you actually deliver the kick—as is the case of the traditional side kick. Instead, you have eliminated many of the unnecessary components of this kick, making it not only easier to unleash but also substantially faster.

| FRONT SIDE KICK 1 | FRONT SIDE KICK 2 | FRONT SIDE KICK 3 |

The Two Styles of Kicking Defense

Once the basic rules of defensive kicking are understood, you can then move on to actually implementing effective defensive kicks in competition. There are two primary methods of defense that the advanced taekwondo practitioner employs while utilizing the kick:

1. The intercepting kick
2. The blocking kick

The Intercepting Kick

The intercepting kick is taekwondo's first line of defensive kicking methodology. In the intercepting kick you drive a defensive kick into your opponent before his kicking or punching attack can be fully actualized.

At the most elementary level, the intercepting kick defense witnesses you delivering a basic front kick, side kick, or roundhouse kick to an open vital strike point on your opponent as he is in the process of launching an aggressive attack toward you. Because targeting is very important with this style of kicking defense, you will want to aim at a location on his body that you are assured of impacting. Furthermore, you will want to target a location that, once you have made contact, will cause his attack to immediately stop. The primary target locations for this style of interceptive kicking defense, in the case of sanctioned taekwondo matches, are the solar plexus, under the chin, and the face.

This style of interceptive kicking counterattack can also be used to intercept the punching assault of your opponent. In this case, you would target a front kick at his inner shoulder—just as he is recoiling to punch. With the impact, not only will his initial attack be halted, but also he will be left open for further counterassault as necessary.

The Intercepting Side Kick

The intercepting side kick is not limited to debilitating first-line kicking counterattacks. For example, an interceptive side kick delivered to the midsection of your attacker will instantly stop any assault he is unleashing.

The defensive intercepting side kick can be most rapidly deployed from your lead leg. This is especially true when your opponent is launching an offensive kicking technique from his rear leg. As his kick rises, you simply deliver a powerful side kick to his side, under his arm, and he will be sent back, often to the ground.

The intercepting side kick is also very effective against the punching assault of an attacker. As his punch is launched, you powerfully deliver a midlevel side kick to his body. His punching attack will be intercepted, due to the fact that not only is the reach of your leg longer than his arm, but it is also substantially more powerful.

The Blocking Kick

The second level of taekwondo's defensive kick is the blocking kick. In this style of defense, you interrupt your opponent's kick by blocking it with a kick of your own. To achieve this, your kick must be faster than your opponent's and halt his attack as close to its point of origin as possible. In this way, his kick will not have gained the necessary momentum to knock you off-balance before you can stop his attack.

The Blocking Side Kick

Delivering a low side kick to the ankle or shin section of your opponent's kicking leg as he attempts to unleash his offensive techniques ideally represents the blocking side kick. This style of defensive kick will immediately interrupt his attack and leave him open to further counterattack.

Follow Up

Once you have intercepted or blocked your opponent's attack with a kicking technique, you must immediately follow up with a secondary counterstrike or his assault will continue. The style of secondary attack you will unleash is predominately defined by the type of kicking defense you initially utilized. For example, if you intercepted an assault with a midlevel side kick to your opponent's stomach or side, then you can immediately use your free hands to deliver a straight punch to his face. If you have blocked his oncoming kick with a side kick to his ankle, you may wish to continue with your kicking defense by immediately retracting your kicking leg and delivering a secondary side kick to a higher level on his body.

The most important thing to remember is that your follow-up technique must occur instantaneously after your initial defensive technique has successfully intercepted your opponent's assault. Additionally, your secondary counterattack must be able to travel rapidly—striking your opponent to a debilitating location, thus, keeping the bout from continuing further.

The advanced taekwondo kick is much more than simply an offensive weapon. When used properly, it can not only aid you in your overall self-defense, but it can also lead you to victory in any physical confrontation.

MASTERING TAEKWONDO'S SPINNING BACK KICKS

The spinning back kicks of taekwondo are not only an advanced offensive weapon but also a strategic defensive tool. Their power is derived from the momentum that is acquired through the spinning of your body and the snapping out of your leg. And, they possess the ability to deliver a very powerful strike, when used correctly, in either offensive or defensive application.

Understanding the Taekwondo Spinning Back Kick

As a strategic weapon, the usage of taekwondo's spinning back kicks is highly effective due to the fact that most confrontational or fighting situations are face-to-face encounters. By spinning and turning, not only have you realigned the fight structure to your own advantage, but you have also created the element of surprise to an unknowing opponent.

In terms of implementation, the most important factor in any of the taekwondo spinning kicks is to keep your eye on the opponent. This is accomplished by pivoting your head before the actual execution of the kick itself. Though this may sound awkward, and you may assume it would give the opponent time to react, this is not the case. For through continued practice, this pivoting of the head first is done so rapidly and naturally that virtually no time elapses between the pivot and the performance of the kick.

The reason it is necessary to pivot your head first, and keep your eyes on your adversary, is that this allows you to watch your opponent for movement from his original positioning. If your eyes are taken off of a competent fighter for very long, he will no doubt move and redirect his location to facilitate his own attack positioning. If this occurs, you must adapt your own offense or defense to be most effective. By keeping your eyes on your opponent, you maintain that ability.

Performing the Spinning Taekwondo Back Kick

Taekwondo's spinning back kick techniques are performed by pivoting on the ball of the foot of your base leg. Pivoting on the ball of the foot keeps the ankle from incurring damage. The knee of the base leg is always slightly bent. This keeps it from hyperextending.

In examining taekwondo's spinning back kicks, we must begin with the most elemental one, which is the straight back kick. Though this may well be the easiest to master, it is still by far one of the most effective kicking techniques in terms of both defense and offense.

The Straight Back Kick

The straight back kick's execution is very similar in style and structure to the common side kick. The difference is that one pivots one's head, then one's body to deliver the kick from the rear, instead of straight from the side as is the case with the standard side kick.

Offensively, the straight back kick, when performed correctly, is one of the most effective aggressive offensive kicking techniques in taekwondo's arsenal. This has been proven time and time again in Olympic competitions.

When used as an offensive mechanism, the kick is performed in a rapid-fire continuation from one straight back kick and to the next, if necessary or desired. One, two, three, or four of these back kicks may be used consecutively with varying legs. This is an excellent method of striking an opponent or driving him back.

The advantages that this kick has is that not only is one's back exposed to the opponent, which allows him little effective space for counterattacking, but also the driving force of the straight back kick, launched generally into the adversary's midsection, is quite a devastating blow.

Off of the Ground

As one progresses in competence with this straight back kicking technique, often it becomes advisable to raise the body up off of the ground while this technique is performed. This is known as the jumping back kick. In essence, to accomplish this, it is the same force of motion that allows the straight back kick itself to be so effective. The momentum of spinning back is added to the thrusting up of the base leg, which then gives one added height for higher striking positioning with this kick.

The raising of one's body from the ground not only aids one in higher impact points on the opponent, but it also allows one the ability to avoid low-level attacks from the opponent in the form of low-sweep kicks and similar techniques.

Proper development of the ability to easily vary a kick from the ground position to a jumping version is very important. The majority of those who perform these jumping techniques use their own exaggerated body momentum or a forced bending down on the base leg knee and then jump up to give the kick more spring to achieve the desired height. Both of these incorrect methods not only alert your opponent to the oncoming jumping, spinning kicking technique, but they also allow these techniques to be easily defended against. This is where much of the aforementioned controversy was born. Therefore, it is imperative to make the jumping versions of any spinning kick as unnoticeable as possible. To develop this ability not only takes dedicated practice of the technique but also the development of certain muscles in the leg and ankle.

The key points of development for the most effective execution of these jumping kicking techniques are the muscles just above the knees and the muscles and tendons surrounding the ankles. It is unnecessary to go into a long discussion of orthopedics and biology; it is quite simple for the practitioner to come to an understanding of how these areas of the body are affected by simply performing the jumping versions of these kicks a few times and then witnessing what part of the body feels the tension.

The quickest and most effective way to strengthen the appropriate muscles so that these advanced taekwondo jumping kicking techniques may be properly developed is to stand next to a wall with your arms stretched upward, on your tip toes, and jump as high as possible, touching the wall with your hands. Do this a few times at first. Then, as your muscles become used to it, increase your practice time. This jumping technique aids in the development of the necessary muscle groups near the knee and strengthens them around the affected ankle tendons.

Through dedicated mirror practice and continued development of the appropriate muscle groups, the jumping versions of taekwondo's spinning back kick can be added to your martial art arsenal and be performed without giving any warning to your opponent.

The Spinning Heel Kick

A close variation of the straight back kick is the spinning heel kick. No doubt this is one of the most powerful and devastating techniques among taekwondo's spinning back kicks. The momentum this kick develops can have a devastating effect on any object that it encounters.

The spinning heel kick is most properly performed by pivoting first your head, then your body. You bend the knee of your kicking leg, make a hook with it, and finally snap it into its final strike with the heel catching your opponent's head or other targeted area. Not only does the movement of your pivot add to the strength of this kick, but also the snapping of the striking leg increases its power immensely.

Keeping the striking leg at least slightly bent upon impact in this kicking technique prevents knee injury. If the kick were to be performed with the striking leg straight, on impact with the target, the knee would be bent against itself, perhaps breaking it.

Though this kick is a devastating technique, as has been proven in numerous taekwondo sparring matches, it still has met with much criticism because many martial artists believe this kick is easily defended against.

SPINNING HEEL KICK

Defending Against the Spinning Heel Kick

Many martial arts systems, including taekwondo, have developed necessary defensive movements to counter the enormous power of this kick. One of the key elements in defense of this technique is to simply step back and out of the way of the onslaught of the spinning heel kick. This is no doubt one of the most effective ways to easily deal with the oncoming spinning heel kick because once this kick has missed, the person performing it continues to spin through with the momentum he has developed, thus leaving himself wide open for a counterstrike. These counterstrikes are as simple as performing a straight front kick to the opponent's midsection or a straight punch to his face. This may instantly change the outcome of the confrontation.

The second and equally effective method of counteracting the power of the spinning heel kick, though this defense is a bit more complicated, is to step inside of the kick's attack. This is accomplished by quickly sliding in close and then behind the opponent who is performing this spinning heel technique.

Because a capable opponent has the ability to step inside of any of these spinning back kicks and thus come around the back and counterstrike the technician who is executing them, yet another case for maintaining eye contact is made. For if this situation arises, you must take further evasive action and position yourself for a counterstrike.

With this deeper understanding of the defensive intricacies of the spinning heel kick, you now understand why you must be able either to alter the strike positioning of the attack or to alter the technique altogether if necessary, in response to your opponent's movements. Though these defensive maneuvers may be the reason that some tend to criticize the spinning heel kick, with proper execution of the technique defense against its power is close to impossible. Furthermore, the competent practitioner, who understands these defensive methods, can counteract them at any moment.

Now that you understand the previous two defensive applications, it is necessary to make sure that your opponent will remain in place when a spinning heel kick is performed. This is accomplished by one of two methods:

The first of these methods is accomplished by allowing your opponent to attack and then deflecting his oncoming punch or kick. Once this has been accomplished, you grab onto him and lightly hold your opponent's limb in place until the kick is fully in progress.

The second method in making the spinning heel kick most effective is to step inside of your opponent's own offensive technique—especially if this is a roundhouse kick or similar type of attack—and launch your spinning heel kick before your opponent's kick has the opportunity to strike. Doing this not only leaves your opponent in the vulnerable position of being halfway through his attack but also ensures that he will not possess the ability to move and change his position. Thus, he is open to taking the full impact of the kick.

As detailed, the spinning heel kick is quite effective as a defensive technique, once the opponent's offense has been neutralized. It is also very effective as an offensive technique. In this application it most efficiently follows a lead-in technique such as a roundhouse kick, straight punch, or back fist. Using one of these techniques first forces your opponent back and hopefully puts him off-balance in the mode of his own counterattack. At this time, while he is locked in this indecisive position, the spinning heel kick easily penetrates his defenses and can deliver a devastating blow.

In combat, the spinning heel kick is almost universally directed at the opponent's head because the strike is executed in this technique with the heel. Though this may cause minor damage to other parts of the opponent's body, such as the chest, the back, or the shoulder, the impact will not be as greatly felt as an impact to the head.

GROUND LEVEL SPINNING HEEL KICK 1

The Ground-Level Spinning Heel Kick

For the advanced practitioner of taekwondo, there is a variation of the spinning heel kick that is sometime brought into play. That is the ground-level spinning heel kick. The ideal use of the ground-level spinning heel kick is to bring an opponent to the ground. To achieve this, the advanced practitioner drops to one knee as he or she is launching the kick. The spinning heel kick is then delivered to the ankles or knees of the opponent, who is sent to the ground from the impact.

The ground-level spinning heel must be delivered in a very rapid and precise movement to make it effective. For this reason, it is only used by the advanced practitioner who has mastered its delivery.

The Jumping Spinning Heel Kick

The taekwondo jumping spinning heel kick has become quite popular, mostly due to its use in many martial art movies. But the taekwondo jumping spinning heel kick is also a very effective advanced kicking technique when it is performed properly.

The common flaw that many have when performing this technique is to physically reveal their intentions to their opponent before the technique is performed. Often it is revealed by pivoting one's body in the opposite direction and then snapping it out in order to gain momentum to raise the body up off the ground. This can be a devastating mistake, because any trained opponent will then see the technique coming.

GROUND LEVEL SPINNING HEEL KICK 2

GROUND LEVEL SPINNING HEEL KICK 3

GROUND LEVEL SPINNING HEEL KICK 4

GROUND LEVEL SPINNING HEEL KICK 5

Key among all of taekwondo's spinning kicking techniques, as discussed earlier, is to not reveal what you are about to do. This is paramount in the case of the jumping spinning heel kick.

The jumping spinning heel kick is slower to execute than the ground-based spinning heel kick, and to be effective, it must not be perceived by the opponent as the technique that is oncoming. There must not be any pronounced movement; it must become quite natural.

To use this kick as an effective offensive or defensive technique, the base leg must become the central point where your body pivots upward and pushes off. The jumping spinning heel kick is properly executed by achieving, through practice, a heightened momentum of the spin standard to the ground-based spinning heel kick and then adding to it the impetus that raises your body up from the ground. This is aided by a slight push upward with the base leg (which has been developed by the appropriate exercises, as discussed earlier).

The jumping spinning heel kick, like all other taekwondo spinning kicks, must have a stationary target in mind or it will not be effective. A trained opponent will not wait for the kick to arrive. Achieving a stationary target is most effectively accomplished when the opponent is in motion with a technique that has just been performed and missed its intended strike point on your body. At that moment, as he is regaining his balance, he is most vulnerable.

JUMPING SPINNING HEEL KICK 1   JUMPING SPINNING HEEL KICK 2

The Spinning Axe Kick

The spinning axe kick is equaled by few other kicking techniques in terms of its ability to penetrate an opponent's defenses. This kick however, is very dangerous because it impacts the opponent's shoulder. This bone is quite easily broken, so all care must be taken when practicing with this technique.

To properly use the spinning axe kick, the opponent must be first trapped or diverted, as discussed with previous kicks, then you pivot your head and body as you raise your striking leg up, then bring the heel forcefully down on your adversary's shoulder.

The more common circular crescent kick—where the striking leg is bent and impact with the opponent is made with the side of the foot not the heel—is not generally used in taekwondo. This kick is believed to leave the knee too vulnerable to damage. The axe kick, though similar, does not pose this threat.

Advancing into the use of the jumping spinning axe kick is similar in application and practice to executing the jumping spinning heel kick. The difference between the two is that the jumping spinning axe kick is performed in much more of a linear fashion. The leg goes up and the heel strikes down. It is much faster and less noticeable than that of the jumping spinning heel kick. It is generally put into practice when the circular structure of the jumping spinning heel kick would either easily be intercepted by the opponent or the fighting situation does not allow for such broad movement.

Through the use of taekwondo's spinning back kick, the advanced taekwondo practitioner learns how, with conscious practice and proper application, one can take these seemingly flamboyant kicking techniques and place them in the realms of usable self-defense.

Part Three
Advanced Taekwondo Techniques

Chapter 7
Poomse: The Foundation of Taekwondo

Forms are one of the most essential elements of taekwondo training. Forms are made up of a prescribed set of defensive and offensive movements. These techniques are put together in an order that will train the beginning and the advanced taekwondo practitioner in methods of how to effortlessly transition from one technique onto the next and the next.

The forms of taekwondo were originally known by the Korean word *kyung*. As time progressed, and the evolution of taekwondo continued, they became known by the Korean word *poomse*.

Many modern practitioners of the combat-orientated styles of the martial arts question the need to practice forms. They feel that these routines are better left to the earlier stages of martial arts development. There are also those advanced taekwondo practitioners who fall away from the practice of forms, believing that they no longer need this seemingly elementary level of training.

In both of these cases, these practitioners are missing the point of forms training. The purpose of forms training is more than simply combat practice. Forms training is a method for the taekwondo practitioner to refine the subtle elements of his or her techniques and, in fact, enter into a higher state of meditative mind while they are being performed. To this end, forms training should never be left behind, even by the most advanced practitioners of taekwondo. As a method of physical and mental technique development and refinement, forms remain an essential part of taekwondo at all levels of expertise.

THE TYPES OF FORMS IN TAEKWONDO

There are two primary sets of forms practiced in taekwondo today. They are the *Chon Ji* and the *Taeguek* forms.

The first set of forms to be formalized in the evolution of taekwondo, in post–World War II Korea, was the Chon Ji set. These forms were devised under the direction of General Choi, Hong Hi. Within this set of forms there are twenty-four patterns. The number twenty-four was used to represent the twenty-four hours in a day—depicting a ever-repeating cycle of life, representing eternity.

The patterns of the Chon Ji system are: *Chon Ji, Dan Gun, Do San, Won Hyo, Yul Gok, Joong Gun, Toi Gye, Hwa Rang, Choong Moo, Kwang Gae, Po Eun, Ge Baek, Eui, Am, Choong Jang, Ju Che, Sam Il, Yoo Sin, Choi Yong, Yong Gae, Ul Ji, Moon Moo, So, San, Se Jong, Tong Il, Saju Jirugi,* and *Saju Makgi.*

The next set of forms to be developed was done so in association with the Korea Taekwondo Association and World Taekwondo Federation. This set was known as the Palgwe system. This system of forms has been left behind, however. And, very few remaining instructors teach it today.

The reason the Palgwe forms were abandoned was that as taekwondo continued to evolve, the leaders of the Korean kwans wanted to move away from the Japanese influence on taekwondo. The Palgwe forms were very close in style and structure to their Japanese predecessors. Therefore, a new set of forms was developed. They are known as the Taeguek forms.

The Korean word *taeguek* means "great eternity" or "great unity of energies." This is also the word used for the South Korean flag. It is believed that these forms most closely define taekwondo as it is practiced today and provide a new cultural and ideological identity to the forms practiced in taekwondo.

TAEGUEK FORMS AND THE I CHING

The Taeguek forms base their structure and movement on the ancient Chinese book of character known as the *I Ching*. The historic foundation of the I Ching can be traced to the third century A.D. in China. During this period a religious sect, Yin Yang Chia, "The Yin and Yang Sect," came into prominence as the central focus of philosophic understanding among the elite and set the standards for religious and philosophic idea dissemination throughout China. This school adopted the ancient Chinese philosophic concept of yin and yang (*um* and *yang* in Korean) and taught that the universe arose from the interplay of these two energies, both on the physical and spiritual level.

YIN AND YANG

Yin and yang literally translated from Chinese means "shade and light." In its most ancient format, yin and yang were used to define the fact of whether or not there was sunlight on the fertile mountain slopes where farming took place. Yang was used to denote the mountain slope that faced the sun and yin to define the slope of the mountain facing away from the sun. As time progressed in ancient China, the concept of yin and yang took on a much more philosophic understanding of defining the polarizing elements of the universe: white and black, positive and negative, light and heavy, female and male, heaven and earth.

The first written document detailing yin and yang occurred in the oracular Chinese text *I Ching*, commonly known as *The Book of Changes*. This text was created in approximately 1100 B.C., during the transition between the Yin and the Chou dynasties. The *I Ching* was one of the few Chinese texts to survive the burning of all ancient manuscripts, ordered by the first historic emperor of China, Chin Shih Huang-ti, in A.D. 213.

The *I Ching* is a text made up of three-line characters, known as trigrams. These characters detail the interplay between yin and yang. The lines that are broken represent yin energy. The lines that are unbroken represent yang energy. These three-line characters are prominent throughout East Asian culture. Four of these symbols appear on the South Korean flag.

There are eight foundational symbols defined in the *I Ching*. From these eight, a total of sixty-four symbols are used as a means of meditation and fortune telling.

Each of the eight primary symbols is understood to possess a specific energy and cosmic understanding. When the forms of taekwondo were devised, these eight primary symbols were used as a means of physical and mental focus for the taekwondo practitioners as they performed the forms.

Taeguek 1—Heaven ☰
In the first form of the Taeguek system the energy of heaven is embraced. Heaven is understood to be the beginning of all creation in this universe. Thus, at this level the practitioner is beginning to walk the path of taekwondo.

Taeguek 2—Inner Firmness and Outer Softness ☱
This form is an expression of the yin and yang—expressing two elements of the universe: strength and elasticity. This form trains the practitioner to be both powerful yet subtle in his techniques.

Taeguek 3—Fire ☲
This form is expressive of sun or fire. Both the sun and fire are powerful vibrant entities, which emanate heat, warmth, and extended power. Just as with the taekwondo practitioner who understands how to unleash focused ki with each technique, this form trains the student how to release power through each technique.

Taeguek 4—Thunder ☳
The power of thunder is released in a rapid burst of powerful energy. This form is designed to train the taekwondo practitioner in using a rapid burst of released energy.

Taeguek 5—Wind ☴
The wind is both a calming and a destructive force in nature. This form trains the practitioner to be both powerful when necessary and relaxed and reflective.

Taeguek 6—Water ☵
Water possesses both a constant flow of softness and a powerful destructive force. This form trains the taekwondo practitioner in how to harness both of these energies.

Taeguek 7—Mountain ☶
This form symbolizes the mountain, because the mountain is firm and long lasting. This form trains the taekwondo practitioner in how to be unmoving.

Taeguek 8—Earth ☷
The earth is the source of all human existence. From the earth, the tree and the plants that feed us grow. Therefore, this form trains the taekwondo practitioner to embrace the source of humanity.

THE BLACK BELT FORMS

At the black belt level the taekwondo practitioner is understood to have mastered the fundamentals of the art. But, there is still much to learn.

Koryo—1st Dan Black Belt

Koryo is the name of the ancient Korean kingdom. Because this is the foundational form in black belt training, its name is in reference to the ancient Korean culture that gave birth to modern taekwondo.

The term Koryo symbolized a wise man that is characterized by a strong spirit and a righteous nature. This is energy that emanates from the practitioner of this form: strength and honor.

Koryo Form
1. Ready position.
2. Pivot left, back stance, double knife hand middle block.
3. Low side kick right leg.
4. High side kick right leg.
5. Right front stance, knife hand middle block right hand.
6. Reverse middle punch left hand.

KORYO 1   KORYO 2   KORYO 3

KORYO 4   KORYO 5   KORYO 6

KORYO 7

KORYO 8

KORYO 9

KORYO 10

KORYO 11

KORYO 12

KORYO 13

KORYO 14

KORYO 15

KORYO 16

KORYO 17

KORYO 18

7. Right back stance, in-to-out fist block.
8. Pivot 180 degrees, right back stance, double knife hand block.
9. Low side kick left leg.
10. High side kick right leg.
11. Left front stance, knife hand middle block left hand.
12. Reverse middle punch right hand.
13. Left back stance, in-to-out block left hand.
14. Pivot 90 degrees to the left, left front stance, knife hand low block left.
15. Reverse circle hand right.
16. Right front kick.
17. Right front stance, knife hand low block right.
18. Reverse circle hand left.
19. Left front kick.
20. Left front stance, low knife hand block.
21. Reverse circle hand right.
22. Right front kick.
23. Right front stance, knee break.
24. In-to-out double middle block.
25. Left front kick.
26. Left front stance, knee break.

KORYO 19 KORYO 20 KORYO 21 KORYO 22

KORYO 23 KORYO 24 KORYO 25 KORYO 26

KORYO 27

KORYO 28

KORYO 29

KORYO 30A

KORYO 30B

KORYO 31

KORYO 32

KORYO 33

KORYO 34

KORYO 35

KORYO 36

KORYO 37A

27. In-to-out double middle block.
28. Pivot to left, back stance, knife hand middle block.
29. Target pull punch.
30. Stepping left side kick.
31. Pivot 180 degrees, right front stance, low knife hand strike.
32. Right walking stance, down block right.
33. Right back stance, circular palm block.
34. Right horse stance, right elbow strike.
35. Knife hand middle block.
36. Target pull punch.
37. Stepping right side kick.
38. Pivot 180 degrees, left front stance, low knife hand strike.
39. Left walking stance, down block.
40. Left back stance, circular palm block.
41. Left horse stance, left elbow strike.
42. Parallel stance, hammer fist.
43. Pivot 180 degrees, left front stance, knife hand strike left.
44. Low knife hand block left.
45. Right front stance, knife hand strike right.

KORYO 37B   KORYO 38   KORYO 39   KORYO 40

KORYO 41   KORYO 42A   KORYO 42B   KORYO 43A

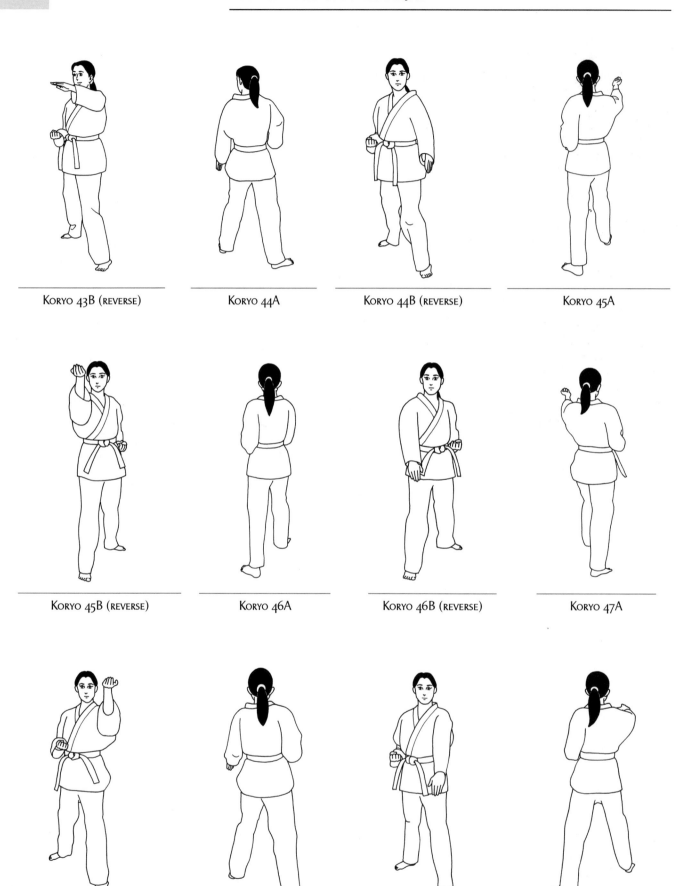

KORYO 43B (REVERSE)   KORYO 44A   KORYO 44B (REVERSE)   KORYO 45A

KORYO 45B (REVERSE)   KORYO 46A   KORYO 46B (REVERSE)   KORYO 47A

KORYO 47B (REVERSE)   KORYO 48A   KORYO 48B (REVERSE)   KORYO 49A

KORYO 49B (REVERSE)	KORYO 50

46. Low knife hand block right.
47. Left front stance, knife hand strike left.
48. Low knife hand block left.
49. Right front stance, circle hand strike right.
50. Ready position.

Keum Gang—2nd Dan Black Belt

The Korean phrase keum gang means "diamond." This form signifies the strength and the beauty possessed by the diamond.

Keum gang is also used in reference to the Keum Gang mountain in Korea. This mountain is considered the central focus of the national spirit of the Korean peninsula. Therefore, the energy emulated in this form is also representative of a quality of balance.

Keum Gang Form
1. Ready position.
2. Left front stance, double in-to-out middle block.
3. Right front stance, palm strike right.
4. Left front stance, palm strike left.

KEUM GANG 1

KEUM GANG 2	KEUM GANG 3	KEUM GANG 4

KEUM GANG 5

KEUM GANG 6

KEUM GANG 7

KEUM GANG 8

KEUM GANG 9

KEUM GANG 10

KEUM GANG 11A

KEUM GANG 11B

KEUM GANG 12

KEUM GANG 13A

KEUM GANG 13B

KEUM GANG 14

5. Right front stance, palm strike right.
6. Left back stance, knife hand middle block left.
7. Right back stance, knife hand middle block right.
8. Left back stance, knife hand middle block left.
9. Pivot 90 degrees left, diamond block, single leg stance.
10. Left horse stance, reverse hook punch left.
11. Pivot 360 degrees, left horse stance, reverse hook punch left.
12. Pivot 90 degrees, left horse stance, high double in-to-out block.
13. Pivot 180 degrees, right horse stance, middle double in-to-out block.
14. Double low block.
15. Pivot 180 degrees, right horse stance, high double in-to-out block.
16. Pivot 90 degrees right, diamond block, single leg stance.
17. Right horse stance, reverse hook punch left.
18. Pivot 360 degrees, left horse stance, reverse hook punch left.
19. Pivot 90 degrees right, diamond block, single leg stance.

KEUM GANG 15A

KEUM GANG 15B

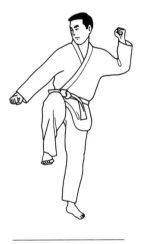

KEUM GANG 16

KEUM GANG 17

KEUM GANG 18A

KEUM GANG 18B

KEUM GANG 19

KEUM GANG 20

KEUM GANG 21A

KEUM GANG 21B

KEUM GANG 22

KEUM GANG 23A

KEUM GANG 23B

KEUM GANG 24

KEUM GANG 25

KEUM GANG 26

KEUM GANG 27

KEUM GANG 28A

KEUM GANG 28B

KEUM GANG 29

20. Right horse stance, reverse hook punch left.
21. Pivot 360 degrees, left horse stance, reverse hook punch left.
22. Pivot 180 degrees, left horse stance, high double in-to-out block.
23. Pivot 180 degrees, right horse stance, middle double in-to-out block.
24. Double low block.
25. Pivot 180 degrees, left horse stance, high double in-to-out block.
26. Pivot 90 degrees left, diamond block, single leg stance.
27. Left horse stance, reverse hook punch right.
28. Pivot 360 degrees, reverse hook punch right.
29. Ready position.

Tae Baek—3rd Dan Black Belt

Tae Baek is a legendary mountain that gave birth to Korean culture. The word *tae baek* actually means "bright light." The Chinese character that is used to symbolize this form is the symbol for the bridge between heaven and earth. The energy in this form is transitional from grounded to ethereal.

Tae Baek Form
1. Ready position.
2. Left cat stance, low double knife hand block.
3. Front kick right.
4. Right front stance, middle punch.
5. Reverse middle punch.

TAE BAEK 1

TAE BAEK 2A

TAE BAEK 2B

TAE BAEK 3

TAE BAEK 4

TAE BAEK 5

TAE BAEK 6A   TAE BAEK 6B   TAE BAEK 7   TAE BAEK 8

TAE BAEK 9   TAE BAEK 10   TAE BAEK 11   TAE BAEK 12

TAE BAEK 13   TAE BAEK 14   TAE BAEK 15   TAE BAEK 16

6. Pivot 180 degrees, right cat stance, low double knife hand block.
7. Front kick left.
8. Left front stance, middle punch.
9. Reverse middle punch.
10. Pivot 90 degrees, left front stance, knife hand high block.
11. Reverse palm hand block right.
12. Right front stance, reverse middle punch left.
13. Reverse palm hand block left.
14. Left front stance, reverse middle punch right.
15. Reverse palm hand block right.
16. Right front stance, reverse middle punch left.
17. Pivot 90 degrees, left back stance, diamond middle block left.
18. Pull and reverse uppercut left.
19. Left horse stance, side punch left.
20. Left side kick.
21. Left front stance, elbow strike right.
22. Pivot 180 degrees, right back stance, diamond middle block right.
23. Pull reverse uppercut right.
24. Right horse stance, side punch right.

| TAE BAEK 17 | TAE BAEK 18 | TAE BAEK 19 | TAE BAEK 20 |

| TAE BAEK 21 | TAE BAEK 22 | TAE BAEK 23 | TAE BAEK 24 |

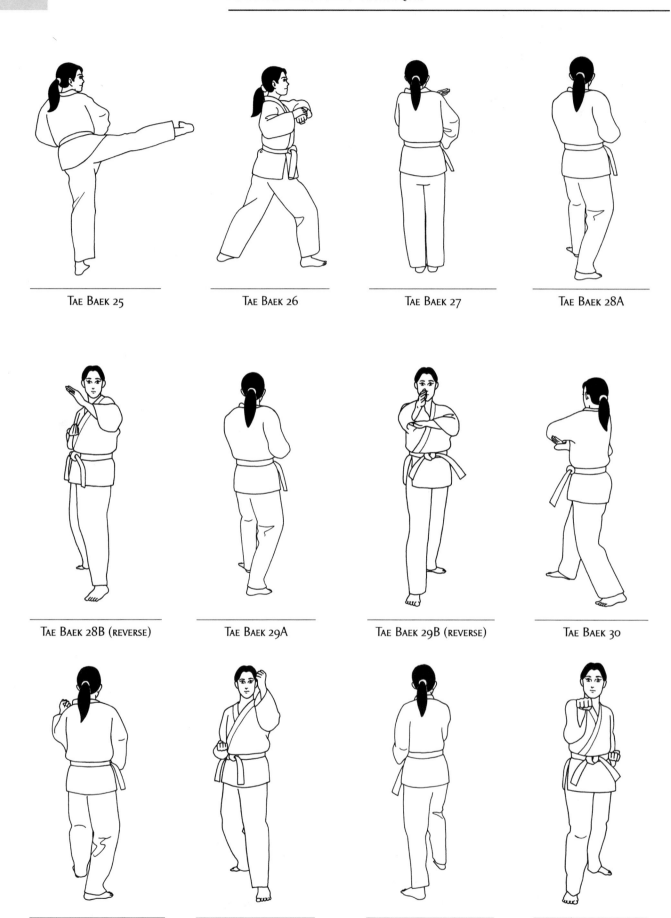

TAE BAEK 25

TAE BAEK 26

TAE BAEK 27

TAE BAEK 28A

TAE BAEK 28B (REVERSE)

TAE BAEK 29A

TAE BAEK 29B (REVERSE)

TAE BAEK 30

TAE BAEK 31A

TAE BAEK 31B (REVERSE)

TAE BAEK 32A

TAE BAEK 32B (REVERSE)

25. Side kick right.
26. Right front stance, elbow strike left.
27. Pivot 90 degrees, feet together.
28. Left back stance, knife hand middle block left.
29. Right front stance, knife hand thrust.
30. Back stance right, spear hand and back fist strike.
31. Left back stance, side fist strike.
32. Right front stance, middle punch.
33. Pivot 90 degrees, left front stance scissor block.
34. Front kick right.
35. Right front stance, middle punch right.
36. Reverse middle punch left.
37. Pivot 180 degrees, right front stance, scissor block.
38. Front kick left.
39. Left front stance, middle punch left.
40. Reverse middle punch right.
41. Ready position.

TAE BAEK 33

TAE BAEK 34

TAE BAEK 35

TAE BAEK 36

TAE BAEK 37

TAE BAEK 38

TAE BAEK 39

TAE BAEK 40

TAE BAEK 41

Pyong Won 4th—Dan Black Belt

The Korean word *pyong won* means "vast plain." On this plain there are under-stood to be all forms of life. From this interaction comes a struggle for survival. Therefore, the energy visualized by the practitioner of this from is used to invoke supremacy over struggle, brought about by concentration, a dedicated focus.

Pyong Won Form
1. Ready position.
2. Standing position, double low knife hand block.
3. Push the mountain.
4. Pivot 90 degrees, right back stance, knife hand low block right.
5. Pivot 180 degrees, left back stance, knife hand middle block left.
6. Left front stance, reverse elbow strike right.
7. Left front kick.
8. Pivot 360 degrees, spinning side kick left.
9. Pivot 90 degrees, right back stance, knife hand middle block right.
10. Right back stance, knife hand low block right.

| PYONG WON 1 | PYONG WON 2A | PYONG WON 2B | PYONG WON 3 |

| PYONG WON 4 | PYONG WON 5 | PYONG WON 6 | PYONG WON 7 |

11. Horse stance, double hand middle block right.
12. Pivot horse stance to front, side fist right.
13. Side fist left.
14. Cross stance, double elbow strike.
15. Stepping right horse stance, double hand high block.

PYONG WON 8A

PYONG WON 8B

PYONG WON 9

PYONG WON 10A

PYONG WON 10B

PYONG WON 11

PYONG WON 12A

PYONG WON 12B

PYONG WON 13

PYONG WON 14

PYONG WON 15A

PYONG WON 15B

PYONG WON 16   PYONG WON 17   PYONG WON 18   PYONG WON 19

PYONG WON 20A   PYONG WON 20B   PYONG WON 21   PYONG WON 22A

PYONG WON 22B   PYONG WON 23   PYONG WON 24   PYONG WON 25

16. One leg stance, diamond block right.
17. Side kick right.
18. Right front stance, reverse elbow strike.
19. Front kick left.
20. Pivot 360 degrees, spinning side kick right.
21. Left back stance, knife hand middle block.
22. Knife hand low block.
23. Horse stance, double hand middle block left.
24. Pivot horse stance to front, side fist left.
25. Side rist right.
26. Horse stance, double hand high block left.
27. One leg stance, diamond block left.
28. Side kick left.
29. Right front stance, elbow strike right.
30. Ready position.

PYONG WON 26A   PYONG WON 26B   PYONG WON 27

PYONG WON 28   PYONG WON 29   PYONG WON 30

Sip Jin—5th Dan Black Belt

The Korean word *sip jin* means "decimal." This form details the ten factors that bring about longevity: the sun, the moon, the mountains, water, stones, the pine tree, the secret herb of eternal youth, the tortoise, the deer, and the crane. This combination is made up of two heavenly bodies, three natural resources, two plants, and three animals.

The Chinese character that symbolizes this form is the straight line. This signifies ceaseless development. Therefore, the energy of this form signifies the bringing together of all the essential elements of life and releasing them in the form of ceaseless energy.

Sip Jin Form

1. Ready position.
2. Standing stance, overhead mountain block.
3. Pivot 90 degrees, left back stance, hand-supported middle block left.
4. Left front stance, reverse knife hand thrust right.
5. Knife hand thrust right.
6. Middle punch left.
7. Reverse middle punch right.
8. Swing rear leg forward into horse stance, overhead mountain block.
9. Walking horse stance, side punch right.

SIP JIN 1   SIP JIN 2A   SIP JIN 2B   SIP JIN 3

SIP JIN 4   SIP JIN 5   SIP JIN 6   SIP JIN 7

10. Pivot 180 degrees, double elbow strike.
11. Right front stance, hand-supported middle block right.
12. Right front stance, knife hand thrust right.
13. Reverse knife hand thrust left.
14. Middle punch right.

SIP JIN 8

SIP JIN 9A

SIP JIN 9B

SIP JIN 10

SIP JIN 11A

SIP JIN 11B

SIP JIN 12

SIP JIN 13

SIP JIN 14

SIP JIN 15

SIP JIN 16

SIP JIN 17

SIP JIN 18

SIP JIN 19A

SIP JIN 19B (REVERSE)

SIP JIN 20 (REVERSE)

SIP JIN 21 (REVERSE)

SIP JIN 22 (REVERSE)

SIP JIN 23

SIP JIN 24 (REVERSE)

SIP JIN 25 (REVERSE)

15. Reverse middle punch left.
16. Pivot 90 degrees, horse stance, mountain block.
17. Horse stance side punch left.
18. Pivot 180 degrees, double elbow strike.
19. Pivot 90 degrees, right back stance, middle block right.
20. Left front stance, knife hand thrust right.
21. Reverse knife hand thrust left.
22. Middle punch right.
23. Reverse middle punch left.
24. Left back stance, knife hand low block.
25. Right front stance, boulder push.
26. Pivot 90 degrees, horse stance, double knife hand middle block.
27. Double knife hand down block.
28. Clinched fists.
29. Pivot 90 degrees, left front stance, boulder push.
30. Right front kick.
31. Right front stance, middle punch.
32. Left front kick.
33. Left front stance, middle punch.

| SIP JIN 26 | SIP JIN 27 | SIP JIN 28 | SIP JIN 29 |

| SIP JIN 30 | SIP JIN 31 | SIP JIN 32 | SIP JIN 33 |

34. Right front kick.
35. Cross leg stance, overhead fist.
36. Pivot 180 degrees, left front stance, boulder push.
37. Low knife hand cross block.
38. Right back stance, knife hand middle block.
39. Left stepping stance, two-fisted punch.
40. Right stepping stance, two-fisted punch.
41. Ready position.

| SIP JIN 34 | SIP JIN 35 | SIP JIN 36 (REVERSE) | SIP JIN 37 |

| SIP JIN 38 | SIP JIN 39 | SIP JIN 40 | SIP JIN 41 |

Ji Tae—6th Dan Black Belt

The Korean phrase *ji tae* is representative of a man standing on the ground with his eyes fixed on the sky. This form symbolizes a person fighting for existence but with his or her mind on the higher good. Therefore, the energy focused upon while performing this for is positive energy for overcoming human struggle.

Chon Kwon—7th Dan Black Belt

The Korean phrase *chon kwon* means "great heaven." This word is representative of the origin of the universe from which all energy and humanity arise from. The energy of this form, therefore, is representative of this vast universal energy.

Hansu—8th Dan Black Belt

Hansu means "water." As water represents universal flow, the energy of this form depicts this neverending, continuous movement.

Il Yeo—9th Dan Black Belt

The Korean phrase *il yeo* represents the thought of the legendary Buddhist priest of the Silla Dynasty, Saint Wonhyo. He is considered the ideal illustration of Buddhahood. He is understood to have possessed a oneness with this universe. This final form of the black belt level is designed to have the advanced taekwondo practitioner become one with the moves of this form and ultimately reach a oneness with self and the universe.

Chapter 8
Training Methods

Through training in taekwondo practitioners continue to hone their skills, develop new mastery of their body, and refine their combative skills to exacting levels. In the early stages of training, a taekwondo student is taught the fundamentals of the art: the basic blocking, punching, and kicking techniques. As one progresses through the ranks of taekwondo, these foundational elements are never left behind. An advancing taekwondo practitioner continues to practice all techniques from the most basic onward, in order not only to gain new understandings and new mastery of each technique but also to build upon these foundations and become a more competent practitioner of the art.

An essential rule to all taekwondo practitioners is, "There is no advanced practitioner who was not once a beginner. In some schools of taekwondo this statement is recited at the beginning of each class. This is done in order not only to make the novice student understand that the practice of taekwondo causes each individual to continually grow in the art, but also to remind the advanced practitioner that he too was once a novice. He must continually remind himself of this fact in order not to let the ego of advancing rank take hold of him and make him falsely believe that there is no more to learn.

The process of advancing in taekwondo is accomplished by continually working from the most basic techniques onward. This is what has caused this art to evolve over the decades and become one of the most sophisticated systems of self-defense on the planet. If the masters of this art had not traced each technique back to its roots, advancing and redefining each movement, taekwondo would have stagnated and not evolved.

Each advancing practitioner must employ this same philosophy. Each technique must be practiced, repracticed, and refined, not only be performed in the way dictated by the art. Each technique must be mastered and uniquely understood by each advancing practitioner. From this, the advanced taekwondo practitioner will come to intuitively understand how his or her own body can unleash each technique in the most effective manner possible.

By continually practicing and refining each technique, the advancing tae-kwondo practitioner is also able to view what techniques his or her own body can most easily and effectively execute, because each person's body has a unique set of parameters. Each individual's size, the length of his or her limbs, muscle mass, and elasticity are all different. Advancing practitioners come to understand that though they practice and continue to develop each technique in the taekwondo arsenal, there will be some that they will be able to do with ease, while there will be others that they will be not able to perform with absolute certainty. This too is the process of advancing in taekwondo—knowing what techniques you can and cannot perform.

In order to continue ongoing development, the advancing taekwondo prac-titioner begins to utilize more and more exacting training methods in order to fine-tune his or her skills. The basic practices of unleashing the fundamental tech-niques are never left behind; they are simply integrated with more refined meth-ods of personal development.

The training drills that follow are advanced methods by which the tae-kwondo practitioner can gain cardioaerobic conditioning, while also training the body in timing, focus, and impact skills. Each drill is designed to work with a spe-cific technique or a specific set of techniques in order to allow the advancing tae-kwondo practitioner to gain new skills and new areas of personal realization about the art of taekwondo.

SOLO TRAINING DRILLS

Solo Training Kicking Drills are ideal methods for you to train your body and mind in the subtle realms of taekwondo's offensive combat. Not only are they an ideal means for you to maintain your cardioaerobic conditioning, but also, through their performance, you take your taekwondo kicking mastery to a new level. As you perform these techniques, your body and mind form a new compre-hension, and you allow yourself to become a more refined practitioner. From these techniques, you expose yourself to new and unique methods of unleashing the taekwondo kick. With this, you master new methods of taekwondo kicking that may be used in specific realms of combat. Solo training kicking drills are an ideal method to hone your kicking skills while you keep your body trained and focused.

The Four Point Kicking Drill

To perform The Four Point Kicking Drill you begin in a fighting stance with your focus directly in front of you. When you feel that you are centered and your foundation is strong you begin by unleashing a front kick toward an imaginary target directly in front of you. (See Four Point Kicking Drill 1.)

The front kick is performed by launching your rear leg forward, by rapidly raising the knee of your striking leg up to approximately your hip level. The lower section of your striking leg is then immediately snapped outward in the direction of the kicking target. The front kick's power is developed by a combination of upper-leg muscle strength and lower-leg snapping momentum. The impact of the front kick is made with the ball of your foot. The ideal strike points for a front kick are your opponent's shins, his groin, his solar plexus, under his jaw or his face. (See Four Point Kicking Drill 2 and 3.)

Once this front kick has been unleashed, you do not immediately place your leg down in front of you or retract it to its original position, as is the case when this kick is performed as a solo technique. Instead, you retract the lower half of your kicking leg and leave it elevated from the ground. You now look to your right side, locate an imaginary target, and immediately launch a side kick directly to your right side. (See Four Point Kicking Drill 4.)

The side kick is performed by shifting 75 percent of your body weight to your forward base leg as your rear striking leg raises up with a bent knee to waist level. As your striking leg rises, you pivot on the ball of your base foot 180 degrees, as the hip of your striking leg turns toward its target. Your body leans sideways toward the ground as your striking leg is extended toward your target. Impact is made with the heel or outside ridge of your foot.

When the side kick is unleashed in this training drill, you simply allow it to be launched directly from where you are standing. Thus, you do not have to pivot excessively on the ball of your foot. You simply allow your side kick to strike outward directly to your side.

As in the case with the previous front kick, you do not plant your kicking leg on the ground once your kick has been completed. Instead, you retract it to a cocked position and hold it up from the ground.

You now train your focus to your left side. You visualize your imaginary target. By pivoting slightly on the ball of the foot of your base leg, you unleash a front kick to your left side. You retract the kick, holding your leg suspended in the air.

You now look over your right shoulder. You see your imaginary target and you unleash a back kick. (See Four Point Kicking Drill 5A and 5B (Reverse).)

The back kick is structurally similar to the side kick. It is executed by first turning your head around behind yourself, thus, keeping an eye on your target. This head turning is performed as you simultaneously pivot your body on the ball of the foot of your lead base leg 180-degrees. Your kicking technique is then launched from rear leg positioning—in side kick fashion.

The back kick is a muscle-driven technique. In this kick impact is made with the heel or the outside ridge of your foot. The ideal targets for the back kick are your opponent's knee, his midsection, or his head.

Once your back kick has been unleashed, you return to your forward position, place your kicking leg on the ground behind your forward leg, and return to a ready fighting stance.

Once you have initially performed this drill, you will want to rest and take conscious notice of your body's placement and how well you performed each technique. It is essential that when you begin to train with this drill you do not simply unleash these basic kicks and assume that you are performing them correctly. As an advancing practitioner of taekwondo, you must master the subtle elements of all aspects of the basic kicks and of the training drill, which will allow you to reach the master level of performance. If you simply perform any technique with the necessary consciousness assigned to it, you may continue on your path as a better practitioner, but you will never reach the level of a master because a master is acutely conscious of each movement associated with each technique. To this end, you must continually make conscious appraisals of each and every offensive and defensive movement you perform. Training drills are no different.

Once you have taken stock of your initial performance in association with this training drill, you will want to perform it again. Upon its completion, again, you will want to assess your performance. You should then perform it for a third time.

Once you have performed three sessions with The Four Point Kicking Drill, shift sides and perform it for three sessions using your other leg as the primary kicking tool. Between each performance, assess your competence with the technique, retune your kicks, and unleash the drill in a more refined manner.

As you perfect this drill, you can increase the speed at which it is performed and the number of times you perform in succession. Ultimately, you will want to reach a point where you can perform this drill ten times with each leg in a rapid and very conscious manner.

FOUR POINT KICKING DRILL 1   FOUR POINT KICKING DRILL 2   FOUR POINT KICKING DRILL 3

FOUR POINT KICKING DRILL 4   FOUR POINT KICKING DRILL 5A   FOUR POINT KICKING DRILL 5B
                                                                              (REVERSE)

Benefits

The primary benefit of The Four Point Kicking Drill is that your keep your body in a constant state of movement while unleashing the four kicks associated with this drill. This trains your body and your mind to rapidly be able to shift from one technique to the next and the next and the next. As physical combat and competition are virtually never limited to one offensive technique, it is essential that your body learns to move rapidly from one technique onto the next. This drill is a great tool in training your body to do just that.

Precautions

While performing The Four Point Kicking Drill, you must remain very conscious of two things. The first is your focus. As is the case with all kicking drills, it is common for the practitioner to simply unleash a kick in a random, haphazard manner—allowing the kick to simply be as high as the individual's stretch and allowing the leg to go by the power developed by the unleashing of the kick. This style of training is not only detrimental to the body, because it can cause muscle tearing, but it also does little to focus and develop the precision of the advancing taekwondo practitioner. For this reason, it is essential that one remain vigilante in the focus of each kicking technique unleashed in association with this drill. You must focus on an imaginary target and then drive each kick as closely toward this target as possible.

The second precaution that must be observed while performing this drill is that you should not simply randomly cause your kicking leg to cross your body—driven solely by momentum. Because the kicks associated with this training drill are unleashed in four unique manners, each technique must be performed with a very conscious focus on your body and how it is reacting to each technique. If you do not remain vigilant through this process, you might damage you joints, which is to no one's advantage.

Therefore, as with all advanced taekwondo training drills, you must perform each technique as consciously as possible. From this, you will not only gain new mastery of the techniques of this art, but you will also become a more refined practitioner.

The Forward Slide Side Kick Drill

The side kick is one of the most essential tools in the taekwondo arsenal of self-defense. The side kick is performed by initially shifting 75 percent of your body weight to your forward base leg as your rear striking leg raises up with a bent knee to waist level. As your striking leg rises, you pivot on the ball of your base foot 180 degrees, as the hip of your striking leg turns toward its target. Your body leans sideways toward the ground as your striking leg is extended toward your target. Impact is made with the heel or outside ridge of your foot.

To perform the Forward Slide Side Kick Drill, you begin by taking a fighting stance. When you are ready to begin the drill, you unleash your first side kick to an imaginary target directly in front of you. In the the traditional side kick, you anchor your base leg to the ground as the side kick is performed. While performing this drill, however, you allow the momentum that this forward-driven, linear kick initiates to drag your base foot slightly forward along the ground. This motion causes you to transverse a bit more distance than this kick commonly covers.

Upon the completion of the traditional side kick, you would immediately lower your kicking leg and place it down directly in front of you. In the Forward Slide Side Kick Drill, however, instead of placing your kicking leg on the ground, you simply lower into a half-cocked position.

At the point where you have reestablished your balance, you immediately launch a side kick for the second time. Again, allowing your base foot to be dragged slightly forward along the ground. How many repetitions you actually perform with this kicking drill and how far you actually travel is solely defined by your personal level of balance and how much space you have to practice.

All advanced taekwondo kicking drills are designed not only to refine your kicking arsenal but also to make you a more balanced and focused practitioner. Therefore, when you perform this kicking drill, it is essential that you do not simply throw a side kick wildly into the air, allowing it to strike at any point your momentum and personal body elasticity will allow it to travel to. Every technique must be performed with precision. To this end, as you unleash each kick in this training drill, it must be focused upon an imaginary target in front of you. You must then drive the kick to encounter that imaginary target. If you do not perform the training drills in this exacting manner, you are not truly taking advantage of the precise knowledge of body dynamics and offensive focusing that they have to offer.

When you begin to practice this exercise, you should also not simply unleash one sliding side kick after the next until you either fall down from lack of balance or reach the end of your training area. After you unleash the first kick, you must retract your leg and take very conscious notice of your balance and how the kick felt when it was unleashed—how precise was your targeting and how effectively did you perform the side kicking technique? Once you have reached your conclusion, only then do you perform the second and third kicking element of this exercise.

When you perform the Forward Slide Side Kick Drill, it is essential that you perform it first with one of your legs as the kicking element of this technique and then with your other leg. Even though it is natural that you will be more powerful and precise with the dominant side of your body, you must perform all training drills utilizing both sides of your body to develop your kicking techniques into becoming the most powerful and acutely focused weapons that they can be.

Benefits

The Forward Slide Side Kick Drill is an ideal method to train your body to move toward your opponent, utilizing the least amount of expended energy and meeting your opponent with the most excessive amount of force possible. This drill ideally trains your body to continue forward with a side kicking technique, even if your opponent is retreating.

As is universally understood in taekwondo, "No energy should be wasted." This training drill allows you to come to understand how to keep your body moving forward with the power and the momentum of your offensive techniques. By allowing your body to continue moving forward with the technique you have unleashed, you will not need to resettle, reform, and redesign a secondary technique if your opponent moves slightly out of the range of your oncoming side kick. If your opponent remains in place, this kicking drill trains your body to unleash added force with your side kicking techniques. You allow your body to move in slightly closer; thereby, the unleashed power of your side kick is magnified because you are closer to your opponent when it is unleashed.

Precautions

The Forward Slide Side Kick Drill causes your body to move forward with your own developed momentum. As you continue to master this training drill, you will be able to move forward over greater distances. In the initial stages of training with the techniques, however, your body may not be accustomed to moving forward in this manner, and you may unconsciously lock your knee in place.

As is always the case with all advanced kicking techniques in taekwondo, the knee of both your base leg and your kicking leg should remain slightly bent to keep the knee from locking in against itself. This is especially true with a momentum-driven kicking drill. Therefore, when you begin to practice the Forward Slide Side Kick Drill, only allow your body to be driven forward is small increments. Do not attempt to allow the momentum of your kick to drag you forward in an unnatural, unbalanced manner because this will increase the possibility of damaging your knee.

Supplement

You can add to your training in the Forward Slide Side Kick Drill by adding one or two additional side kicks to each segment of the drill. This is to say, you can begin by launching a low side kick, then a midlevel side kick, and finish off with a high side kick as you slide in toward your next location. By making the Forward Slide Side Kick Drill a three-part exercise, not only do you add additional side kick targeting to your routine, but you also refine your side kick targeting ability.

The Forward Slide Roundhouse Kicking Drill

As is the case with the side kick, detailed in the previous training drill, the roundhouse kick is another essential element in the taekwondo arsenal of self-defense. The roundhouse kick is launched from your rear leg. It is directed, in a circular fashion, from its point of origin to its target. This movement is accomplished by pivoting 180 degrees on the ball of the foot of your base leg, as the kick continues to travel toward its target. The roundhouse kick is a muscle- and momentum-driven weapon. Power is added to it with a snapping out of your knee, just before the kick has reached its impact point. Impact with the roundhouse kick is made with the instep or ball of the foot.

In the Forward Slide Roundhouse Kicking Drill, you entering into a fighting stance as you ready yourself for this technique. Once you are centered and feel you are ready, you begin this technique by launching your roundhouse kick. Normally, when a roundhouse kick is launched, your kicking leg is either rapidly placed down directly in front of your body or it is retracted and placed in its original rear leg positioning. With this drill, however, the kick is not performed in this manner.

To perform the Forward Slide Roundhouse Kicking Drill, you unleash your roundhouse kick. There are two important elements to this training drill that are not employed when the taekwondo basic roundhouse kick is unleashed. First of all, when you unleash a traditional roundhouse kick, the common method of practice is to allow your kick to travel though your imaginary opponent. In this way, you are assured of developing appropriate momentum and power to penetrate any object that is struck by this kick. When practicing this drill, however, your roundhouse kick is not driven through your imaginary target, because this would result in your kicking leg needing to reestablish itself on the ground before a secondary kick could be launched.

In this training drill, your roundhouse kick is launched at your imaginary target. Instead of passing though it, your kick is only guided to meet this placement.

The second element to this training drill, which is in contrast to the execution of the traditional roundhouse kick, is that instead of locking your base leg to the ground, you allow the momentum this kick develops to move you forward—causing your base foot to slide slightly forward. In addition, as detailed, while practicing this training drill you do not return your kicking leg to the ground once your kick has been completed. Instead, you simply retract it to a cocked positioning, held in midair.

Once you have unleashed the initial roundhouse kick, associated with this kicking drill, you must remain standing on one leg and reset your balance before you launch a secondary kick. Once you feel that you have regained your footing, launch a secondary kick. With this kick, as with the previous example, allow your base foot to be dragged slightly forward along the ground.

As you begin this training drill, perform the roundhouse kick three to five times in a very slow and controlled manner on each side of your body. This will allow your body to become naturally accustomed to this drill and will cause your body to become aware of the amount of balance you will need while performing this technique.

This method of initial warm-up should be performed no matter how many times you have performed this training drill. As every advanced practitioner of taekwondo understands, warming up is the most essential method for keeping your body free from injury.

Once you have performed the warming-up stage of this training drill several times, you may then increase the speed of the drill and the power with which your kicking technique is unleashed. How many repetitions you actually perform with this kicking drill and how far you travel will be defined by your personal level of cardioaerobic endurance and balance, and how much space you have to practice.

The Forward Slide Roundhouse Kicking Drill is designed as a method for you to train your body and mind to gain an enhanced sense of balance and body dynamics. Because this is a very exacting training drill, it is essential that you focus on an imaginary target and cause your foot to strike it.

It is common for novice students of taekwondo to attempt to drive their kick as high in the air as their current state of stretching allows the kicking leg to travel. Though this is a common practice, it is not a good practice. By performing any technique in this manner, you are not taking control over the technique; it is taking control over you. At the advanced level of taekwondo, this method of training cannot be employed because it does not lead to the overall refinement of your offensive and defensive techniques. Therefore, when you perform the Forward Slide Side Kicking Drill, focus your kicks on a target that is naturally reachable with your kicking leg. By performing the drill in this fashion, not only do you heighten your level of focus expertise, but also you come to understand what level of technique your body is most comfortable at. By understanding this, you will not be prone to unleashing unnatural techniques during combat, which may well not only result in your being defeated but possibly also cause self-injury to your body.

Benefits

As with the case of the Forward Slide Side Kicking Drill, The Forward Slide Roundhouse Kicking Drill trains your body to move in a forward-driven pattern, while maintaining control over your kick. Whereas the side kick is a linear tool of offense, the roundhouse kick bases its energy on circular energy. This kicking drill therefore trains your body and mind in the method of isolating circular energy and converting it to linear movement. As with the case of The Forward Slide Side Kicking Drill, this drill teaches you to bring your fighting techniques in closer to your opponent, without the need to restructure and redefine your offensive attack if your opponent retreats.

Precautions

When you begin to perform The Forward Slide Roundhouse Kicking Drill, upon completion of your first kick, you will undoubtedly sense that your body is not fully balanced as you remain with your leg suspended in the air. You should never perform any taekwondo technique if your body is not in a state of balance, as this may cause you to bring unnecessary injury to your body. It is very easy to become unconsciously wrapped up in the moment when performing a training drill such as the Forward Slide Roundhouse Kicking Drill. You may assume that you are balanced, when you are not. This may cause you to injure your knee because of the momentum-driven nature of this kick or it may cause you to fall to the ground. Therefore, it is essential that you perform this training drill in a slow and controlled manner, until you have mastered the subtle elements of this technique.

Supplement

Just as in the case of the Forward Slide Side Kicking Drill, you can add additional kicks to your training regimen with The Forward Slide Roundhouse Kicking Drill. You can begin by launching a low roundhouse kick to the approximate level of an opponent's knee. You can then follow through with a high roundhouse kick as your momentum causes you to move forward. If you desire, you can also add a midlevel roundhouse kick to this training before you finish off with your high roundhouse kick.

With each additional kick, you add additional movements to your routine. Not only does this cause you to keep your heart rate up, thereby giving you additional cardioaerobic stimulation, but you also hone your skills in multiple-kick methodology.

The Repeated Spinning Roundhouse Kicking Drill

The roundhouse kick is launched from your rear leg. It is directed, in a circular fashion, from its point of origin to its target. This movement is accomplished by pivoting 180 degrees on the ball of the foot of your base leg, as the kick continues to travel toward its target.

The roundhouse kick is a muscle- and momentum-driven weapon. Power is added to it with a snapping out of your knee, just before the kick has reached its impact point.

Impact with the roundhouse kick is made with the instep or ball of the foot. The roundhouse kick is ideally targeted at your opponent's knee, thigh, midsection, or head.

The Repeated Spinning Roundhouse Kicking Drill witnesses you launching four consecutive roundhouse kicks from one location. To achieve this, you must allow your body to pivot freely on the ball of the foot of your base leg. This will take some practice, because the taekwondo practitioner normally performs this kick in a much more stable fashion, due to the power this kick is able to release.

The Repeated Spinning Roundhouse Kicking Drill begins by your taking a fighting stance. You focus on an imaginary target directly in front of you. When you are ready, you launch your first roundhouse kick—targeted at this imaginary focal point directly in front of you. Now, instead of placing your leg down directly in front of you, as is the case when you normally practice this kicking technique, you instead retract your leg to half-kick position.

Once you have found your balance in this position, you launch a secondary roundhouse kick across your body. This roundhouse kick is directed to an imaginary target directly to your side. To accomplish this, you must allow the ball of the foot of your base leg to pivot in a less-anchored fashion than when this kick is normally performed. Once this roundhouse kick has been performed, you again retract your leg to a half-kick position and regain your balance. A roundhouse kick is then immediately launched toward what has now become your side. Once this kick is completed, you again find your balance, and you launch your final roundhouse kick to your side.

As you begin to master this training drill, the rapidness of unleashing each kick will naturally increase. It is essential at the beginning stages of practicing this technique that you perform it in a very conscious and precise manner. Because, as any advancing taekwondo practitioner understands, it is essential to maintain control and focus with each kicking technique. You must always control a kick as opposed to letting the power or momentum of the kick control you. To this end, in the beginning stages of training with this kicking drill, you must very consciously unleash each kick and then very precisely bring your leg back to ready position before you continue forward with the next stage of this training drill.

When you begin training with this solo kicking drill, you should begin with one full set before you come back to your original position and rest. This means that you will launch the roundhouse kick into its full position and then return to your beginning location and rest in your fighting stance. Upon retuning to your original position, you will want to take conscious notice of your place and the structure and firmness of your stance. You will need to stabilize yourself before you move forward and perform the training drill for the second time.

At the early stages of working with this solo training drill, you will want to work up to three full sets of sound roundhouse kicks before you come to a resting position. The three full sets regimen will allow you to master and refine this kicking technique without putting undue strain upon your ankles, knees, and legs.

As you master this technique, you can move the amount of repetitions up to any number you feel is appropriate to your training level. As in all cases with taekwondo training, it is essential that you only train at your own level of expertise, thus keeping yourself free from injury.

It is essential that you perform this kicking drill with both of your legs as the kicking tool. If you only use your dominant leg to perform this drill, you will not advance your overall understanding of body balance, and one of your kicking legs will remain in a dormant state as opposed to becoming fully developed.

Benefits
The benefits of the Repeated Spinning Roundhouse Kicking Drill stem from the rapid, unhindered movement. Whereas many of the elementary taekwondo kicks and training drills teach the practitioners to anchor their body firmly on the ground, to enhance the power and velocity of their kicks, this training drill allows advancing practitioners to become much more fluid in their movements, while enhancing their ability to focus their kicks and develop power while in a state of movement.

Precautions
Pivoting on the ball of your foot will become a very natural action once you have practiced this technique slowly over a period of time. Practitioners who attempt to perform this drill in a rapid manner before they have developed the mental and

physical attitude for it can easily injure their ankle, their knee, their hip, or the ball of their foot. For this reason, when you first begin to perform this advanced training drill, you must be very conscious of each movement. Do your first kick. Relocate and reposition your body, and only then perform the second kick in the series. Once this kick is performed, regain your balance and mentally focus before you launch the third and fourth elements of this kicking drill.

It is essential to keep in mind that all taekwondo training is based on methodical offensive and defensive foundations. This too is the basis of advanced kicking drills. To this end, take the time to master the fundamentals of each drill before you attempt to take them to the advanced level.

You must also never allow your roundhouse kicks to be launched in a random, undirected fashion when performing this training drill. Focus is one of the essential elements to all taekwondo training. This is particularly the case with advanced training drills. If you perform this training drill in a haphazard manner, allowing your kicks to simply drive you to wherever their momentum will take your body, you will lose one of the essential elements of this training drill, focus. For this reason, you must control your kicks as you perform this, or any other advanced training drill. From this, you will gain a new sense of advanced mastery not only of the taekwondo kick arsenal but of your overall body dynamics, as well.

The Repeated Spinning Heel Kicking Drill

The spinning heel kick is one of the most powerful techniques in a taekwondo kicking arsenal. The momentum this kick develops can have a devastating effect upon any object it impacts.

The spinning heel kick is executed by turning your head to look behind yourself, to make sure that your target has not moved, as you simultaneously pivot 180 degrees on the ball of the foot of your forward leg. Your rear leg lifts up off of the ground and proceeds toward its target in a circular fashion. This kick impacts its target with the back of your heel. The spinning heel kick is ideally targeted at the midsection or head of your attacker.

When you deliver the spinning heel kick, it is important to drive your kick through your target. This is to say, if your target is central to your body, do not plan to halt your kick at this location. Instead, allow your kick to powerfully drive through the target, coming to a conclusion at a much deeper point. From this, your spinning heel kick develops substantially more power and is much more difficult to defend against.

The Repeated Spinning Heel Kicking Drill starts with your taking a fighting stance. You imagine a target in front of your body. When you feel that you are centered and prepared, you begin to unleash this training drill.

It is essential when you perform this training drill that you do not simply spin around striking to various imaginary locations in the air. You must stay centered and focused with a keen since of hitting the same imaginary point in the air with each unleashing of this kick.

When you begin to practice the Repeated Spinning Heel Kicking Drill, you should perform three consecutive spinning heel kicks. Once these three kicks have been performed, you should return to your original fighting stance and take conscious note of how your body has reacted to this technique. Be conscious of how your body feels once you have returned to your original ready stance and notice if your feet are planted firmly upon the ground.

At the point you feel you are very consciously aware of your body and the technique you are about to perform, unleash this training drill for the second time. Upon its completion, take note of yourself—how you feel, how your body has reacted, and the sturdiness of your stance.

When you begin to practice this training drill, you should perform three sets of three spinning heel kicks in a very controlled and slow manner. This is to say, you should not attempt to throw the spinning heel kick as fast as you possibly can. Though this training drill may appear to be pretty when performed in a very rapid manner, this style of training will help you master not only the subtle elements of the spinning heel kick but also the more refined elements of your bodily movement dynamics.

In addition, when you begin to perform this training drill, it is essential that you perform it with both of your legs. Because one side of your body will always be the dominant, it will be natural for you to begin with this side. But, as an advancing practitioner of taekwondo, you must very consciously develop both sides of your body to their greatest potential if you hope to be the best competitor and self-defense technician that you can be. Therefore, once you have performed this training drill with your right leg, it is essential that you change sides and perform it three times with your left leg.

As you advance with this training drill and become more acquainted with the sensation of spinning through multiple spinning heel kicks, you can increase both the speed and the number of repetitions of this drill. Ideally, you may wish to work up to ten rapid spinning heel kicks before you stop and reestablish your footing.

Benefits

The Repeated Spinning Heel Kicking Drill is an ideal tool to not only create spinning heel kick focus but also to develop an enhanced sense of bodily balance—as you are performing the kick in a repeated manner.

In many ways, this drill allows you to gain an enhanced sense known to few taekwondo practitioners. Just as ballet dancers or whirling dervishes learn to focus on one point as they spin and to not become dizzy, advanced taekwondo practitioners also learn how to focus their spin in a manner that will keep them from becoming overtly dizzy while performing this technique.

Because the spinning heel kick is commonly performed only once, with impact made with the first blow, many taekwondo practitioners never perform this kick in a multiple fashion. The reason that this drill is an essential element for the ongoing training of the advancing taekwondo practitioner is that if your opponent moves out of the path of your first spinning heel kick attack, you will need to immediately develop a secondary plan of attack. If, on the other hand, you have developed the ability to quickly launch a secondary, and perhaps a tertiary spinning heel kick, you will not need to change your course of offense; you will simply need to relaunch the same technique until it has made contact with your opponent.

Precautions

It is important when you begin to train with the Repeated Spinning Heel Kicking Drill that you do not allow yourself to become dizzy and lose control of your body and fall down. The essence of all advanced taekwondo training drills is to make you a better practitioner—with improved techniques. To this end, each training drill you practice must be done with acute focus as to your intended target and with a clear sense of body dynamics. For this reason, this technique is never unleashed as a method to simply see how many times you can spin around before you fall down from dizziness.

Repeated Spinning Heel/Roundhouse Kicking Drill

As detailed with the previous two training exercises: through the practice of the Repeated Spinning Roundhouse Kicking Drill and the Repeated Spinning Heel Kicking Drill, the advancing taekwondo practitioner is allowed to gain new knowledge about target focusing, body dynamics, and fluidity of moments. To take these two training drills to the next level, the advancing taekwondo practitioner can combine them. From this, the practitioner will gain new insight into body dynamics by his or her ability to unleash a variance of kicking techniques in a rapid manner.

The Repeated Spinning Heel/Roundhouse Kicking Drill begins with you taking a fighting stance. Ready yourself and when you feel you are prepared, begin by launching three consecutive roundhouse kicking techniques. The moment you have completed this element of the exercise, immediately launch four roundhouse kicks in the manner prescribed in "The Repeated Spinning Roundhouse Kicking Drill." This is to say, you will launch your first roundhouse kicking technique the way you are facing. The next one will be launched to what was originally your side. The following one to what was originally your back. You will finish up by launching one to what was your other side, before you come to rest.

Upon the completion of the first stage of this multiple kicking drill, it is essential that you come to rest in your original position and analyze the proficiency of your techniques and how your body felt unleashing these techniques. As in all cases of performing advanced taekwondo training drills, simply the ability to perform a specific kicking technique is never enough to aid you in the mastery of this technique. You must perform it from a very conscious perspective if you wish to obtain a complete understanding of all elements of taekwondo's kicking arsenal.

The Repeated Spinning Heel/Roundhouse Kicking Drill causes you to move in two completely different planes of motion. The first segment of the drill has you spin around three times, performing the spinning heel kick. The second segment of this drill, the roundhouse kick portion, has you interrupt the flow you instigated with the spinning heel kicks and turn in the opposite direction. In this segment, you unleash four very defined roundhouse kicks. From this uninterrupted flow, you train your body and mind how to alter your pattern of movement, while remaining in constant motion, unleashing offensive kicking techniques.

To execute this kicking drill properly, you must be very conscious of all elements of your body and your movement. When you are rotating through the spinning heel kick segment, it is very easy to allow the momentum you develop by unleashing these kicks to cause your body to spin in an almost unrestricted manner—driven solely by momentum. This is a mistake, however, for it is the essence of taekwondo that you maintain control over all of your physical movements. Therefore, as you perform the spinning heel kick segment, you must unleash every kick with a profound consciousness of each action.

At the point you have performed your three consecutive spinning heel kicks, it is a natural response to stop, rearrange your body, and at the point when you feel you are settled, and only then, launch into your roundhouse kicks. This is, however, an incorrect way of practicing this drill.

To perform this drill correctly, you must train your body to make the transition from the first part to the second part in a seamless manner. Certainly, this will take practice. But, this is what taekwondo's advanced training drills are designed to do—provide you with the ability to move forward and develop new skills.

As you train with this drill, you will want to ultimately perform at least five full sets of techniques. This is to say, you will want to perform five full sets of spinning heel kicks intermingled with five full sets of roundhouse kicks. Upon the completion of this series, you will want to shift sides and perform this drill using your opposite leg.

Benefits

The benefits of the Repeated Spinning Heel/Roundhouse Kicking Drill are many. As detailed, you train your body to immediately shift from one pattern of movement and instantly move forward into a second pattern. This is an ideal method of training your body and mind to adapt to combat situations, where you can never anticipate what your opponent may unleash and, therefore, you must possess the ability to immediately revamp your offensive and defensive methodology as necessary.

This training drill is also an ideal method to train your body and your mind in the various forms of movement. Because the two kicking techniques are very different in their application and execution, you come to understand and redefine new elements of your own personal body dynamics and your body's reactions to specific sets of movement.

Precautions

As in all cases, it is easy to overperform this training drill before you have mastered the subtleties of its techniques. Therefore, in the early stages of training with this drill, it is essential that you perform it slowly and consciously. With this approach, you will master the subtle elements of this movement before you speed it up and perform it in a rapid manner.

As is the case with all spinning kicks, your knee can easily be damaged if you do not allow your body to correctly spin on the ball of your foot. This is especially the case with a technique that can be performed in a rapid manner such as this one. To this end, you must remain not only very conscious but also very light on your feet while performing this training drill. You must allow your body to freely move and compensate for its constant repositioning.

The Multiple Jumping Front Kick Drill

The jumping front kick is generally the first offensive jumping kick a taekwondo student is taught. The traditional jumping front kick is launched by snapping the rear leg forward and up in order to gain enough momentum that your body is lifted from the ground so that your other leg can snap forward in an aerial front kick fashion. Though this is the accepted method of delivering this jumping kick, this is not the method an advanced taekwondo practitioner employs when unleashing this kick.

The jumping front kick, when delivered in a traditional fashion, is not only a very obvious kicking technique, but it is also a very slow offensive technique. The advanced taekwondo practitioner uses a slightly redesigned version of this kicking technique to make it not only faster but also a more effective weapon.

To begin to redesign the jumping front kick, ready yourself in a fighting stance. Visualize an imaginary target several feet directly in front of you. Just as you are about to launch the jumping front kick, allow the knee of your base leg to bend down very slightly. Now, kick your rear leg powerfully forward in front kick fashion. Do this as you simultaneously allow your slightly bent base leg to launch you upward, off the ground. Allow the momentum of this technique to drive you deeply in forward, toward your imaginary target.

What you have achieved is a jumping front kick that does not rely upon the multiple leg kicks used in the traditional jumping front kick. With this approach, not only have you simplified the jumping front kick technique, but you have made it substantially faster and much more difficult to defend against.

To perform the Multiple Jumping Front Kick Drill, you first ready yourself in a fighting stance. When you feel that you are ready, launch a jumping front kick toward an imaginary target directly in front of you. The moment you land, instead of simply repositioning yourself, you must immediately launch a jumping front kick from your opposite leg. Once you have landed, again, you must launch another jumping front kick from your original leg. This kicking drill can go forward from there, limited solely by your level of endurance and how much space you have to practice.

It is essential in the early stages of training with this drill that you launch each technique in a very defined manner. You must ready yourself, launch your kick, land, reposition yourself, and then move forward with additional techniques. The essence of this drill is to train your body and mind in rapid jumping front kick penetration techniques. If you simply haphazardly jump from one kick to the next, you will not refine your understanding of the subtle elements of this kicking drill. Therefore, even once you have mastered this kicking technique and this kicking drill, when you begin, you must perform it in a slow and controlled manner for the first few segments. This allows you to take conscious note of how your body is reacting on the particular day you are training with the drill and how well you are unleashing the technique.

JUMPING FRONT KICK DRILL

Benefits

The Multiple Jumping Front Kick Drill causes your body to move forward in a dynamic and defined pattern of offensive action. This drill trains your body in an ideal fighting tool for attack on an opponent who is at some distance from you or one who is retreating. This drill develops your ability to rapidly progress from one jumping front kick to the next with little thought, thereby, providing you with the ability to quickly move in on an opponent and penetrate his defenses in all combative situations.

Precautions

Any time you lift your body off of the ground, you have the ability to damage your feet, your ankles, your knees, or your hips when you land. For this reason, it is essential that you do not allow the momentum and adrenaline that is generated by performing this drill to overpower your better judgment and cause you to jump when your body or mind is not ready. Many advanced practitioners damage their own bodies simply because they believe they have performed a technique so many times that they understand it and will never be injured in its performance. This is a mistake you should never make. Always warm up, and perform any jumping technique in a slow and controlled manner in its initial stages. Additionally, if you ever feel off-balance, again, stop performing the technique and take time to recenter yourself. This is also the case if you are in the middle of a class, for it is far better for an instructor to scold you than for you to injure your body, which may force you to stop training altogether for an undefined period of time.

The Standing Jumping Side Kick Drill

The traditional jumping side kick is initially performed by entering into a fighting stance. As the kick is unleashed, your rear leg steps forward as a means to propel your body up and off of the ground. Your striking leg is then sent forward, as you push your body upward from your base leg, and your kick is driven in toward your target in side kick fashion.

As you begin training with the Standing Jumping Side Kick Drill, your side kick will be executed in a similar manner to the traditional jumping side kick. The difference will be that you will add the stepping-in motion, which commonly propels you from the ground.

Begin by entering into a fighting stance. Instead of focusing on a target directly in front of you, look to your right side. You will now bend your knees slightly, to aid in propelling yourself into the air. Once you feel that you are ready, push your body up and off the ground, extending your jumping side kick to an imaginary target to your side. Immediately upon the execution of this kick retract your leg and land in approximately the same position you began.

When you land, take very conscious notice of your balance and how it felt to unleash a jumping side kick without the aid of the momentum that is developed by stepping into it—as in the case of the traditional jumping side kick. Assuredly, this will be a new experience and should be studied completely.

The first time you perform this kicking drill, you will obviously not possess the understanding to propel yourself high into the air. This should not concern you, because this exercise, as is the case with all training drills, is designed to make you a more complete and more competent taekwondo technician.

Once you have assessed how you performed your first technique and how you may improve upon it, launch into a second technique, and then a third. Each time you perform this drill, do so in an increasingly conscious and precise manner, performing each new kick more precisely.

When you first begin to practice the Standing Jumping Side Kick Drill, it will be more of an experience of discovering a new method of launching a kick than simply a training drill. As you progress with your understanding of your own body dynamic, this drill will provide you with a method to add a new and very viable weapon to your offensive arsenal.

The Standing Jumping Side Kick Drill should initially be performed in limited increments, with only two or three jumping side kicks, from each side of your body, in each segment. The subtle training elements of this drill take time to develop, and you should be careful not to unduly strain or damage your knees and ankles until you have become very accustomed to the effects of this training drill.

When you have developed an acute understanding of this drill through the slow development stage, this drill becomes an ideal tool for leg muscle development and for focus training. At this point, you will want to take this drill to the level where it can also aid you in your cardioaerobic development.

To use the Standing Jumping Side Kick Drill not only as a focusing tool but also as a cardioaerobic drill as well, you will want to ready yourself in a fighting stance. When you are ready, you will locate an imaginary target to your right side and launch into at least five repetitive jumping side kicks, in the method described, with your right leg. The moment you have completed this segment of the drill, you will want to reposition yourself and immediately find your focal point to your left side and then unleash the drill five times from your left leg. As you progress with understanding and cardioaerobic development with this drill, the process of shifting sides and performing the drill can be increased up to five times.

Benefits
The benefits of the Standing Jumping Side Kick Drill are that you train your body in new and unique methods of propelling yourself from the ground and unleashing an offensive technique. This training drill coaches you in methods that may help you in combat when you have to strike an opponent who is moving in very close to you.

Precautions
As is the case with all jumping techniques, you increase the chances of self-injury, because you are lifting yourself off of the ground. For this reason, and particularly with the Standing Jumping Side Kick Drill, you must take time to develop your understanding of this drill before you perform it in a rapid and repetitive manner.

PARTNER TRAINING DRILLS
Advanced taekwondo partner training drills are designed to refine your combative skills on all levels. Performing drills with a partner trains your body and mind in the advanced elements of focus, combative strategy, and offensive technique execution. Whereas the beginning taekwondo student focuses his training upon developing the basic skills, advanced taekwondo practitioners focus their ongoing martial art development on how to execute each technique in the most efficient and effective manner possible. To achieve this end, partner training is an absolute necessity—because you need not only to refine your own personal techniques but also to understand how an opponent will move in physical combat.

More than simply personal development, partner training allows you to add the element of scrutiny to your training. As you work with a training partner, you must allow him or her to observe the level of your technique and comment on what may make it better. As your partner is the one viewing your actual technique execution, he or she will possess the ability to view flaws that you may not have noticed. For this reason, advanced taekwondo partner training is not about being the best; it is about becoming the best. Ego must be put aside and you must allow your training partner to help you to become a more proficient practitioner by receiving constructive criticism. Advanced taekwondo one-on-one training drills require no equipment. They simply require you to face off with a partner and perform a precise set of movements.

The Front Kick Body Slide Drill
To begin, face off with your training partner. When you have both acknowledged that you are ready, you will launch a front kick from your right rear leg toward your opponent's mid-body, in a slow and controlled fashion. As you do this, your

partner will slide directly out of the path of your oncoming kick, in a linear motion, directly to his or her right side. Upon the completion of your initial kick, you will retract your kicking leg to its original positioning. In a low jumping fashion, you will now place your left leg to the rear, as your training partner reestablishes his or her frontal positioning. You will now launch your next front kick from your left leg, as your partner slides to his or her left.

It is essential in the early stages of this drill to perform it in a slow and controlled manner. This allows both you and your training partner to develop the understanding of how to use the least amount of energy while unleashing a kick and moving out of its path.

Begin this drill by rapidly kicking at your opponent, forcing him or her to rapidly move out of your path, which diminishes the educational aspects of this drill. Therefore, no matter how many times you have practiced this technique, you should always begin by delivering your kick in a slow and controlled manner.

Prior to beginning this training drill, set a number of kicks you will perform in a very slow manner. Ideally this will be from between five and ten, depending on how much time you have to perform this drill. Once you have performed the predetermined number, speed up the drill. Again, perform the drill at a more rapid rate, for the prescribed number of times. At the point of completion, speed the drill up again; bring it to a very fast pace. Each stage of this training drill will cause both you and your training partner to develop a new understanding of the mechanics associated with physical combat

It is essential when practicing this drill that you do so from both the offensive and defensive position. If you only perform this drill from the offensive position, you will not develop a keen understanding of how to quickly and effectively move out of the path of an oncoming kick.

There are two ways you can change offensive and defensive positioning with your training partner while performing this drill. The first is that you can progress from the slow, to medium, to fast performance of the front kick while remaining the offensive opponent. The second is that you can change positions during the drill. This is to say, you will perform the front kick in a slow and controlled manner, and then your opponent will take over. In the next stage you will perform the mid-speed kick and then allow your training partner to take over the offensive position. Ultimately, you practice this drill in both manners and determine what works best for you.

Benefits

As detailed, the purpose of the Front Kick Body Slide Drill is to provide a lesson in development for both the offensive and defensive training partners. For the offensive opponent, it trains the eye to watch for the movement of an opponent—because when you're in combat with a trained adversary, it is very common that he will possess the ability to rapidly slide out of the path of your oncoming offensive technique. For the defensive opponent, this drill trains the eyes how to rapidly and efficiently move out of the path of an attack, thereby, training the mind how to react to the onslaught of an attack without thinking—by simply reacting.

Precautions

It is very easy for the offensive opponent in this training drill to launch a kick and strike the training partner before they are ready or prepared to move out of the way. It is also easy for the offensive opponent to sneak in a fast kick when the training partner is expecting a slower kick.

The purpose of this drill is to train the body and the mind in the subtle realms of combat. To this end, it serves no purpose to hit an opponent unnecessarily. For this reason, you must always remain respectful of your training partner and not attempt to strike him or her unnecessarily.

Supplement

A supplemental technique you can add to this training drill is that once the defensive opponent has slid out of the path of the oncoming attack, he can add a counter defensive technique, such as a straight punch or a spinning heel kick to the body of the training partner. By adding a secondary element to this training drill, it will cause both of the participants to gain new insight into physical combat and body mechanics.

Again, as it is easy to strike a training partner who is not anticipating a powerful and expected counterattack, it is essential that you lay the groundwork for this element of the drill before you proceed to add this supplemental element to it.

The Standing Hook Kick Drill

The Standing Hook Kick Drill begins with you facing off with your training partner. You inform your training partner of which leg you will be using as your kicking leg. Your training partner will then inform you of which leg he or she will use.

When you are both ready, you inform your partner that you are about to unleash your kick. You then perform a hook kick toward the head of your opponent. As your kick travels toward its target, your partner's feet remain locked into position but he or she leans backward, out of the path of the oncoming hook kick. Once the kick misses, you quickly reposition yourself, and your training partner launches a hook kick toward your head. As the kick approaches, you lean backward, out of the path of this oncoming hook kick.

The moment this kick has missed, your training partner repositions himself or herself. You then launch another hook kick toward your partner's head. Your partner leans out of the path of this kick, as he or she did with the previous one. You regain your defensive footing and your partner unleashes another kick toward your head.

When beginning the Standing Hook Kick Drill, each kick is unleashed in a very slow and controlled manner. Initially, it is a good idea to not actually target your opponent's head, but to focus your kick a few inches in front of your partner. As you begin to develop a feel for this drill, your kicks may then be speeded up to the maximum level, where you and your training partner are both comfortable.

Ideally, you will perform this drill for twenty repetitions. Not only will you have given your body a cardioaerobic workout, but you will also have used your body to perform a specific kick numerous times—something that may actually occur in a sparring match.

The reason that this drill is performed for a maximum of twenty repetitions is that if you perform more repetitions, your kicks may tend to get sloppy and you may strike your opponent. For this reason, a twenty-kick drill is an ideal number to train toward. But, it must be understood, that if at any point you feel your body being strained or you are losing your focus, then this drill should be discontinued, because you do not want to injure your training partner.

Benefits

No matter what level of taekwondo practitioner you are, you begin the Standing Hook Kick Drill by unleashing your hook kicks in a very slow and controlled manner. This reveals the subtle elements necessary for mastering this kick. In addition, you are able to gain substantial insight into hook kick targeting.

From the defensive perspective, you will develop the ability to see an oncoming kick and move just enough out of its path. From this, you will learn how to conserve energy while in combat. Plus, you will master how to immediately launch a counterattack once an offensive technique has missed you. In addition, by not forcefully blocking the kick, you save yourself from a possible blocking injury. This will make you a more proficient practitioner both in the ring and on the street.

Precautions

Because the hook kick is a very powerful weapon, it is essential not to kick your training partner. For this reason, from an offensive perspective, you must possess the ability to truly control your kicks. From a defensive perspective, you must understand how to quickly and precisely lean out of the path of the oncoming kick.

One of the main problems that occurs when this drill is practiced is that the defensive partner will wait too long to move out of the path of the kick. When this happens, he or she is struck in the head by this weapon.

At no level is taekwondo a game. For this reason, this drill, and in fact all advanced taekwondo training drills, must be performed from a very conscious state of mind. Do not wait to see how close your training partner's kick can come to your face!

The Standing Roundhouse Kick and Hook Kick Drill

The Standing Roundhouse Kick and Hook Kick Drill begins in the same way as the Standing Hook Kick Drill. You face off with your training partner. When you are both ready, instead of launching a hook kick at the head of your partner, you launch a roundhouse kick. Your partner leans out of the path of this oncoming kick. Once your roundhouse kick has missed, you immediately launch a hook kick. Again, your partner leans slightly out of the path of this kick. The moment your second kick has missed, you quickly reposition yourself. Your training partner now launches the same two kicks toward your head.

In the beginning stages of working with this training drill, you will want to launch your roundhouse kick from a rear leg position, driving powerfully through your target, landing your kicking leg on the ground, before you relaunch your secondary hook kick. As you progress with this training drill, you may wish to develop the ability to launch your roundhouse kick from a midair position, before your kicking leg touches the ground.

As is the case with the Standing Hook Kick Drill, this drill begins with you launching your kicks in a very slow and controlled manner. This trains you in the body dynamics of unleashing multiple kicks from the same position. As you and your training partner begin to become more comfortable with this drill and can anticipate each other's movements, you may speed up your kicks as you both feel is appropriate.

The Standing Roundhouse Kick and Hook Kick Drill should be performed for no more than twenty repetitions. This allows both you and your training partner to remain very conscious of each offensive and defensive action and keeps you from becoming sloppy with your techniques.

Benefits

There are two very essential benefits of the Standing Roundhouse Kick and Hook Kick Drill. First of all, from a defensive perspective, you train your body to lean out of the path of multiple oncoming kicks, while exerting the least amount of energy possible. From an offensive perspective, you train yourself to target and unleash multiple kicking techniques at your opponent.

It is natural to see a target and unleash a kick with the intent of it making contact. The reality of combat, however, is that your opponent may move out of the path of this initial attack. This drill trains you to immediately launch into a secondary attack without the need to reposition your body. Your opponent in the ring or the street may not expect or be prepared for this instantaneous secondary attack.

Precautions

As in all taekwondo training, it is essential that you remain very alert while performing the Standing Roundhouse Kick and Hook Kick Drill. In this drill, you must, first and foremost, remain conscious of your partner's positioning, because you do not want to accidentally kick him or her. You must also remain conscious of your own body.

Because you are quickly changing from one kicking technique to another, you can injure your own body. The knee, hip, and ankle of your base leg can all be injured while performing this drill. The knee of your kicking leg can also be injured if you snap either your roundhouse or your hook kick too rapidly. For this reason, you must remain very alert while performing this drill.

FOCUS TRAINING DRILLS

An essential element of advanced taekwondo is striking your target with precision. As you progress through the ranks of this art, at each level, you become more and more proficient with not only the powerful delivery of your kicks but also the precision in which they are unleashed.

At the advanced level, the taekwondo practitioner never throws kicks wildly into the air. Each technique, even while warming up, is unleashed with a highly specific purpose and point of impact in mind. For this reason, the advanced practitioner trains with the sole purpose of taking techniques to new levels of excellence. At the advanced level, focus training is one of the primary elements of ongoing taekwondo training.

The Focus Glove

There is no greater tool in developing your advanced taekwondo kicking focus and kicking strategy than the focus glove. There are many varieties of focus gloves. They are all similar in design, however, in that they slip onto the hand—similar to a glove. On one side of the focus glove is a padded surface. This surface is an ideal target to refine both your ever-advancing taekwondo punching and kicking techniques.

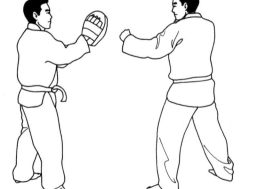

FOCUS GLOVE DRILL 1

The reason that the focus glove is such an essential element of advanced taekwondo partner training is that it is not a stationary target such as a hanging bag. Because it is allowed to move and change its positioning, dictated solely by the choices of your training partner, the focus glove is the closest you can come to the actual realities of physical combat—because your opponent will virtually never remain locked into a single position. Partner training with a focus glove forces you to remain in a constant state of movement, analyzing and redefining each of your offensive techniques as necessary.

FOCUS GLOVE DRILL 2

The Repeated Spinning Heel Kicking Drill

As detailed in the previous section, the Repeated Spinning Heel Kicking Drill witnesses you focusing on an imaginary target and performing the spinning heel kick multiple times. You can supplement the Repeated Spinning Heel Kicking Drill with partner training. This not only enhances your own mastery of the spinning heel kick but also allows you to gain new insight into focus and targeting.

To begin this training drill, have your training partner locate himself or herself in front of you with a focus glove. You will then proceed to perform the drill by impacting the glove.

Once you have become comfortable with this element of the training drill, you can ask your partner to periodically move the glove higher or lower as you spin. This will aid you in compensating for the movement of your opponent. You can also have your training partner move the glove either closer to or farther from your body. This will also allow you to train your ability to strike a moving target with this explosive kicking technique.

FOCUS GLOVE DRILL 3

Benefits
The benefits of training with the Repeated Spinning Heel Kicking Drill in association with a focus glove are that not only do you develop the ability to spin with continuous of energy, but you also gain the ability to focus your spinning heel kick with a new level of precision. This drill allows you to become confident when spinning around to look behind yourself, and trains you to adjust your movement if your opponent moves from his or her original positioning prior to your kick being unleashed.

Precautions
The basic problem with performing the Repeated Spinning Heel Kicking Drill against a focus glove is that you can drive your kick forward with too much speed before you have developed the precision and understanding of your own body dynamics to perform it correctly. As a result, you can injure the knee of your base leg. For this reason, you must maintain very conscious control over your body while performing this technique, to keep yourself free from injury.

The Side-to-Side Roundhouse Kick Drill

To perform the Side-to-Side Roundhouse Kick Drill, you will face off with your training partner, who has a focus glove on each hand. Your training partner will hold a focus glove out in front of himself or herself for your targeting. When you are both ready, you will unleash a roundhouse kick directed at the focus glove. Your training partner will immediately step back and present the second focus glove, and you will deliver a roundhouse kick, using your other leg, to that glove. This process will continue until your partner has backed up as far as he or she can—defined solely by your training space.

Once your partner has retreated as far as possible, he or she will signal you to reverse the direction of your attack and will begin to move in toward you. You will unleash a roundhouse kick. Once this kick has made contact, you will move back instead of moving forward, as in the previous segment of this drill. You will continue the process of unleashing a roundhouse kick with each leg, as you retreat, until you have backed up as far as you can.

Benefits

The Side-to-Side Roundhouse Kick Drill is an ideal way not only to develop your roundhouse kick focus but also to prepare yourself for actual combat.

When you are in competition or in street combat, your opponent will virtually never stay locked into one position. He will be in a mode of either retreat or advancement. This drill trains you to deliver powerful roundhouse kicks in both the advancing and retreating modes of combat.

Precautions

In the early stages of training with this drill, it is very easy to lose focus and simply unleash your roundhouse kick without definite targeting in mind. When this happens, you can easily strike your training partner.

In all advanced taekwondo training, it is essential that you remain very conscious and very focused. No technique should ever be unleashed without a precise impact point in mind.

While performing this drill, it is essential that you keep your eyes focused on the target. Because this drill is all about coordinating your eyes and your kick, no kick should be wasted. Therefore, if your training partner moves the target, and you do not feel that you can properly strike it, it is far better to maintain control over your body, regain your focus, and then unleash the kick. In this way, your training will remain focused, and you will not waste your energy unnecessarily.

The Random Punch Kick Drill

The Random Punch Kick Drill has your training partner placing a focus glove on each hand. You face off with your partner. When you both have signaled that you are ready, your partner will begin to move. As your partner moves, he or she shifts one focus glove to the front. You then deliver a punch or a kick that you feel is appropriate for the glove's position. You partner will then move the second glove forward to a new location, and you will deliver a technique you feel is appropriate.

While performing this drill, you will randomly shift between a punching and a kicking attack, varying your techniques in a manner that you feel is appropriate to the placement of the focus glove.

The Random Punch Kick Drill should be performed for three-minute intervals. Because this is the length of a round in a sanctioned taekwondo match, this is the ideal amount of time to work on this drill.

Benefits

The benefits of the Random Punch Kick Drill are that you learn to coordinate your various punching and kicking techniques in association with the movement of your opponent. This drill is an ideal tool to train you in focus targeting for actual combat.

In addition to hand-eye coordination training, this drill is also a great form of cardioaerobic exercise. Because you are constantly moving while performing this drill, you drive your heart rate up and maintain it at that level for as long as you perform the drill.

Precautions

When performing the Random Punch Kick Drill, it is very easy to allow the momentum of your movement to overpower your focus. This is particularly true two minutes or so into the drill. Because you are becoming winded or tired, it is a natural response to lose your focus or power.

As this is a drill and not actual competition, it is essential that you do not allow this to happen. You are not going to get hit if you let your guard down. But, you will lose critical developmental skills if you become lazy or sloppy. For this reason, it is essential that you drive yourself to train very hard with this drill and do not let yourself slack off, at any level, while performing the three-minute segments of this training drill.

Supplement

An ideal supplement that can be added to the Random Punch Kick Drill is to have your training partner tell you what technique to unleash—be it a roundhouse kick, spinning heel kick, front kick, straight punch, or roundhouse punch. What this style of training does is to force you to develop and unleash techniques that you may not be all that comfortable with.

In taekwondo, there are certain techniques that each of us performs better than other techniques. It is a natural reaction, as one advances through the ranks, to continually train with the techniques that you can perform most easily and exactly and to veer away from other techniques. If your training partner is guiding you to perform unchosen techniques, you are then forced to develop a deeper understanding and, in fact, more proficiency with these lesser-used offensive strikes. From this, you will become a more competent combatant.

The Training Shield

A training shield is larger than a focus glove. Training shields vary in size, but their dimensions are approximately 2 feet by 3 feet in diameter. They are held with two hands and are braced against your training partner's body.

The extra padding possessed by a training shield allows them to become an ideal tool to not only hone your targeting focus on your opponent's body but to deliver more powerful kicking techniques.

The Back Kick Drill

The taekwondo back kick is an ideal defensive and offensive weapon. Because you are spinning to your rear when you perform this kick, you can counteract forward attacks such as the axe kick, or you can drive into your opponent's midsection.

From a competitive standpoint, this kick is ideally suited for Olympic competition because strikes only count if they are delivered to the front section of the body. Because you have spun so that your back is to your opponent, you have

BACK KICK DRILL 1

BACK KICK DRILL 2

BACK KICK DRILL 3

BACK KICK DRILL 4

BACK KICK DRILL 5

limited your opponent's ability to hit a scoreable target. This is the reason to train in the Back Kick Drill.

To perform the Back Kick Drill, face off with your opponent, who is holding a training shield (see Back Kick Drill 1). When you have both signaled that you are ready, drive forward with several back kicks, launched from alternate legs, as your training partner moves backward (see Back Kick Drill 2–5).

The ideal number of kicks to perform during this drill is defined solely by your training space. In a competitive situation, you can expect to deliver approximately three or four before you either score or drive your opponent from the ring. So, the ultimate number you perform is defined solely by you.

Benefits

The benefits of the Back Kick Drill are that you train yourself to rapidly penetrate your opponent's defense and strike to his midsection. This drill educates you in the understanding of how to focus your attack and then target your opponent as you are alternating from side to side.

Precautions

It is essential while performing the Back Kick Drill to keep your eyes focused on the target and never unleash your technique until you actually see your target. It is a common mistake to simply unleash your kick and expect your target to be there. If you perform the back kick in this manner, what occurs when you spin around to the rear and find that your target has moved? Commonly, it is too late for you to retract the kick, because it has already been unleashed. For this reason it is essential to develop the understanding that you must look first before your kick is unleashed.

FOOTWORK DRILLS

Footwork drills train you to move in toward your opponent or retreat from an attack in the most efficient manner possible. The reason that training with footwork drills is an essential tool in the ongoing development of the advanced taekwondo practitioner is that they allow you to come to a deeper understanding about how to move in the most efficient and energy-conserving manner possible. From this, not only do you become a better combatant, but you also become a better overall practitioner of taekwondo.

Understanding Taekwondo Footwork

Footwork refers to your ability to place yourself where you want to be in the midst of competition and to move yourself out of locations you determine are less than appropriate in the most expedient and energy-efficient manner possible. To the average martial artist, footwork is just a random set of movements that causes them to move in or move out of a particular situation. To the advanced taekwondo practitioner, however, footwork is a science.

There are four primary styles of footwork used in taekwondo:

1. Forward footwork
2. Reverse footwork
3. Lateral footwork
4. Pivoting footwork

For each of these methods of footwork, there are training drills that can advance your understanding of each of these movements.

Forward Footwork

Forward footwork teaches you to rapidly move in toward your opponent with one very direct linear movement and attack. This forward motion can either take the form of a step or a slide. An ideal example of this is that when a match begins, you immediately slide in toward your opponent and deliver a front kick to his or her midsection, under your opponent's guard.

The Forward Slide Drill

To begin the Forward Slide Drill, face off with your training partner and enter into a fighting stance. When you have both signaled that you are ready, you may begin the drill.

To perform this drill, you will slide in toward your partner by leaving your lead leg in its forward position. To achieve this you will keep the foot of your lead leg pointing in toward your opponent. You will then raise it just slightly off of the ground. You will allow your lead leg to propel you forward.

In this first stage of this drill, you will rapidly move in on your training partner, using the previously described method. You will then rapidly retreat by pushing yourself back off the ball of the foot of your lead leg. You should perform this drill several times before you change off with your training partner.

The second stage of this drill has you more separated from your training partner. Again, you face off in a fighting stance. As your partner is farther away from you than in the previous drill, you will be forced to do two things. First of all, you will have to use more muscle to drive your rear leg forcefully to push you in toward your partner. Secondarily, you will need to make two or three actual movements to close the range between the two of you.

As with the previous example of this drill, once you have come into contact range with your training partner, you will then rapidly retreat to your orginal position.

Benefits

The benefits of the Forward Slide Drill are that it trains you to move directly in at your opponent in a rapid and unceasing manner. This will allow you to close the distance between your opponent and yourself in an extremely efficient manner, either in the ring or on the street.

This drill also trains you to retreat in an effective and efficient manner if an opponent ever rapidly closes in on you. From this, you will learn to maintain your balance and be able to launch a counterattack once you have repositioned yourself.

Reverse Footwork

Reverse footwork witnesses you rapidly moving back, away from the onslaught of an opponent, in a linear pattern. As in the case of forward footwork, this movement may take the form of a step or a slide. A jump back is also added to your possible actions in regard to reverse footwork.

The common time for retreating in this fashion is when your opponent has launched an attack at you. Instead of blocking it, you wish to reposition yourself to launch a counterattack. An ideal example of this is in the case of an axe kick being launched in your direction. You slide back out of its path and then immediately counter with a roundhouse kick.

The Jump Back Drill

To begin the Jump Back Drill, you will face off with your training partner. You will both take fighting stances. Your partner will then launch a linear attack at you, such as a front kick, axe kick, or a straight punch. The moment that this attack is launched, you will allow the ball of your foot of your lead leg to lift you just slightly off the ground and drive you back. Once in this retreat positioning, you will immediately launch a counterattack toward your training partner, such as a front kick to his midsection.

You should perfom this training drill several times before you switch positions with your training partner. From this, you will gain new insight into lateral reverse body movement and your ability to launch an appropriate counterattack.

Benefits
The benefits of the Jump Back Drill are that you train your body to instantly retreat when an attack is launched in your direction, in the most rapid and energy-efficient manner possible. You learn that you do not need to lift yourself too far off the ground to make a successful retreat. And you learn how to land in a stance that will assist you in launching an appropriate counterattack.

Lateral Footwork
The next style of footwork that an advanced taekwondo practitioner must master is lateral footwork. In lateral footwork you move from side to side.

The basic application of the lateral footwork has you simply slide or step to the side when a linear attack has been launched against you. This action is performed in order that you reposition yourself for a counterstrike. An example of this would be if your opponent has attempted a side kick. You would simply slide to one side, out of the path of the attack, and then immediately counterstrike your opponent with a roundhouse kick or other appropriate technique.

The Lateral Footwork Drill
Face off with your training partner. When you have both signaled that you are ready, have your training partner launch a slow front kick toward you. As it is executed, slide to the inside of it. This is to say, if your partner launches a front kick with his or her right leg, you will move to your right.

Moving Inside a Kick
The reason that you always move inside of a kick is that, initially, this protects you from having the kick make contact. If you move to the outside, this places you in, much closer to the kick. With a rapid technique such as the front kick, this may cause you to be struck by it.

The second reason that you always move inside a kick is that it provides you with a clearer opening to drive a counterattack in toward your opponent. In the case of the front kick, the head and midsection of your opponent will be open for attack.

Continuing With The Lateral Footwork Drill
Once you have slid out of the path of your partner's intitial kick, immediately return to your central positioning and have your partner launch a secondary front kick at you from the opposite leg. Again move inside of your partner's kick.

The moment each kick has missed, immediately return to your original positioning and slide out of the path of continuing front kicks launched by your partner. These kicks should be launched in an increasing rapid manner.

Benefits
The benefits of the Lateral Footwork Drill is that you train your body to witness the oncoming stage of an opponent's unleashing a kick toward you. From this, you gain the ability to quickly and efficiently move out of the path of a kick before it has the chance to strike you. Along with this, you prepare yourself to launch appropriate counterattacks in the ring or on the street.

Turning Footwork

Turning footwork is the most advanced level of footwork employed by the tae-kwondo practitioner. With turning footwork, you actually spin out of the path of an attack, continue on, and launch your own offensive assault. For example, say that your opponent attempts to kick you with an axe kick. You pivot out of the path of the attack on the ball of your foot. You then continue spinning through, delivering a spinning heel kick to your opponent's head. This level of footwork is only employed by the most advanced practitioner of taekwondo, who understands his or her own offensive speed and capabilities.

The Turning Footwork Drill

Face off with your training partner. When you have both signaled your readiness, have your partner launch a slow front kick with his or her left leg. As your part-ner's kick is executed, spin around and deliver a slow and controlled spinning heel kick to the back of his or her head.

The reason that this drill must be unleashed in a very slow and controlled manner is that the spinning heel kick is a very powerful weapon. As such, if you strike your training partner with this kick, you could injure him or her. Because training with kicking drills is just that, training, you do not want to injure your partner. Therefore, this training drill is only used by the advanced practitioner and, then, is only to be used in a controlled manner.

Once this initial stage of the drill has been completed, return to your original positioning and perform the drill for a total of five to ten segments. Once you have completed these segments, change legs and perform the drill for a total of three to ten times using the other side of your body.

Benefits

The benefits of the Turning Footwork Drill are that you train your body to wit-ness oncoming attacks. Instead of retreating or blocking these attacks, you develop the ability to encounter them by using a method of attack. From this, you become not only a more proficient competitor but also a more exacting self-defense practitioner.

Part Four
Advanced Applications—
Taking Your Practice to the Next Level

Chapter 9
Sparring and Competition

Competition has been one of the primary elements of personal development employed in taekwondo since its inception. From the beginning to the most advanced levels, competition is a way for the practitioner to hone and to test his skills. Whereas the novice student of taekwondo enters into a sparring match and unleashes whatever block or offensive technique that randomly comes to mind, the advanced practitioner makes every unleashed technique a science.

Sparring competition is an ongoing process of learning and development. The ever-advancing practitioner makes this development a science. He comes to master the various techniques of the art and comes to learn what can be expected from the opponent. From participating in numerous sparring matches, the advanced practitioner of taekwondo has taken taekwondo competitive training to a new level of excellence—making it an exacting science of combative self-defense.

COMPETITION PRELIMINARIES

The most basic understanding about taekwondo competition, both at the Olympic and non-Olympic level, that the taekwondo practitioner must come to comprehend is that competition is not about ego. Competition is not defined by who can beat up whom—as is so often the case in the realms of professional boxing, where the competitors insult one another at press conferences prior to their match.

Taekwondo has been developed to bring the practitioner to a new and unique understanding of self—both physical and mental. From training in taekwondo, practitioners are guided along a path where they raise their physical and mental understanding of the combative arts to a level never embraced by the average individual.

Each school of taekwondo and each master of the art has a unique and personal understanding of the elements that make up this advanced system of self-defense. Thus, each instructor has something unique to teach each student. As the taekwondo practitioner advances through the ranks of the art, he or she also emerges with a unique understanding. These two elements, that of training and that of personal understanding, are what each individual practitioner brings to the arena of competition.

The advanced taekwondo practitioner rises above the limitations of the ego of "I have won" or "I have lost" and makes each competitive experience a learning experience. Each competition, be it a win or a lose, thereby becomes the foundation for a new understanding on how to become an overall more proficient practitioner of taekwondo.

Ultimately, taekwondo competition is about becoming better: better at understanding what physical attacks an opponent may unleash toward you. Better at understanding how you can countermand and defend yourself against these various attacks. And, better at understanding the definitions of this system of martial arts.

COMPETITION TRAINING

Training for competition begins the moment the new student walks into the taekwondo dojang for the first time. From the moment the student is taught the first kick and the first block, he or she is being groomed to become a competitive fighter.

All schools of taekwondo emphasize the need for interactive sparring, whether this is no-contact sparring, which takes place at the beginning levels; light contact sparring, which takes place at the intermediate levels; or full contact sparring, which is witnessed at the advanced levels; the art of taekwondo is based on the rudimentary concept of becoming proficient in physical combat.

Other systems of martial arts born on the Korean peninsula, such as hapkido, do not teach the exacting system of competitive combat that is embraced by taekwondo. The advancing taekwondo practitioner understands that to truly comprehend what physical contact is, one must actually participate in a sparring match with an equally trained opponent. From this the taekwondo practitioner comes to understand the true nature of physical combat, thereby becoming a proficient proponent of the art.

The Basics

At the root of competitive training in taekwondo are the basics that are taught to every student of the art. The blocks, the punches, the kicks are what define taekwondo competition. Therefore, even the most advanced practitioner of taekwondo never leaves behind the most rudimentary element of training—the taekwondo class.

Each time an advanced practitioner performs even the most basic of kicks, he or she develops a deeper understanding of the technique and a new realization about how it can be utilized. It is for this reason that many of the advanced practitioners of the art, who focus their training upon the competitive aspects of taekwondo, begin each training session by standing in front of a mirror and performing each of the basic kicking techniques very slowly. They continue forward, as they slowly increase the speed at which each kick is unleashed. They do this until they reach maximum velocity and speed. This training practice is performed to train the body and the mind in the subtle aspects of each technique, thereby making the practitioner a true master of each of taekwondo's offensive maneuvers.

Mastery of a competitive technique is based upon a deep understanding of the technique. This can only come through regimented practice. For this reason, even the most advanced master of the art never leaves behind the basics.

Cardioaerobic Training

Cardioaerobic training is one of the most essential elements for the advanced taekwondo practitioner who wishes to enter competition. It only takes a few seconds in the ring with an opponent to realize how truly important this element of training is to the competitor.

Running is the option that most taekwondo practitioners add to their training regimen when they enter the world of competition. This is so because there are few activities that are as directly linked to cardiovascular fitness as running. In addition, running develops additional leg strength, which can add muscle development and in turn add to the power of the taekwondo kick.

The competitor in training will normally run 2 miles, five days a week, when not in preparation for an upcoming match. Two miles a day keeps the body in shape and allows the taekwondo practitioner to remain healthy, while maintaining the fitness level necessary to push the body to the next level when an upcoming competition is iminent.

When the taekwondo practitioner is preparing for a competition, intense training usually begins four to six weeks before the event. At this stage, taekwondo practitioners brings his or her body up to the level where he or she can easily run four miles a day. By jogging this distance, you will be on the road from between thirty to forty-five minutes. This is plenty of time for your body to gain the cardiovascular workout needed to prepare you for competition.

If you are in training for an upcoming competition, you should also add what is known as "the Boxer's Run" to your training regimen. The boxer's run is a common training method used by boxers who are preparing for an upcoming bout.

Because each round in a boxing or taekwondo match is three minutes, what the boxer's run prescribes is that after you have warmed up, after about a mile of jogging, you sprint for three minutes. Once this time has elapsed, you will return to your slower pace. You will then jog for three more minutes, then sprint for three minutes. At this point, you will then return to your jogging pace and finally perform the sprint for one last three-minute session. You will finish your run at a jogging pace.

The boxer's run is an ideal way to prepare your body for the endurance needed in a taekwondo match. It is an ideal method to learn what it feels like to bring your heart rate way up, as if you were sparring, and then allow it to slow down somewhat, while still remaining elevated.

Skill Training

There is no more essential element to entering into the ring with an opponent than your ability to efficiently unleash an attack. From the moment you began your taekwondo training, you have developed and redeveloped your ability to unleash the various techniques possessed by this system of martial arts.

At the competitive level, the techniques of taekwondo must be extremely efficient and easily unleashed. To compete, you must know how to unleash the various kicks. You must know which ones you can unleash with precision and must discard all that you cannot perform with excellence, because if you cannot release a kick with power and accuracy in training, you are not going to be able to unleash the kick with any proficiency in competition. To this end, all of the classes, all of the focus drills, and all of the mirror training you have gone through over the years defines what techniques you will use in competition.

If you are an expert with a front kick, use it. If you can unleash a perfect axe kick, use it. If you are clumsy with performing a spinning heel kick, discard it form your arsenal while in competition.

One on One

The primary training method to advance your skills in competition is to train with an opponent. To begin to raise your competitive skill, set up a predetermined set of techniques and then unleash them in the direction of your training partner. At this level of training, contact is not made with these techniques. Instead, a prescribed number of competition-orientated techniques are unleashed near the intended target in order that the taekwondo practitioner in training gets the feel for what techniques are ideally suited to be delivered to an opponent in competition. This also gives the practitioner the ability to develop focus and timing with these techniques.

In taekwondo competition, it is rare that more than three out of four techniques will be unleashed before a point is scored or a competitor is driven from the ring. For this reason, a set of three or four techniques is used in this exercise.

As each advanced taekwondo practitioner has come to learn, through experience, which techniques he or she is most suited to deliver and which ones have the most penetrating effect, the set of techniques used in this practice are defined by each individual practitioner. This is not to say that new techniques or ones that have not been mastered should not be performed, because this training drill is an ideal method of refining your understanding of new techniques.

An example of a set of prescribed techniques to be launched at a training partner is the roundhouse kick, left leg; roundhouse kick, right leg; inside axe kick, left leg; spinning heel kick, right leg.

In this practice drill, once the set of techniques has been defined, it is then performed. Once the initial techniques have been delivered, one's training partner performs the same set of techniques.

This style of training is an ideal warm-up to be undertaken prior to sparring training. This practice segment not only accelerates the heart rate, but also causes one's training partner to begin to move and dodge oncoming attacks.

Sparring

There is no better way to prepare yourself for an upcoming taekwondo tournament than by sparring with a competent opponent. With the advent of the protective gear now worn in sanctioned taekwondo events, this style of full contact training has become far less damaging to the body of the practitioner than in the days of taekwondo before this equipment was available.

As an advancing taekwondo practitioner, you will, no doubt, be sparring with training partners continually. These types of casual sparring matches are not necessarily gearing you toward the type of competition that will take place in a sanctioned match, however. They are most likely simply a means to keep you active and keep your skills honed. As you move toward the date of the event, however, you will want to take your training to a new level. Again, this element of training should begin four to six weeks prior to the event.

The ideal training method to employ at this point is to spar several times a day with a competent opponent. You should break your matches up into rounds—just as is the case in a sanctioned match. If you spar for several minutes with no defined clock, you will not develop the ability to mentally define the length of a round. By sparring to the clock, you will allow yourself the ability to define how much energy to expend at each point during the round. From this, you can learn to pace yourself.

The Study of Movement

The next thing that you must do during sparring training, as you move toward an event, is to acutely study the movement of your partner. If you have advanced up the ranks of the taekwondo competitive ladder, and you are training with highly schooled fighters, you will be able to learn much from their movements, and your sparring training will be very rewarding. If you are training with members of your school, you will, nonetheless, want to become very aware of how they move before each style of technique is unleashed and how they react once it has made impact or has missed. From this, you will gain new insight into how to interrupt an oncoming attack and possibly score a point.

Strategy

Competition strategy is the game plan you design in order to emerge victorious from a competitive bout. There is no one strategy that the taekwondo competitor utilizes to win sanctioned matches. Strategy is a unique, individual perspective designed to utilize the best of what you can bring to the ring.

For some competitors who possess the ability to drive forward with powerful, continuing assaults, their ideal strategy is to do just that—be a very aggressive fighter. For others, who possess the ability to accurately read an opponent, theirs may be to dodge oncoming attacks, and then deliver powerful counterattacks, thereby scoring points.

There is no better tool to define your own level of offensive and defensive strategy than sparring. Sparring is the only way to come to understand what works for you.

It is very common in the realms of advanced taekwondo competition training that your instructor or coach will try to guide you to perform certain techniques in a certain manner in order for you not only to develop new skills but also to address new areas of your training which need development.

Many times when a coach is leading a taekwondo competitor through the offensive and defensive mechanics of a sparring bout, the coach will tell the competitor to act and to react in a certain way. Many coaches have been advanced competitors themselves. From this knowledge, they attempt to make their pupils fight in the same manner that has worked for them. Though training your body to do new things and learning how to react to new methods is an ideal form of advanced taekwondo training, it is you who must ultimately define what works best for you in the realms of competition. Because each person is different, each person performs techniques in a slightly different manner and with a slightly different level of precision. Understanding this, the advanced practitioner of taekwondo learns what he or she can from each instructor and coach and then moves forward, defining his or her own strategy for competition.

Footwork

Footwork refers to your ability to place yourself where you want to be in the midst of competition and to move yourself out of locations you determine are less than appropriate. As mentioned earlier, to the average individual, footwork is just a random set of movements that causes one to move in or move out of a particular situation. To the advanced practitioner of taekwondo, however, footwork is an exact science.

There are four basic types of footwork used in taekwondo sparring: forward, reverse, lateral, and circular or turning. Within the realms of this defined footwork, the advanced competitor trains his body to move in the most appropriate manner in association with both attack and defense.

Forward Footwork

Forward footwork teaches you to rapidly move in toward your opponent with one very direct linear movement and attack. This forward motion can either take the form of a step or a slide. An ideal example of this is when a match begins, you immediately slide in toward your opponent and deliver a front kick to the opponent's midsection, under his or her guard.

Reverse Footwork

Reverse footwork is used to move you rapidly back, away from an attacking opponent, in a linear pattern. As in the case of forward footwork, this movement may take the form of a step or a slide. You can also jump back as part of your reverse footwork.

The common reason for retreating in this fashion is when your opponent has launched an attack at you. Instead of blocking it, you wish to reposition yourself to launch a counterattack. An ideal example of this is when an axe kick is launched in your direction. You slide back out of its path and then immediately counterattack your opponent with a front kick.

Lateral Footwork

Lateral footwork is the next level of movement that the advanced taekwondo practitioner utilizes to position himself or herself in the appropriate location during a sparring match. A lateral footwork technique witnesses you moving from side to side while in competition.

The basic application of the lateral footwork has you simply slide or step to the side when an attack has been launched at you. This movement is performed so that you reposition yourself for a counterstrike. An example of this would be if your opponent has attempted a side kick. You would simply slide to one side, out of the path of the attack, and then immediately counterstrike with a round-house kick to your opponent's mid-body.

Turning or Circular Footwork

Turning or circular footwork is the most advanced level of footwork, employed by the advanced taekwondo combatant. With turning footwork you actually spin out of the path of an attack, continue on, and launch your own offensive assault. For example, say that your opponent attempts to kick you with an axe kick. You pivot out of the path of the attack on the ball of your foot. You then continue spinning through, delivering a spinning heel kick to his head.

The Feint

Taekwondo footwork is not solely designed to be utilized in offensive and defensive applications. Taekwondo footwork is also a means to lure your opponent into assuming that you are about to launch one type of attack, when, in fact, you intend on launching something completely different.

A feint is a deceptive movement, intended to distract your opponent's attention. For example, you can simply rapidly jump forward in the direction of your opponent and stomp your lead foot as it lands on the ground. This will distract your opponent for a second. In this moment of indecision, you can launch a powerful secondary attack, such as a rear leg front kick—thereby scoring a point.

A feint is not simply a forward-driven stomping movement. As you develop your techniques as a competitive strategist, you will learn more subtle ways to lure your opponent into thinking that you are going to perform one movement when you, in fact, are going to launch another. Simply raising your lead leg may be enough to make your opponent jerk. Or by twisting your body and by lifting your lead arm as if you were going to deliver a roundhouse punch may cause your opponent to anticipate the wrong attack.

Each opponent is different and will react to an opponent's movement and feints differently. For this reason, the moment you enter the ring with an opponent is the time to begin to make mental notes about each of your opponent's actions. In some cases, an opponent will fall for the same trick over and over again. In other cases, you may attempt to try the same feint a second time, and your opponent will immediately rush in at you with a powerful attack. For this reason, though a feint is a necessary tool to master in your competitive training, you cannot rely on it to win matches.

Developing Footwork

The development and application of footwork is a personal process for the taekwondo practitioner. It is something that is actualized over time and with extensive amounts of practice.

It is essential to understand that each opponent will deal with footwork in his or her own unique manner. Therefore, the style of footwork that will cause you to emerge victorious from a match with one competitor may not work with another. For this reason, you must first develop an overall pattern of utilizing footwork, which works with your body type and level of competition. You must then be willing to alter this pattern to deal with the specific type of opponent you are fighting.

Weight Shifting

Hand in hand with footwork development, advanced practitioners of taekwondo use the subtle techniques of weight shifting not only to position themselves to launch more powerful kicking techniques but also to be able to move forward or retreat in the most rapid and effective manner possible.

Weight shifting starts with your taking a fighting stance. You then move the weight of your body slightly back on your rear leg or slightly forward on your front leg. What this does is set you up to launch the most appropriate style of movement in your sparring competition. For example, if your weight is placed predominately on your rear leg, you can then use the rear leg to propel you forward as you rapidly move in on your opponent and deliver a powerful straight punch.

The more an advancing practitioner of taekwondo becomes experienced with weight shifting, the more subtle and less noticeable this process becomes. As you have advanced through your competitive training, your eyes have become your best first line of defense. From this, you come to witness all of the actions of an opponent. For example, if you see that your opponent shifting his weight back to his or her rear leg, you will become very aware that your opponent is about to launch an attack.

For this reason, as you advance through your competitive training, you can gain the ability to move your weight less consciously. You can also develop the ability to weight shift very quickly in order to advance or retreat.

CLOSING THE DISTANCE: MOVEMENT FROM LONG TO SHORT RANGE

Competitive matches never begin with you nose to nose with your opponent. The distance between your opponent and yourself does not need to be your enemy. As you develop your competitive strategy, you can learn how to effectively close any gap between your opponent and yourself and not only strike your opponent first, but also continue forward with effective offensive techniques that will help you to emerge victorious from the match.

To understand how to effectively close the distance between your opponent and yourself there are two issues you need to study. The first is how to rapidly penetrate your opponent's defenses and make the initial strike. The second is how to successfully defend against an opponent who is attacking you from a distance.

To view this from a more scientific standpoint, when you view your opponent at a distance, he or she is obviously awaiting your attack. Generally, your opponent will be standing in a ready fighting position, with his or her fists at chest level. What you can observe by studying your opponent's stance is that his or her lower extremities are open for attack.

The Front Kick

To launch a successful attack and beat the possible blocking arm techniques of your opponent, you need to move in quickly and powerfully. One of the best ways to achieve this is to instantly extend a front kick to your opponent's solar plexus.

Many traditional taekwondo practitioners extend their front kicks very obviously from their hip. When the front kick is delivered in traditional fashion, it is snapped out and up. This type of traditional front kick is not an effective form of competitive offense, especially when your opponent is at any distance from you. This is so because when the front kick is performed in the traditional manner, it has no ability to achieve distance and its energy is expended in upward movement—which your opponent can simply lean back from and the attack will miss.

The more effective front kick, especially when there is a need to cover distance, is to not focus the kick in an upward fashion but to extend it from your rear leg outward in the direction of your opponent. By performing the front kick in this fashion, you can gain enormous distance with it, because the kick's own momentum drives you deeply forward; it also will penetrate under your opponent's traditional fighting stance.

Once you have made initial contact with this front kick and possibly scored a point, you can now simply halt your attack. If a point was not scored, you must immediately continue forward with additional offensive attacks. By fighting in this fashion, your opponent does not have the opportunity to successfully counterstrike at you.

The Axe Kick

Another penetrating offensive technique, which is effectively launched at your opponent, is to perform a stepping axe kick to his or her shoulder the moment the match begins. The stepping axe kick not only quickly covers much distance, but also its impact is devastating to your opponent. Because your opponent will no doubt be waiting in a fighting position, the stepping axe kick easily penetrates your opponent's defenses by going over him or her.

The stepping axe kick is effectively performed by rapidly placing your rear leg behind your forward leg; thus giving you added distance. As this movement is performed, you will raise your forward leg straight up. Once you have achieved your desired location, close to your opponent, you powerfully bring your axe kick down onto his shoulder.

Closing the Distance

Closing the distance between your opponent and yourself is not difficult when executed properly. The important thing to remember is one technique is rarely enough to emerge victorious from a match. Therefore, additional techniques to seal your opponent's fate should always be performed.

Because there are no guarantees that you will be the first to move on your opponent, you must also study effective methods to defend against your opponent's oncoming assault at you from a distance.

The Stepping Side Kick

The stepping side kick is no doubt one of the universally most powerful techniques in taekwondo's arsenal. Additionally, it is an excellent method to close the distance on your opponent. Knowing this, what happens if your opponent launches this attack technique at you?

The stepping side kick, by its very design, is very linear. It is performed by placing your rear leg behind your front leg and rapidly extending your front leg in side kick fashion. As powerful as this kicking technique is, its linear nature is its weakness. This sets the stage for how it can be defended against.

Defensive Methodology When You Are Attacked From a Distance

Your opponent attempts to perform a stepping side kick at you. You slide your body to one side; the impact of the kick thereby misses its target on your body. While sidestepping the kick, you should be deflecting it, as well, with a cross arm block. The need for this added deflection arises, because by deflecting the kick you also momentarily take control over your opponent's kicking leg and thereby keep him from rapidly grounding it and perhaps back fist punching you.

Once you have sidestepped and deflected the stepping side kick, the next course of action you should take is to powerfully hand strike your opponent. Though hand strikes in a taekwondo competition are obviously not an effective tool to win a match, they nonetheless are a rapid striking technique.

If you have sidestepped a stepping side kick, due to your close proximity to your opponent, unleashing a rapid and penetrating kicking technique may not be your best form of secondary defense. Therefore, a body punch may be your answer.

There is one exception to this rule. If you have sidestepped your opponent's stepping side kick, you may be able to immediately launch a roundhouse kick to his or her midsection.

As in all cases in competition, what technique you unleash is defined by your placement in relation to your opponent, how skilled your opponent is in recovering from his or her last technique, and how quickly you can deliver a secondary form of offense. To this end, it is essential to keep your techniques simple and only launch them if they have a calculably high probability of making contact.

The Jumping Side Kick

Another very effective distance gainer is the jumping side kick. This kick is launched by stepping your rear leg in front of your forward leg, jumping off of it, and side kicking your opponent. Though this kick is very distance penetrating and powerful, it has the same flaw as the stepping side kick—its linear nature. Additionally, the jumping side kick is more pronounced and slower than the stepping side kick. Therefore, if your opponent attempts to attack you with it, your initial defense is to sidestep.

As you remove yourself from the path of the jumping side kick, you should simultaneously launch a straight punch or roundhouse kick to your opponent's midsection. Because the jumping side kick is a momentum-driven kick, your opponent does not have the ability to effectively stop it once it is launched. As well, once this kick is in progress and you have sidestepped it, your opponent is left open for an effective first punch strike.

Understanding Distance

As you have come to understand, distance between your opponent and yourself does not have to be a disadvantage. You can either launch the first attack, closing the distance, or if your opponent is first out of the gate, you can effectively defend against his or her attack.

By making distance fighting a science and by studying its elements, you can come to an understanding of how to effectively use it to your advantage.

Chapter 10
Self-Defense

At the heart of taekwondo is an exacting system of self-defense. Throughout the evolution of this art, the practicalities of self-defense have been continually refined and redesigned in order to make the taekwondo practitioner more competent and confident in whatever type of physical altercation he or she may encounter.

To come to better understand how the advanced practitioners of taekwondo embrace the science of self-defense, we can view some of these advanced teachings. From this, we can come to understand how the advanced taekwondo practitioner continually refines his or her self-defense methodology and becomes a more competent proponent of the art.

Within each system of self-defense there are root elements that define the art. Taekwondo is no different. In taekwondo, there are also subtle teachings, beyond the basics, which are only revealed to the advanced practitioner of the art. It is understood that only the advanced practitioners, who have trained in the art for an extended period of time, possess the deeper knowledge of taekwondo necessary to truly comprehend these teachings.

ADVANCED SELF-DEFENSE METHODS

Taekwondo is a linear, hard-style system of self-defense. This is to say that all of its techniques are designed around the principle of directly encountering any form of assault.

Linear combat does not mean that there are no circular movements in taekwondo. It simply dictates that every technique, both offensive and defensive, is designed to encounter an attacker in the most direct and efficient manner possible. Whereas the Korean art of hapkido uses deflection of an opponent's energy as its primary method of self-defense, taekwondo uses forceful blocks, powerful strikes, and immediate counterattacks as its primary methodology of self-defense, thereby making it a hard-style system of self-defense.

The First-Strike Advantage

At the root of taekwondo's self-defense methodology is a powerful offense. This is to say, that at the advanced levels of taekwondo, the practitioner prefers to anticipate an opponent's attack and strike first—as opposed to initially blocking and then counterattacking in response to any form of attack.

An ideal example of this style of self-defense is seen when an advanced taekwondo practitioner faces off with an opponent. Rather than simply allowing this altercation to begin, the advanced practitioner will immediately launch a powerful, direct, and very rapid attack. This style of preemptive assault is commonly seen in a driving front kick to the opponent's groin or midsection. This style of defense is known as the first-strike advantage.

The reason that the advanced taekwondo practitioner utilizes the first-strike advantage is that he or she understands that the first person to be powerfully hit in any combative situation is most commonly the one who will lose the confrontation. This is so because once a person is powerfully stricken, not only is he or she more prone to being struck a second and a third time, but also the person most probably has become disoriented by the initial strike and is less likely to possess the ability to come back and launch his or her own powerful attack. To this end, the first-strike advantage is one of the most commonly used tools of self-defense by the advanced practitioners of taekwondo (see Appendix D for illustrations of the Rear and Frontal Attack Positions).

The Taekwondo Kick as a Method of Self-Defense

The essence of taekwondo's art of self-defense is the use of the legs and feet. No other martial art in the world has the elaborate level of advanced kicking techniques possessed by taekwondo.

Because the kick is at the heart of taekwondo's offensive arsenal, it is also the heart of its self-defense methodology. The reason the kick has been designed to be such an exacting weapon in taekwondo is the very effective and powerful striking ability of the legs.

Understanding the Taekwondo Kick

The human legs are developed from birth to be the tools on which we walk. By the very design of the human body, the legs are powerful enough to hold us erect, allow us to walk, and for those fitness-prone individuals, provide us with the ability to run for an untold number of miles. As the legs develop naturally through a human being's life to be powerful tools, they are naturally very effective weapons of offense and defense when they are trained through the techniques of taekwondo. In addition, the length of the legs, when they have been trained to be used effectively in combat, possess a greater reach than the arms. Therefore, the exacting use of the legs greatly enhances an advanced taekwondo practitioner's range of self-defense techniques.

Taekwondo Kicking Self-Defense versus Competition

All of the taekwondo kicks have continued to go through an ever-expanding evolution. This continuing evolution is ever refining the taekwondo kick, making it a very exacting tool of self-defense.

Whereas Olympic sport taekwondo has limited the targeting of the taekwondo kick to above the waistline, this is not the case with taekwondo self-defense. The very powerful taekwondo kick can be targeted to any location on an opponent's body, whether above or below the belt, in order that the practitioner may emerge victorious from any altercation that has occurred.

As a means of self-defense, the first-strike advantage can be initiated by the taekwondo practitioner by unleashing a powerful kick to the ankles, knees, groin, or any other location on an attacker's body that will disable him. Because no rules apply to street combat, the advanced taekwondo practitioner possesses the ability to unleash his or her kick to the most debilitating location possible on his or her opponent.

Jumping Kicks and Taekwondo Self-Defense

As can be seen in any class on taekwondo or at any taekwondo demonstration, this art possesses some of the most beautiful and elaborate kicking techniques ever witnessed. Though the jumping kicks of taekwondo can be developed to be very powerful weapons, in street combat, the advanced practitioner rarely uses these kicks. The reason for this is that it is understood by the advanced practitioner that the moment you jump off the ground, you expose yourself to a plethora of potentially devastating defensive techniques that could not be used against you if you had remained on the ground. Not only do you open yourself up to additional self-defense techniques from your opponent, there are also many other disadvantages to jumping into the air during actual physical combat. The first and perhaps the most self-debilitating is landing incorrectly. If you land incorrectly from your jumping kick, you could easily cause injury to yourself. This is a fact that can be attested to by an untold number of practitioners who have done just that during a taekwondo class or a demonstration.

If you injure yourself while in the midst of combat, you will obviously limit your self-defense effectiveness. Thus, it is understood by all advanced practitioners that there is no advantage to jumping off of the ground simply because you have mastery over a specific jumping technique while in the taekwondo studio.

From a self-defense perspective, the main reason that you do not want to perform an elaborate jumping kick, while in combat, is that these kicks are much slower than a low and precisely targeted kick directed from the ground. As the jumping kicks are slower and more obvious, your opponent may reposition himself while you are in the midst of unleashing this technique. With this, not only will your jumping kick become ineffective, but it will also be difficult to reposition yourself and launch into a secondary assault before your adversary counterattacks you.

To this end, the advanced practitioner understands that the elaborate jumping kicks of taekwondo are best left to the realms of studio and to demonstrations. The jumping kicks that are used in actual self-defense applications are restricted to those that are very direct and very easy to unleash, such as the jumping front kick directed toward an opponent's midsection.

The Taekwondo Punch in Self-Defense

In Olympic-style taekwondo competition, the punch is never allowed to be delivered to an opponent's face or head. Punching techniques are restricted solely to an opponent's body. With the inauguration of the sport of taekwondo, this formality has caused many fundamental taekwondo teachers to veer their teaching away from sport taekwondo. The reason for this is that many believe that training practitioners to focus their striking techniques solely on the body of an opponent hinders their natural ability to strike to the more debilitating locations on an opponent's neck and head if they are ever faced with real combat.

Hidden Inside the Forms of Taekwondo

It must be understood that taekwondo was developed to utilize all elements of the practitioner's body in the most efficient and effective manner possible. Simply by looking at the forms of taekwondo, one immediately sees that there are low kicks to the legs, punches to the head, knife hands to the throat, and elbow strikes to the temples. With the dawning of Olympic sport taekwondo, some teachers have moved away from training their students in the actual self-defense applications detailed in these forms. Instead, they have left the low kicks and the various hand strikes to be practiced only during the forms segment of a taekwondo class. This has caused much speculation on the part of many taekwondo students as to how to actually use the techniques detailed in the forms. This has given birth to the school of thought that there are secret elements, known only to the masters, hidden in the forms of taekwondo.

The only reason this myth persists is based in the fact that many of the modern taekwondo teachers no longer embrace the essential self-defense applications detailed in the forms of taekwondo. They have shifted their focus to training their students in the limited applications of sport taekwondo.

By not embracing the entire system of self-defense detailed in the original delineation of taekwondo, many students have been left with a less than adequate understanding of self-defense. To overcome this problem, the entire system of taekwondo self-defense training, must be embraced, thereby, making all taekwondo practitioners the most competent and well-rounded technicians possible.

Joint Locks and Self-Defense in Taekwondo

Self-defense in taekwondo is not limited to punching and kicking. In the original system of taekwondo, joint locks were an essential element to defend against the grabbing attack of an opponent. Though the joint lock methodology of taekwondo is not as elaborate as its cousin hapkido, nonetheless, joint locks are taught and used by all advanced practitioners of taekwondo as a means of self-defense.

In taekwondo, a joint lock is commonly applied just before or just after a powerful defensive strike has been unleashed. The reason a powerful hit commonly precedes the taekwondo joint lock is that this hit will cause a grabbing opponent to loosen his hold—even if just for a moment. This allows the advanced taekwondo practitioner to then powerfully joint lock the attacking opponent.

The advanced taekwondo practitioner also commonly unleashes a powerful defensive strike, once he has locked his attacker with a joint lock. The reason for this defensive methodology is that a joint lock cannot be held indefinitely. To emerge victorious in any combative situation, a secondary technique must be unleashed. To this end, once an opponent has been restrained, a powerful strike is often made to completely disable the attacker.

One- and Three-Step Sparring

Both beginning and advanced practitioners of taekwondo refine their understanding of self-defense by performing what is known in taekwondo as one- and three-step sparring. One-step sparring witnesses a taekwondo class breaking up into pairs. The students face off. The offensive student performs a front stance, low block, followed by a front stance, middle punch, as he ki haps. The defending student then follows up with the same process. Once the defending student has signaled his or her readiness, the offensive student unleashes a single punch

MAKING A JOINT LOCK EFFECTIVE

The key element that makes all joint locks effective is to move a joint in a direction that it does not naturally travel. By manipulating a joint against itself, you invariably come to a superior degree of control over your opponent—much more so than you could obtain by simply struggling with him muscle to muscle.

To begin your understanding of proper joint-locking techniques, simply take your hand and bend one of your fingers backward in the direction it is not supposed to go. The obvious reaction to this is discomfort. Imagine the reaction you would obtain if you were to perform this finger-bending technique, very aggressively, against an attacking opponent.

To understand how this finger joint-locking technique can be effectively used, simply have a training partner grab your throat with one of his hands. You rapidly reach up to his grip. With your hand and fingers, you dislodge one of his fingers from his grasp. Immediately, you rapidly and powerfully bend that finger back, toward him. Due to the pain you are inflicting on his finger, he instantly releases his grasp on your neck. Thus, you are freed from his chokehold and you may have broken his finger in the process—depending on how powerfully you bent it back. Once you have a controlling hold of your opponent's finger, you can easily dominate his motions by maintaining pressure on that finger, or effortlessly throw him to the ground by simply bending his finger back further toward his own arm and directing him in the direction of the ground.

Though the bending back of the finger is a very simple illustration, it is not only a highly viable joint-locking technique, but it is a very pointed example of how easily control over your opponent can be maintained by locking his joints—leaving him in a submissive position, where he cannot readily come back at you with a further attack.

or kick. The defensive student then defends against that attack in a predetermined manner.

One-step sparring is made up of predetermined offensive and defensive applications. For example, the offensive student will perform "straight punch, number 1." The defensive student will then counteract that attack with a specific block and counterstriking measure. The students will then switch and the other student will defend against the attack. The pair of students will then move forward onto "straight punch, number 2." This process will continue until they have worked through all of the one-step sparring techniques appropriate to their belt level.

One-step sparring teaches the beginning taekwondo practitioner how to defend against the onslaught of a punching or kicking attack in the most efficient manner possible. The student is then capable of taking this knowledge to the streets if the need ever arises.

In three-step sparring, pairs of students face off. In this drill, once the defending student has signaled his or her readiness with a down block, middle punch, and ki hap, the offensive student unleashes three consecutive offensive techniques. These may include three kicks, three punches, or a combination of both kicks and punches.

Three-step sparring allows the student to develop an understanding of combination techniques. It also teaches the student, through actual experience, which offensive technique most easily follows the previous applications.

Both one- and three-step sparring are ideal tools for even the advanced practitioner to continue to refine his or her understanding of taekwondo's self-defense methodology. These predetermined sets of offensive and defensive maneuvers are far too sterile for the type of combat that takes place on the street, however. For this reason, the advanced practitioner of taekwondo comes to understand that these maneuvers are simply a basis for defensive action in an actual street fight and therefore studies and comes to embrace the more refined level of physical combat.

UNDERSTANDING PHYSICAL COMBAT

The first thing a new student of taekwondo is taught is how to perform the basic blocks, punches, and kicks of the art. As one progresses through the middle ranks of the art, he begins to refine these techniques and begins to evolve into a more refined practitioner—utilizing the various self-defense techniques with less thought and more instinctive dynamics. A practitioner does not move onto the advanced level of the art, however, until he comes to understand some very subtle elements of physical combat.

At the advanced level, the taekwondo practitioner must master taekwondo's economy of motion, theories of continuous motion, and the control of distance. Once these understandings have been mastered, the taekwondo practitioner will possess a unique knowledge of physical combat never understood by most combatants. This will provide the practitioner with a distant advantage, increases his or her chances of emerging victorious from any combative situation.

Taekwondo Self-Defense and The Economy of Motion

In any self-defense-orientated physical confrontation, there is one and only one ultimate goal: survival by the most rapid means possible. What this entails is to overcome any style of attack that your opponent launches against you and deliver the first debilitating blow—never allowing your opponent to possess the first-strike advantage.

This style of advanced taekwondo self-defense is accomplished by initially becoming aware of and utilizing the shortest distance between the two most important points in the confrontation: your fist, foot, elbow, or knee and a debilitating targeted area on your opponent—in other words, defense that is offense. This concept is known in taekwondo as "economy of motion."

Conventional Training Versus The Economy of Motion

In the early stages of taekwondo training, the student is taught how to block, where best to target strikes, and how to get out of the way of an oncoming assault. Generally, the novice taekwondo practitioner chooses to take a lengthy, round-about way to achieve these goals, however. Basic taekwondo training teaches the student to initially forcefully block the attack of an adversary and then counter-attack with a prescribed technique. With today's sophisticated fighters, however, this extended method of self-defense is no longer a viable means of protection. Therefore, the advanced practitioner of taekwondo employs an understanding of economy of motion.

Use a Punch as a Block

Here's the most obvious example of this understanding: instead of blocking a kick and then launching a counterassault, simply block the oncoming kick with a punch to your opponent's shin. This is much more expedient and with this, not only have you delivered the first strike, but you have also possibly injured your

> The basic principle of taekwondo's economy of motion dictates that you reduce your physical movement and thereby speed up your ability to strike or counterstrike your opponent. Within this framework every block, strike, or movement you make must have an absolute necessity and a destined goal, or there is no purpose in performing it.

PUNCH BLOCK

opponent's leg in the process. With this style of offensive defense, you have instantly begun your road to victory in the confrontation.

Economy of Motion: Theories of Defense

Taekwondo's economy of motion consists of four primary rules of defense:

1. All defensive techniques must actually be offensive.
2. Step out of the way of any technique rather than encounter it directly.
3. Never anticipate what your opponent may have in mind.
4. Never attempt a technique that you have not fully mastered.

Rule One

Rule number one of taekwondo's economy of motion teaches the advanced taekwondo practitioner to never block a technique with the hopes of following through with a counterattack. All forms of physical combat are very fast and completely unpredictable. You can never know what your opponent will unleash next. For this reason, your ability to follow through with a secondary attack after you have blocked a punch or a kick may never occur. Therefore, it is far better to circumvent any attack with a counteracting punch or kick, such as the previously described punch interception of a kick.

Rule Two

Rule number two teaches the advanced taekwondo practitioner a very simple and self-evident rule of combat—it is far better to step out of the path of a punch or a kick than to attempt to block it. This is so because the impact of blocking any punch or kick can damage your body. As any beginning taekwondo student comes to readily understand, a punch, and particularly a kick, is a very powerful oncoming weapon. When you forcefully block it with your hand or arm, it can easily become bruised and in some cases broken. Thus the advanced practitioner of taekwondo uses economy of motion and never meets an oncoming attack with an unnecessary block—when it is far better to simply move out of the path of an attack and then counterstrike with a powerful punch or kick.

A basic example of this style of defense occurs when your opponent launches a front kick toward you. Simply retreating, in a controlled fashion, means that his kick will not possess the distance to make impact. Once the kick has missed, you can then rapidly move in on your opponent and strike him or her with a powerful punch or kick.

In a more advanced example, your opponent may launch a stepping side kick toward you. In this case, you can simply sidestep the onslaught of this technique. The kick will miss, and you can deliver a powerful technique such as a low side kick to your opponent's knee or a straight punch to his or her face.

Rule Three

The third rule of taekwondo's economy of motion dictates that you can never know what your opponent may have in mind. Therefore, advanced taekwondo practitioners never assume that once they block or intercept a specific technique that they will be able to follow through with a particular and predetermined counterattack.

Physical combat moves at a very rapid pace. Each opponent is unique in his or her fighting abilities and understanding of combat. For this reason, you cannot anticipate what an opponent will do next. Therefore, you must remain fluid in your motion and be able to adjust and readjust to any form of attack or counterattack that may be unleashed.

Through the formal training using one-step and three-step sparring, the taekwondo practitioner is schooled in the various forms of blocking and methods of counterattacking taught in taekwondo. Though this form of traditional training lays the foundation for your ability to defend yourself, these training methods are far too sterile for the type of combat that takes place on the street. Therefore, advanced taekwondo practitioners use the tools learned in their classes to lay the foundation for their self-defense methodology and then move forward and train themselves to readjust any technique to make it the most advantageous to any style of combat they find themselves engulfed within.

Rule Four

The fourth rule of taekwondo's theory of economy of motion teaches that you should never attempt a technique that you have not fully mastered. Though this may sound logical, there are an untold number of practitioners who perform the various taekwondo punching and kicking techniques in the dojang and feel that they understand them—though they have never attempted to use them in actual physical combat. This way of misunderstanding the combat effectiveness of a technique is commonly found in those schools of taekwondo that only train their students in light or no-contact sparring. In these types of sparring matches, the techniques are slowed down immensely, and each technique is delivered in a very controlled and defined fashion. Though this is a fine method to train the novice student in control and provide some of the elemental understanding of fighting, it does little to prepare one for the ferociousness of actual hand-to-hand combat on the street.

With this style of controlled, sterile training, many practitioners may be able to deliver a kicking technique in a very precise fashion with beautiful execution, but in doing so they also come to falsely believe that they have mastered the techniques. Mastery, however, is not simply about how prettily you can execute any given technique. Mastery is your ability to use the technique effectively in combat.

Taekwondo is not ballet. Taekwondo is a precise system of self-defense. Though taekwondo obviously possesses some techniques that are more effective in a demonstration than in combat, each technique is, nonetheless, developed around the principal of personal self-defense. To this end, though you can perform a technique with beautiful execution, this does not necessarily mean that the technique is combat effective. And, this is where many advancing practitioners fall prey to seasoned street fighters.

The Simpler the Better

It is essential to remember that though you may practice a kick a thousand times and be able to deliver it in a stunning fashion in front of the mirror this does not mean that the technique is streetworthy. A streetworthy technique is one that is rapid, precise, and hard to block. In other words, "the simpler the better."

To consider that you have mastered a technique, you must be able to use it efficiently in combat. If you cannot, the technique should never be unleashed in an altercation on the street.

Mastering Taekwondo's Economy of Motion

The best step you can take to integrate the economy of motion into your self-defense arsenal is to delineate what you believe is the appropriate reaction to any given action. Then, try it out with a training partner. If it works, great. If not, remove the technique from your self-defense methodology.

TAEKWONDO AND THE PRINCIPLES OF CONTINUOUS MOTION

Once an adversary has accosted you on the street, attacking with one offensive technique is virtually never enough to emerge victorious from the confrontation. It is uncommon that you will strike with enough force or enough power to completely disable an opponent in one blow. Additionally, if you wait to see your opponent's responses to each hit you deliver, it only gives him the ability to come back and counterattack, perhaps at that point, gaining victory.

Advanced taekwondo practitioners understand that what they must do is to find a conscious continuum from one technique to the next and to the next until their opponent has no chance of coming back and defeating them. This is known as taekwondo's theory of continuous motion.

The Dojang Versus the Streets

As detailed previously, traditional taekwondo training generally teaches a novice student to follow a block with a punch, a punch with a kick, and so on. This style of self-defense is too orchestrated and far too sterile for any confrontation that may occur on the street, or, in fact, for any sanctioned competition which takes place under the watchful eye of judges and referees.

For your defensive and offensive techniques to be effective on the street, your techniques must be performed in an extremely rapid fashion and strike your intended target with a continuous flow from one movement onto the next. This does not mean that you simply block and then strike once. What this entails is that you block your opponent's advance and then strike and continue on with another strike and another one, until he has become completely debilitated.

Though this may sound logical, it is not as easily effected as you may think—for there are many elements that come in play in a physical confrontation that do not exist in the taekwondo studio—certainly not the least of which is your opponent's desire to win. To this end, the advancing taekwondo practitioner studies the elements that make up taekwondo's method of continuous motion. Thereby, making continuous motion a science and not simply a random form of self-defense where techniques are launched simply as they come to mind.

The Three Rules of Continuous Motion

The following are the three rules of continuous motion:

1. Always follow one technique with another.
2. Always strike to the most debilitating and easily accessible target on your opponent.
3. Each defensive and offensive technique you perform must allow you to easily and effectively follow it with another technique.

Rule One

When we view the three rules of taekwondo theory of continuous motion, we see that the first rule is the defining factor in this level of advanced taekwondo self-defense understanding. That rule is to always follow one technique with another. What this means is that one technique, be it defensive or offensive, must always be followed by another, and then another, until you have obtained victory over your opponent.

No Random Acts

To begin to practice this taekwondo theory of continuous motion, you must first understand that continuous motion does not mean your opponent and yourself go at it randomly, throwing whatever technique comes to mind, as is generally the case in a street fight, until one of you emerges the victor. What taekwondo's advanced understanding of continuous motion does teach is that you understand what type of technique effectively follows your last one—allowing you to maintain the advantage and accomplish your objective of winning the confrontation quickly.

In the streets, one technique rapidly follows another one. Whether they are launched with conscious understanding or not is irrelevant. If you do not immediately take control of a street confrontation, the random continuous motion of a savvy street fighter will easily defeat even the most long-trained taekwondo stylist who believes in following the rules of combat as taught in the martial art studio.

The advantage you, as a trained taekwondo stylist, have over the street fighter is that when it comes to the use of continuous motion, you have developed the proper technique in using the various blocks, punches, and kicks. Knowing these techniques, and then placing them in the scientific realm of conscious continuous motion, gives you the advantage in any confrontation.

You may, in fact, be quite well schooled and capable of launching the appropriate block and following it with a powerful strike. The situation many taekwondo stylists fall into, however, is that when the first technique does not prove to be effective, they cannot quickly and easily move forward into a secondary technique. For example, assume that your opponent launches a roundhouse punch at you. Quickly, you step in and block it with a standard in-to-out block, expecting to then counterstrike. In a street fight, it is very common that once your opponent's initial punch has been blocked, he will instantly swing at you with another random striking technique with his other arm. What will your course of action be if you have stepped in too deeply, placing all of your strategy on this one planned block and one planned follow-up? You will, undoubtedly, be hit by his secondary strike.

For this reason, taekwondo's theory of continuous motion teaches that you must remain continually in motion. Do not lock into one defensive technique and expect it to be enough to allow you to counterstrike. Be constantly aware and willing to instantly change your defense strategy to overcome any specific fighting situation.

Rule Two

The streets are not a favorable place to be engaged in any altercation. What takes place there is neither pretty nor fair. If you ever find yourself engaged in a street fight, you must defend yourself at all costs, because you can be certain your opponent will have no mercy on you. Thus, it serves no purpose in your disposal of an attacking opponent to face off with him and go blow to blow as in a sanctioned taekwondo match. This type of fair fighting is for the movies, where the good guy always wins. In the street, any counterattack you unleash must be done so with your ultimate self-preservation in mind. Thus, rule two: "always strike to the most debilitating and easily accessible target on your opponent," should always be employed.

As an advancing taekwondo stylist, you have undergone a large amount of training in where to strike and why to strike. By refining this understanding and making it street oriented, you will possess the advantage in a street confrontation. The obvious preliminary strike points that will quickly debilitate your adversary are the nose, the eyes, the temples, the throat, and the ears. The secondary strike points on an opponent are his groin, knees, kidneys, and ribs. These are the only locations you should even think of launching an attack at during a street altercation. To strike randomly not only wastes your energy but also gives your opponent the ability to take control of the confrontation if he delivers one powerful offensive technique.

Also, you should not aim strikes at your opponent's body in a street confrontation with the hope that such continual hits will eventually have the effect of disabling him—as is sometimes the case in sanctioned boxing or kickboxing matches. This type of attack strategy gives the trained opponent too much time to launch a debilitating attack on your person. Therefore, any strike you make must be very precise and be unleashed with a debilitating power to the primary strike zones.

The majority of the first-strike points are to your opponent's head. Knowing this, what striking instrument reaches those points most quickly? Obviously your hands. Therefore, even though taekwondo has a great array of kicking techniques, they should not necessarily be used in close-contact street fighting. Straight punches, back fists, palm strikes, and to a slightly lesser degree, knife hands and elbows are the first-strike weapons of choice for the advanced practitioner of taekwondo in a street altercation, because they are not only the closest to his head but also require a great deal less aim and timing than does a taekwondo kicking technique to your opponent's head.

Understanding the Continuous Motion of Your Opponent

In a street fight, there is no guarantee that any target on your opponent's body will remain in any location long enough for you to be able to focus, set up, and then deliver a powerful strike. This is so because your opponent is continually in motion just as you are. Therefore, though other hand techniques may prove to be effective as secondary strike weapons, the fist assures you of immediate powerful impact. For example, if your first assault does not make contact, the fist is easily redirected and formed into a secondary weapon—be it a block or strike.

Once an initial penetrating strike has been made, the fist also allows you to readily strike again and again, as necessary. This secondary strike can be more creative, as long as your opponent has been properly stunned by your first strike.

Again, however, you must remember that it is unlikely that your first strike will posses enough power to completely debilitate your opponent. With this in mind, the reason you can vary your technique, at the time of your secondary attack, is that the initial stun of a powerful punch will last approximately three seconds. Though this may seem like a very small amount of time, in a street fight it can be the difference between winning and losing. Therefore, you must instantly follow up your first fist strike with an equally powerful blow. This may well be most effectively accomplished by alternating arms and punching to his head again and again several times. You may, however, at this point have the ability to kick him to the groin or deliver a foot to his knee. The key element is to allow whatever fighting techniques to flow naturally and continue until your victory is assured.

Rule Three

A common mistake that many make at the outset of a street confrontation is placing far too much emphasis on one very powerful offensive technique. You may assume that it will cause enough damage to debilitate your opponent. But, what happens if this technique misses its target? A competent street fighter will take advantage of your missing him and rapidly hit you. Here again, you must never expect any particular initial or secondary striking technique to win the battle for you. You must be willing to instantly change your mode of operation at any point in the confrontation.

Do not lock yourself into the last technique that you have performed. By doing this, you only prevent yourself from instantly unleashing a different attack when necessary.

For these reasons, you must allow both your defensive and offensive techniques to be fluid, loose, and free enough that you can quickly move onto secondary or further assault techniques when and if it is necessary.

Move Naturally

To be effective using taekwondo's theory of continuous motion in a street fight, you must perform the strike that comes most naturally in any given situation. For example, if you have just blocked your opponent's oncoming punch, your hands are most likely at approximately shoulder level. What this tells you is that you should continue through, telegraphing a fist strike to your opponent's head quite effortlessly. By immediately striking to his head once his technique has been blocked, not only does your arm not have far to travel, but also your opponent will have had virtually no time to redirect his energy to launch a secondary attack on you. Furthermore, by instantly continuing through with a linear technique, such as a straight punch, you have not allowed your opponent the ability or time to see this type of technique coming. Thus, he will not possess the ability to block it.

Partner Training in Continuous Motion

As there is no time to think and plan out your strategy in a street fight, the blocks and strikes you make must become very natural and follow a flowing pattern. But, how can you achieve this ability, maintain control of a fight, and not allow it to become just a slugfest? Though the answer to this is not simple, the ability to rapidly achieve desired results in a street confrontation comes from a tactical understanding of where and when to hit your opponent. Well-protected partner practice is the ideal way to come to this understanding of how to effectively block and then immediately strike while making all of your techniques very effective.

The most important factor in partner training, in relation to continuous motion, are street-fighting drills. Your training partner and you should not be allowed to know or expect what is coming—for this is the leading problem with most traditional martial arts training.

To become proficient in continuous motion, it is essential that, while in partner practice, you simply allow whatever will happen to happen—with no rules attached. As this is the case in a street fight. From this type of training, you can ascertain what techniques will rapidly allow you to emerge victorious in a street fight.

Remember, in any street confrontation, strike first before your opponent strikes. If this is not achieved, then block and instantly counterstrike with the closest weapon you have to your opponent's head. This is usually a fist, but never rule out any other technique that may be effective. Then, once you have connected with your first strike, you must continue to strike again and again, to the most vulnerable regions on your opponent's body, until he has no ability to recover.

Taekwondo and the Dynamics of Distance

Physical confrontations commonly begin at one of two distances. The first is when you and your opponent are in very close proximity to one another. The second is arguably the most common start point for a confrontation—one that begins when the two of you are at a distance from one another.

Ideally illustrative of this is the altercation that begins when an agitated opponent signals his intentions by calling you names. This style of initial confrontation is actually to your advantage, because at a distance there are many more viable ways of defending yourself than when your opponent has already accosted you and the two of you are face to face.

Keep Your Distance

The first rule of taekwondo distance fighting is to keep your distance. As long as your assailant is not close enough to hit or grab you, you will remain free from injury and not have to forcefully defend yourself by punching or kicking your attacker.

The question always arises, "How do I keep my opponent at bay?" In actuality, this is one of the most readily achievable forms of self-defense. The answer is "keep moving."

This is the same understanding that is used in a taekwondo sparring match. As long as you keep moving, your opponent will not only have difficulty in closing the distance between the two of you, but in certain circumstances he may never be able to make offensive contact with you at all. How you move is the most important element, for if you wish to keep your opponent at a distance, your defensive movements should never be made randomly.

Movement

The first method of consciously keeping your distance from your attacker is to define your environment. Ideally, you will have several feet of space, or more, around you. In these cases, begin to pivot in a circular fashion around your opponent. Using him as your central axis, you should continue to circularly alter your location. As a result, he will not have a direct path of attack.

The reason that you move in a circular fashion is that this allows you to keep your opponent off-balance. Because he is at the center of the circle you are making, he will be forced to pivot around in a very small pattern. This will often cause him not only to remain off-balance but may also cause him to trip over his own feet because he may become somewhat disoriented. Additionally, by moving in a circular pattern, you can slowly and consciously continue to move back and away from him, thereby, increasing your distance. As you do this, he will have to travel farther to actually attack you. Thus, you will have additional time to prepare your defense.

It is essential at this level of self-defense that you do not turn and take your eyes off of your attacking opponent at any time. If you do, this will provide him with an opportunity to charge in at you. Because you may not see his approach, this could be devastating. Therefore, keep your eyes on your attacker at all times, as you continue to move.

Move and Block

Though circular movement is a viable first line of defense, many times an enraged attacker will become agitated at his inability to simply come up and punch you. This is when he may simply run in at you to make contact. At this point, your first line of self-defense is to simply alter your circular pattern and rapidly step back or step to the side of his attack. Because of his momentum-driven run, if you are quick, you will again have foiled his attempted attack.

Of course, this style of defense will not necessarily cause you to emerge victorious from all confrontations. If your opponent persists, your next line of self-defense is to block your opponent's attack when he rushes in at you.

It must be reiterated, however, that your best method of self-defense is to never make contact with an opponent unless it is absolutely necessary. With no contact, there is no possibility of physical injury. The moment that contact is made, the chances of injury are enormous—both by being hit and by delivering your defensive applications. Thus, actual physical contact should be your last level of self-defense when all other methods have failed.

Your first line of blocking self-defense is to rapidly sidestep any rushing attack. The basis for this style of movement can be seen in football when a pass rusher charges in at the quarterback. The quarterback will wait until the last second before impact is made and then rapidly sidestep the onslaught, applying a little deflective push to his opponent. Possession of the ball is maintained, and the individual who attempted the tackle is sent to the ground where he must get up if he hopes to instigate another offense.

The key element to remember in this style of blocking self-defense is to not move until the last possible moment. If you move too soon, your opponent will see this action and have time to recalculate his attack—perhaps making contact with you.

Keep in mind that your attacker is highly adrenalized. Thus, his energy is quickly expended. As long as you can keep him away from you, he will be burning excessive amounts of energy and you, remaining relatively calm, will maintain your energy surplus. Thus, like the competent boxer who allows his opponent to chase him around the ring, you too can conserve your energy and counterattack only when your opponent is worn out.

Tight Quarters

You will not always be in a wide open space when an assailant accosts you. When a large amount of space is not available, many instructors of self-defense teach that you should back yourself up against a wall. This is especially the case if you find yourself in a room. The belief is that if you back yourself up to a wall, your attacker cannot come around behind you. Though there is a logic to this form of self-defense, the biggest downside to it is that once you back yourself up against a wall, your movement is highly limited and your attacker can close in on you and strike with multiple attacks. Additionally, your defensive blocking techniques are highly restricted, with your back against a wall, as you can only move effectively from side to side. If you attempt to push out from the wall, you must then meet the punches of your attacker head on.

For these reasons, moving against a wall should only be employed when it is absolutely to your advantage. This situation would occur when your attacker were rapidly rushing in at you. Then, simply by sidestepping his attack, redirecting his aggressive energy, and guiding his face or body into the wall, you will have saved yourself the necessity of striking out at him, because you have used his own momentum-driven force to cause him to powerfully impact the nearby wall.

In virtually all other cases, it is to your advantage to keep moving if you find yourself accosted in a walled indoor or outdoor location. Even if your movements must be linear, due to the confined configuration of the space, your attacker will still need to chase after you to grab or to strike at you.

When Movement Fails

Movement should always be your first line of defense. Blocking should be your second. But, movement and blocking cannot always be your last line of defense. For this reason, you must be prepared to effectively defend yourself when you come face to face with an attacker.

There are a few very basic, yet very effective, preliminary techniques you can employ when an opponent has closed the distance on you. The first, and perhaps most effective, is to deliver a powerful front kick to his groin, to his midsection, or under his jaw just before he is close enough to make punching or grabbing contact with you. By kicking him in this rapid and penetrating fashion, not only will you have gained the first-strike advantage, but also your surprise attack may debilitate him to the degree that he will not desire or possess the ability to regroup with a secondary attack.

In some cases, this front kick self-defense cannot be administered. Your next line of defense will then be you deflecting the onslaught of his shoving, punching, or grabbing assault. To do this, you must first employ the basic rule of deflection, "get out of the way." The most effective way to do this is simply to sidestep the assault. Then, once his initial attack has missed, you can take control over the altercation by delivering a powerful counterstrike, such as a low side kick to his knee. In other cases, you will want to dominate his movements and send him to the ground, where he cannot effectively launch another attack.

TAEKWONDO KICKS FOR SELF-DEFENSE

Modern taekwondo has entered into a period where the rules of Olympic sport taekwondo have come to dominate the way in which this system of martial arts is taught. Though taekwondo's presence in the Olympics has done much to promote the art, on the whole, the rules inherent with Olympic sporting events are limiting by their very design. Because of this Olympic association, many of the offensive and defensive techniques used in traditional taekwondo have been left behind and are no longer taught by many instructors who focus their training upon the sport application of this art. As taekwondo was first and foremost designed to be an exacting system of self-defense, these lost techniques must be reintegrated into the overall training of the taekwondo practitioner. From this, the advancing taekwondo stylist will become not only more well versed in self-defense applications but also a more complete proponent of the art.

Self-Defense and the Low Kicks of Taekwondo

In Olympic taekwondo, the offensive strike zone on an opponent is limited to locations above the waistline. There are, however, numerous kicking techniques that were once commonly taught in traditional taekwondo, and can be found in the forms, that were targeted at locations well below the waistline. Because these techniques are ideal to use in self-defense applications, they must be rediscovered by advanced practitioners of taekwondo and can be put to use as a means of exacting self-defense.

The Self-Defense-Orientated Front Kick

The front kick is the most easily used self-defense-orientated low-kicking technique in the taekwondo arsenal. As is commonly understood, a front kick to the groin of any man is universally debilitating. There are, however, other less frequently used offensive and defensive applications for the front kick. The first of these is a front kick strike targeted at an opponent's shin.

A shin strike, though obviously not as devastating as a groin strike, is, nonetheless, very effective in deterring an opponent from initially launching an attack. This is especially the case with close-contact infighting. For example, if an opponent moves in at you in an attempt to punch you in your face. By immediately delivering a powerful front kick targeted at his shin, your will halt his attack, and you will have the ability to either follow up with additional countermeasures or leave the situation before the altercation continues on any further.

The Self-Defense Orientated Roundhouse Kick

The low-level roundhouse kick is another taekwondo kick whose self-defense effectiveness becomes substantially enhanced by targeting it at a low location on your opponent's body. At the outset of any confrontation, a roundhouse kick can be most effectively delivered to the outside of your opponent's knee.

Striking to an opponent's knee with a low roundhouse kick will send your opponent off-balance—perhaps to such a degree that he will be knocked to the ground. If your impact is not that substantial, he will at least be set off-balance, and additional techniques, such as a straight punch to his face, will cause you to emerge victorious from the confrontation.

You can also deliver a low roundhouse kick toward your adversary's outer thigh. The impact of this can be used as a prelude to a secondary offensive technique, because the outer thigh strike location will not immediately impair an opponent. Nonetheless, this is an easily targeted location on your opponent's body, and striking it can be used to distract him while you deliver another powerful attack.

The Self-Defense-Orientated Side Kick

As an offensive weapon, the side kick can be effectively delivered to low targets on an opponent such as his shin or his knee. At midlevel, the side kick is ideally targeted at your opponent's midsection. This kick can be used at the outset of a confrontation to impede the progress of an adversarial attack. Or, it can be used at any point during the fight when you are in close proximity to your opponent and need an effective weapon that is very difficult to block.

The low side kick does not need to be launched from the rear leg, as is common with many traditional taekwondo kicking techniques. This kick can be launched from virtually any standing position.

A forward leg, low side kick is virtually impossible for an opponent to defend against. Thus, it is an exceedingly effective offensive weapon.

Defense Against the Taekwondo Kick

In all basic classes in taekwondo the obvious and generally prescribed method to defend against any oncoming kick is to forcefully block it. There are, however, problems with defending against a kick in this manner. First of all, if your opponent develops any power in his kick, its impact to your blocking hand or arm can easily break them. In some cases, when a kick is forcefully blocked, the damage to the blocking components of your body can exceed the damage that may have incurred from the kick actually impacting you into its intended strike point. Therefore, all advanced practitioners of taekwondo understand that it is far better to never allow a kick to strike any part of your body. If it doesn't strike you, there is no chance of the kick injuring you. Understanding this, the advanced practitioner of taekwondo masters new methods of dealing with the onslaught of a kick.

Linear Offense

As detailed earlier, taekwondo is a linear, hard-style system of the martial arts. That is to say that its patterns of assault are based in straight-ahead movements. In fact, taekwondo's entire martial philosophy is that the striking weapons of the body, be they the hand, the arm, the foot, or the leg, directly impact a specific target.

With this understanding, the initial effortless defense used by the advanced practitioner of taekwondo against the kick is to simply move out of the path of the opponent's striking leg. The most elemental example is to simply allow yourself to quickly retreat in either a sliding or stepping back manner, out of the reach of the oncoming kick. Though this may sound exceedingly simple, it is in fact perhaps the quickest, safest, and most applicable way to not be hit by an oncoming kick.

Effortless Defense Against the Roundhouse Kick

Your opponent launches a roundhouse kick at you. When you simply lean back out of the path of the kick, not only does it miss you, but also the momentum it has developed forces your opponent to continue through with the power of the kick itself.

The roundhouse kick by its very nature does not have a deeply penetrating path of attack. This is the case with all circular kicks. Thus, once its target has moved out of the way of its impact, all hope for that specific roundhouse kick to be effective is lost.

By eluding a roundhouse kicking assault in this manner, not only were you not struck by the kick, but you also avoided having to forcefully block it. Once the kick has missed, you now possess the ability to easily counterstrike your adversary whose missed kick has left him in a vulnerable position.

Effortless Defense Against the Spinning Heel Kick

Other circular kicks in the taekwondo arsenal such as the spinning heel kick possess the same structure and fate as the previously discussed roundhouse kick. As they are both circular kicks, once they are launched, simply by moving yourself out of their range, they cannot strike you.

Effortless Defense Against the Linear Kicks of Taekwondo

When we view the basic front and side kick, we see that they are equally limited in their range. Though they are straight kicking techniques, once they are launched, their power has been expended. If you move just slightly back out of their range, your opponent's advances have been nullified, and there is little more your opponent can do in these situations but move onto another technique. In the interim, you have the ability to take countermeasures.

Variations on the basic front and side kick pose a more complicated defense scenario. Advanced taekwondo kicks such as the stepping or jumping front or side kick have much more power, speed, and range than do the previously mentioned simple versions of these kicks. If you are quick, you can rapidly retreat from these advanced kicks. But, due to the speed of these kicking techniques, doing so generally leaves you off-balance and thus in a less than ideal situation to counterstrike. Furthermore, due to the range potential and the ability for your opponent to quickly recover and redirect his energies from these kicking techniques, a straight back retreat is generally not what is best prescribed.

The quickest and easiest way to effectively deal with the onslaught of one of these linear kicks, without having to block it directly, is simply to sidestep it. You now have the opportunity to further defend yourself against your opponent.

Is Movement Enough?

As you now understand, the most effective and effortless method to deal with the two types of taekwondo kicks is to simply move out of their path. But, is simply moving out of the way of the oncoming kick enough, or is it necessary to take further defensive action? That depends on your situation.

In a street confrontation, simply moving out of the way of a kick is probably not enough. Therefore, you must come to understand what options are available to you to continue forward with the appropriate self-defense once the power of the oncoming taekwondo kick has been nullified.

There are two courses of action you can take. The most obvious is to counterstrike your opponent with the most powerful technique available to you once his kick has missed. This may be a kick or a punch to the most exposed part of his body.

To better understand this method of forcefully counterattacking the taekwondo kick, we can look at the roundhouse kick. Once a roundhouse kick has been launched at you, leaning out of the way and allowing your opponent to continue through with his momentum leaves him exposed for you to deliver a powerful counterattack. Two ideal examples of this are an axe kick to his shoulder or a simple straight punch to his head.

In the case of a stepping side kick, your first defense would be to sidestep from the path of its attack. Once the kick has missed, you can immediately deliver a low side kick to the back of your opponent's knee. This will set him off-balance and keep him from launching a secondary attack at you. At this point, you should deliver a secondary strike such as a side kick to his head or a straight punch to his face. By doing so, you will emerge victorious from the confrontation.

A Kick as a Form of Defense

Though these counterstriking techniques against the taekwondo kick can be quite forceful, they can also be performed in an almost toying yet extremely effective manner. For example, no doubt one of the most useful techniques for blocking the straight back kick or spinning heel kick is simply extending a front kick to your opponent's buttocks region once he has begun turning back into the kick. This front kick interception will immediately nullify his offense, and you can continue through with further counterattack techniques as necessary.

Understanding Effortless Self-Defense

The three previous examples detailed how the advanced taekwondo practitioner can effortlessly defend against a kicking attack and then deliver an effective counterstrike on his or her opponent.

The main thing to keep in mind when you perform this style of advanced taekwondo self-defense, however, is that you must immediately take advantage of your opponent's vulnerability and counterstrike him to the most open and debilitating location on his body. This counterstrike must be unleashed at the moment your opponent's kick has missed making contact with its intended target, because this is when he is most off-balance and vulnerable to counterattack.

More Than Self-Defense

More than simply a means of self-defense, rapidly moving out of the path of an oncoming attack and then aggressively counterstriking is often the tool of choice for advanced practitioners in taekwondo tournaments. The reason for this is that they keep the competitor free from injury and are able to rapidly score points.

Stay Aware

Perhaps the leading mistake many taekwondo stylists make when embroiled in a confrontational situation is to witness their opponent preparing to perform a kick and then allowing him to go through with it. If you witness your opponent preparing to kick, should you give him the opportunity to go through with this technique?

Undoubtedly, the simplest and most direct method of counterattacking the taekwondo kick is to never allow it be executed in the first place. This form of advanced self-defense is quite easily achieved by remaining very aware of your opponent's movements.

Your opponent gets in a stance and prepares to kick at you—by immediately rushing in at him and closing the striking distance, you foil his kicking technique by throwing him off-balance. Not giving him the distance needed to continue through and perform his kick keeps his kick from being unleashed. Therefore, you have performed initial self-defense. At this juncture, you will need to take control over the confrontation. By closing in on him and immediately striking him with a fist to his face, you have taken the first-strike advantage in the fight, thus placing you in the dominant position.

Making It a Science

To achieve the ability to defend against the taekwondo kick without ever blocking it directly, the advanced practitioner of taekwondo personally studies each of taekwondo's kicks, thereby making defending against them a science. From this, a new level of self-defense mastery is born, leaving the taekwondo practitioner with a unique understanding of how to defend against these advanced kicking techniques.

Taekwondo Kick Takedowns

Any advanced practitioner of taekwondo possesses no doubt as to the power of the taekwondo kick. The best way to counteract and defeat an opponent who has launched one of these powerful kicking techniques is an ongoing element of study for all advanced practitioners of this art.

Each confrontational situation in which an opponent launches a kicking attack toward you has its own set of circumstances. As detailed previously, at times, a quick retreat from the attack of the kick, followed by a rapid counteroffensive advance may be the best form of self-defense. At other times, the only recourse may be to forcefully block the attack. No matter what method is used to deal with the oncoming taekwondo kick, some type of defensive action must be taken or the power of the taekwondo kick will, undoubtedly, overpower even the most savvy opponent.

Understanding Advanced Kick Defense

It is the practice of the advanced taekwondo practitioner that no defensive technique, be it retreating from an oncoming kick or blocking a kick, should be performed as the sole response. As you now understand, the advanced taekwondo practitioner utilizes the theory of continuous motion. This means that one technique must immediately follow the last. To this end, the advanced taekwondo practitioner will often first defuse a kicking attack as close to its point of inception as possible, and then, immediately, follow through with a technique that will disable the attacker.

Often in physical confrontations you will not possess the ability to simply move out of the path of an oncoming kick and then rapidly move in and counterstrike. For this reason, taekwondo possesses an array of kick interception techniques that possess the ability to rapidly send your opponent to the ground.

The Taekwondo Throw

The techniques of throwing an opponent to the ground have all but been forgotten in many sport-orientated schools of taekwondo. The original art of taekwondo did, however, employ many throws in order to implement additional means of self-defense for the advanced practitioner. To see how the throws of traditional taekwondo are both easily unleashed and very effective, we can view a throw as used in self-defense against the side kick.

The Point of Inception

To begin to understand how to properly send your kicking opponent to the ground, you must first understand how the advanced practitioner properly intercepts an oncoming kick.

Your opponent has faced off with you. He has begun the process of unleashing a roundhouse kick. The roundhouse kick is one of the most powerful techniques in taekwondo's arsenal. If you wait to block this kick until it has been fully actualized, you could be hit very hard with all its power. What often occurs when someone attempts to block a powerful roundhouse kick is that the force of the kick sends the defender's blocking hands and arms smashing back into his or her face and body. Furthermore, by blocking in the traditional manner, you become so locked up in your blocking technique that you will not be able to quickly move into an offensive positioning and unleash a counterattack. Instead, it will be your opponent who will possess the advantage to quickly move on to his next technique.

For this reason, as mentioned previously, the advanced practitioner of tae-kwondo understands that it is a far more effective blocking technique to encounter any kick as close to its point of inception as possible. In this way, the kick will not have developed a powerful velocity, with the possibility of injuring you, even if you do effectively deliver a blocking technique against it.

To properly intercept the roundhouse kick, you must not attempt to block it in a traditional fashion. The proper defense against the roundhouse kick must be studied.

Your opponent is preparing to launch a roundhouse kick at you. This time, instead of waiting for it to be coming in your direction, you move in toward your opponent. By traveling even this slight distance, you lessen the power of this kick, because it will not have the chance to fully develop.

This very slight forward movement does not require much time or energy to complete. The moment you begin this forward motion, you must begin your roundhouse kick block as well. In taekwondo's continuous motion theory we learn that no movement, be it offensive or defensive, is of itself enough to emerge victorious from a confrontation. Therefore, to move in and then begin to block not only slows your entire defensive technique down but also could ultimately lead to the offensive kick making impact with you. You must move into blocking posture immediately, as you begin to move toward the kick.

The Open Hand Block

Though there are several effective roundhouse kick blocking techniques, the leading mistake that many martial artists perform when encountering the round-house kick is to attempt to block the kicking leg of their opponent with an open hand. The roundhouse kick is a very powerful weapon because of the momentum it develops. Blocking it in open-hand fashion can easily lead to broken fingers, if your fingers are snapped back.

The Taekwondo Roundhouse Kick Throw

One of the quickest, easiest, and most effective methods of blocking the mid-body targeted roundhouse kick is to simply continue your movement in toward your opponent's kick and allow his leg to impact you on your chest and his shin to contact you on the biceps region of your arm. The key to making this an effective roundhouse kick block is to not allow the instep of your opponent's foot to make contact with you. This is because the instep is the ideal impact tool of the roundhouse kick, and it is where all of the kick's power is focused.

The most efficient way to not allow your opponent's instep to strike you is to close the distance between you and your opponent by stepping slightly in toward his body as he launches his kick. This roundhouse kicking defense effort-lessly works because you move both in toward the kick and close the distance between your opponent's body and your own. Thus, you will have effortlessly defused the majority of the power of this kick.

Once your opponent's roundhouse kick has been intercepted, you must continue with taekwondo's theory of continuous motion and move forward with additional techniques until your opponent is defeated. In the case of the round-house kick block, you must continue on with additional defensive techniques to ensure your victory.

You have now intercepted the roundhouse kick; instead of allowing your opponent to quickly pull his leg back to regain his footing, you must immediately take control of the confrontation and grab a hold of it. You can most effectively achieve this by wrapping your arm around his leg. Now that you have substantial control over him, you can rapidly step through, behind his leg, and by simply shoving him back at his shoulder level with your free hand, throw him to the ground.

The Taekwondo Spinning Heel Kick Throw

The spinning heel kick is very similar in form and structure to the roundhouse kick. The spinning heel kick is a circular, momentum-driven kick. Thus, it is dealt with in a similar fashion to the roundhouse kick.

The spinning heel kick is one of the most powerful kicks in the taekwondo kicking arsenal. Its impact power comes from making contact with its target. Therefore, with this kick, the heel is the object to avoid.

To avoid being struck by the spinning heel kick, as your opponent launches this kick, you can quickly step in, toward his body (See Spinning Heel Kick Throw 1). By doing this, you will now be inside of the kick's power. Once inside, as the kick travels toward you, you can take control of your opponent, by allowing his leg to continue to travel toward you, as you did with the roundhouse kick. Once the back of his leg has made powerless contact with the biceps region of your forward arm, you can wrap your arm under his kicking leg (See Spinning Heel Kick Throw 2). Now, by sweeping up his nonkicking leg and pushing at his rear shoulder, you can easily send him to the ground (See Spinning Heel Kick Throw 3).

SPINNING HEEL KICK THROW 1   SPINNING HEEL KICK THROW 2   SPINNING HEEL KICK THROW 3

The Taekwondo Front Kick Throw

The front kick, though one of the most basic offensive techniques in the taekwondo kicking arsenal, is no doubt one of the most penetrating and effective. To deal with it, you must first rapidly slide your body back as your opponent attempts to make front kick contact with you. This moves the front kick's target point, and the power of the kick's muscle-driven force will keep it moving upward. As you move back, you should simultaneously perform a cross-arm block to the shin of your opponent.

The cross-arm block is executed by crossing your arms at just below elbow level, and allowing the front kick to impact the point where your two arms meet. Thus, your opponent's front kick will impact into strong bone and muscle mass, which will leave you free from injury.

Once you have stepped back and blocked the oncoming front kick (see Front Kick Throw 1), you must immediately wrap your hands down and around your opponent's kicking leg before he has the ability to get his kicking foot back on the ground. Once you have made this grab, you must instantly lift your opponent's leg up, while forcing his knee back into his body. This will send him flying backward to the ground (see Front Kick Throw 2).

The muscles of the leg are much stronger than those of the arms. Thus, you are actually at a grasping disadvantage when you hold an opponent's leg in this fashion. Therefore, this taekwondo throwing technique must be executed very rapidly for it to become a useful defensive application.

FRONT KICK THROW 1

FRONT KICK THROW 2

Defending Against the Taekwondo Side Kick

The side kick is undoubtedly one of the primary techniques used in taekwondo. To effortlessly defend against a side kick, initially you simply need to sidestep the attack (see Side Kick Throw 1 and 2). Then, by reaching your hand and arm in and locking it around your adversary's neck, you can easily throw him to the ground by pivoting his body over your extended leg (See Side Kick Throw 3 and 4).

The Taekwondo Axe Kick Throw

It is the upward linear thrusting motion of the front kick that gives it its force and power. In the reverse, it is the forceful down motion of the axe kick that allows it to be a devastating tool of offensive destruction.

The axe kick is first forcefully brought up and then powerfully brought down onto an opponent's shoulder. With this impact, the collar bone is easily broken. The general method for dealing with the axe kick is to step out of its path.

SIDE KICK THROW 1

SIDE KICK THROW 2

SIDE KICK THROW 3

SIDE KICK THROW 4

Though this is no doubt one of the best methods of defense against this kick, at times you may need to be more assertive in your handling an aggressive opponent who has launched one of these techniques. When this is the case, the opposite of stepping out of the path of the axe kick is your best counterattacking measure.

Your opponent launches an axe kick at you. As his leg rises up, you rapidly move in on your opponent and place yourself under the path of this kick.

The impact point of the axe kick is made with the heel of the foot. Again, as with the other kicks we have discussed, you must avoid being struck by any kick's actual point of focus.

By rapidly moving in toward your opponent, you impact your shoulder into the calves of his leg—below his heel (See Axe Kick Throw 1 and 2). From here, you must quickly reach around his kicking leg, taking control of it. Because his kicking leg has now been trapped against your shoulder, you forcefully move

AXE KICK THROW 1   AXE KICK THROW 2   AXE KICK THROW 3

closer toward him. With this forward motion, his kicking leg is forced against him. Then, if you release your grasp as you continue to push his leg back, he is easily thrown backward onto the ground (See Axe Kick Throw 3).

Blocking a kick in a traditional method is never the end-all to any confrontation. For this reason, the advanced practitioner of taekwondo takes control over an opponent's kicking leg and sends him forcefully to the ground—where additional offensive actions can be unleashed as necessary.

Get Out Fast

If you find that you did not deliver a kick fast enough or precisely enough to make contact with your opponent and your leg was grabbed in the process, there is an advanced taekwondo method used to quickly remedy this situation. What you do is to shift all of the weight of your body forward, and forcefully shove down on your leg before your opponent has the opportunity to throw you. As is easily remembered from childhood play, jumping and wrestling to get a trapped leg free does not work. Therefore, your freeing actions must be very precise and very dynamic.

In addition to shifting your weight forward and forcing your leg down out of your opponent's grasp, executing a well-placed straight punch to your opponent's face aids in this process.

If your kicking leg is trapped, get out fast. It is the only way to prevent you from being sent forcefully to the ground—which is never to your advantage.

TAEKWONDO'S STRATEGY AGAINST THE STREET PUNCH

The common punch is undoubtedly one of the most universally used offensive weapons you will run up against in a street confrontation. Taekwondo has a number of blocks that are designed to defend against the punch. There is the in-to-out forearm block, the out-to-in forearm block, the one-handed knife hand block, the two-handed knife hand block, and so on. Though most schools of taekwondo teach these various formal blocks to encounter an opponent's launched punch, this type of expected training is far too sterile for the wild and random punches an opponent will throw at you on the street. For this reason, the taekwondo practitioners initially study the various blocking elements of the arm in order to come to a rudimentary understanding of how to block a punch. As they continue on to the advanced levels of this art, practitioners then advance their knowledge and come to master techniques that will actually be effective against the wildly thrown punches they may encounter in a street confrontation.

Studying the Punch

To begin the study of the punch, we must initially view how to most easily deal with the two basic types of punches that exist: the straight punch and the more common roundhouse punch. To achieve this understanding, it is most effective for you to work with a training partner. When you do, first have your partner launch punching attacks at you slowly and then speed them up as you become more familiar with their individual paths of attack, their limitations, and how they are most effectively dealt with.

Understanding the Straight Punch

First of all, have your training partner perform a straight punch directed at your face. What is your initial course of action? What is generally done and is, no doubt, the leading mistake made by most novices and long-trained taekwondo stylists alike? They attempt to forcefully block it. Though this is the generally pre-scribed method in most one-step sparring techniques, there is, however, a problem with this style of self-defense.

Blocking the Straight Punch

To illustrate the folly of attempting to forcefully block your opponent's oncoming straight punch, allow him or her to strike quickly and forcefully at your face with a straight punch technique. Ideally, you will have your opponent wear boxing gloves during this stage of your practice. As your opponent punches, attempt to block the punch with whatever traditional technique you may have been trained in. What happens nine out of ten times, when you attempt to block your opponent's strike in the traditional way, is that you will be hit.

The straight punch by its very nature is linear in design and application. Its force is derived from the expelling of power from the central axis of the body. The well-delivered straight punch is not only one of the most powerful elements in the advanced taekwondo stylist's hand arsenal but also one of the hardest punches to effectively block. And, this fact is true no matter how precisely developed your blocking technique may be. The reason for this is that this punch drives forward on a linear path from a directed central point onto a specific impact point, and it does not require much developed motion to deliver a powerful impact. There are, however, effective defensive methods that the advanced taekwondo practitioner uses in order to effectively deal with the straight punch other than simply blocking it.

Blocking the Straight Punch: A New Understanding

Let's try viewing the oncoming straight punch in a new manner—not simply as something to attempt to forcefully block or get struck by, but simply as an oncoming object that we would avoid.

This time, have your training partner attempt to execute a straight punch at you. Now, instead of directly encountering it with a traditional blocking technique, simply rapidly sidestep the punch while it is moving forward toward you. As you have learned from the advanced taekwondo practice of stepping out of the path of an oncoming kick, this is one of the most effective methods to deal with an oncoming linear technique.

If you sidestep from the path of the straight punch, first of all the punch will miss you. Second, the momentum developed by the force of your opponent's straight punch will cause your opponent to continue through with his or her own momentum, leaving your opponent in a vulnerable position for a counterattack. Because you have stepped out of the way of the oncoming punch, no injury occurred to you or any part of your body, and you used virtually no energy in your defense against it. Now, you can launch a counterattack in the form of a powerful straight punch to your opponent's face or a roundhouse kick to his or her midsection.

Understanding the Roundhouse Punch

Now that you understand the basic elements of the straight punch defense, let's shift our attentions to the most commonly used punch on the street, the roundhouse punch. Have your training partner perform a roundhouse punch, directed at your head. As your opponent performs the punch, quickly step back and out of the range of the oncoming strike. With this, the punch misses you and the momentum your opponent has developed causes him or her to continue through with the power of his own momentum. Again, leaving your opponent vulnerable to a counterattack.

The roundhouse punch develops its power through circular movement. The distance between its initial swing and impact point multiplies its force. Therefore, stepping back out of its range allows the punch to develop full power. Once it has missed its target, the punch's own momentum causes your opponent to clumsily continue through with his or her own motion.

What the advanced practitioner comes to understand from the previous two illustrations is that there is often no need to forcefully block a punching assault from your opponent at all. Just as you learned from advanced taekwondo kicking defense, it is not only simpler but far safer to quickly move out of the way of any oncoming punching technique—allowing it to miss its impact point on your body altogether. Furthermore, by not actually forcefully blocking the punching technique, you have seen how the momentum your opponent developed by launching the assault against you forces your opponent to continue through with his or her own momentum, leaving your opponent open for a rapid counterattack.

Certainly, it must be understood that with the wildly thrown punches that commonly occur in a street confrontation, you may indeed need to forcefully block them at times. But, it must also be understood that this is the last line of defense of the advanced taekwondo practitioner, who chooses to deal with these forms of assaults in a far more expedient manner.

When a Block is Necessary

In the event that a block is necessary against an offensive punching technique, your first attempt should be a punch block that deflects the opponent's energy—rather than directly encountering it. By deflecting your opponent's energy, instead of encountering it head-on, you may again utilize his own expended energy against himself. Which would be to your advantage.

Understanding Punch Deflection

Deflection is accomplished in different ways with different punches. For example, in the case of a straight punch, it is most successfully implemented by initially following the procedure described earlier and simply sidestepping the punch's impending force. As you step slightly forward, toward the outside of your punching opponent, you should deflect the punch with either an in-to-out forearm block or an in-to-out knife hand block—using the arm that is closest to your opponent. The reason that you use the closest arm is that this will be the fastest way to reach his punching arm. In addition, it requires the least amount of expended energy on your part. Once your opponent's straight punch is deflected, he will then continue through because of his own momentum, as previously described.

You should move slightly forward as you deflect a straight punch for three reasons. First, this forward motion aids in keeping your opponent traveling forward with his own developed momentum. Second, it leaves you in the least vulnerable position for him to launch a secondary attack. Finally, it places you in a superior position for counterattacking.

It is imperative when deflecting an opponent's attack that not only is he left in a less than optimum position for launching a secondary attack on you but also that you are left in the superior position to make a successful counterattack on him. Therefore, you have the advantage in a street confrontation when you encounter a punching opponent and deflect his attacks if you have come to understand, through partner practice, what techniques effectively deflect each punch.

Deflection Leads to a Counterattack

Try this example with your training partner. Your training partner throws a roundhouse punch at you. Step slightly back out of the range of the assault, as previously discussed. The moment that the punch has missed you, rapidly move in on him and push his striking arm into his body, at his elbow level. If he attempts to move it, apply more pressure onto it. As you will see, this simple technique allows you a large amount of control over your opponent's body. It additionally allows you to effectively and powerfully counterstrike him, as necessary, because you will be able to hold him in place for a moment.

Deflection Versus Blocking

Certainly no one believes that he or she will always be able to simply step out of the way of a punch or deflect a barrage of oncoming punches from a wildly driven opponent. However, to insure your own safety, as your first line of deflective defense, you should always try to do so. If this is not possible, then your next form of defense should be to deflect oncoming punches. If your opponent continues on with his attack, and your initial deflective defenses have been unsuccessful, then, to save yourself from being hit by impending strikes, block the punches by any means possible.

If simply moving out of the way of a punch is not achievable, and a forceful punch block is necessary, the key element to remember is to always block your opponent at his elbow region, for if you control your opponent's elbow, you control his entire body.

Successful Defense Against the Roundhouse Punch

The design of the roundhouse punch allows it to be seen long before it is actually executed. The power of this punch comes from the momentum it gains from its swing. Therefore, there are times when you will see a roundhouse punch coming and want to block it as near to its inception point as possible.

To gain the proper understanding of the timing involved with actually blocking the roundhouse punch, allow your training partner to strike at you again with a roundhouse punch. This time, do not move back out of the way of the oncoming strike but quickly step into it, blocking the punch in an in-to-out fashion either with a knife hand or forearm block to the inside of your opponent's elbow region. Again, you will witness how you have gained control of your opponent's arm.

To obtain optimum results in directly blocking the roundhouse punch, you must encounter it as close to its point of inception as possible so that your opponent will not have had the opportunity to develop much force in his swing. This makes the block much easier to perform.

When you block a roundhouse punch to the inside of the elbow, as described, your opponent may attempt to strike at you with his other arm. This is a natural reaction in a street fight. Therefore, you must be prepared and be able to move into further defense against another punch, with a similar blocking technique, if necessary.

Moving In
The final way of quickly, easily, and effectively dealing with a punching opponent is to rapidly rush in on top of his attack, thus leaving him no room to punch. By doing this, you not only curtail his ability to develop any power in his punching offense but also throw him off-balance. Because this type of crowding defense is rarely used, few have the ability to quickly recover from it. The drawback to this type of punch defense is that if you do not immediately launch a counterattack, your opponent may grab hold of you and you could end up in a grappling match on the ground, which is to no one's advantage. Therefore, you must rapidly come in, ready to execute a knee attack or perhaps a palm hand strike to your opponent's face.

Advanced Taekwondo and the Punch
At the advanced level of taekwondo, you never perform a defensive technique without immediately launching the appropriate counterassault at your opponent, because a street confrontation is generally never won simply by avoiding or blocking your opponent's attack. For this reason, you must always be prepared to rapidly counterattack your opponent.

It is important to understand how easy and effective these counterattacks can be in punching defense situations. To this end, again square off with your practice opponent and allow him to execute a punch at you. In regard to the straight punch, once you have deflected or sidestepped the punch, you are in an optimum position to easily side kick your opponent to the side of his knee. In the case of the roundhouse punch, once you have stepped from its reach, you can either front kick your opponent to his groin or rapidly move in on him, checking his elbow and throwing a straight punch to his face.

Dealing with Multiple Punches
If your initial counterattack is ineffective or if your adversary continues on with a barrage of punches, you must rapidly deal with the situation so that his continued strikes at you will not have the cumulative effect of his winning the confrontation. Therefore, if a wild punching attack ensues, step rapidly back away from the impact of the continued punches, allowing at least one punch to pass in front of you. From there, rapidly move in and powerfully strike him with your

most powerful hand or leg technique, for letting a confrontation continue longer than is necessary is only to the advantage of the aggressor.

As you now see, once you understand the elements that make up the various street punches, they are easily and effectively dealt with. For this reason, all advanced taekwondo practitioners make self-defense a science and do not simply learn contrived techniques to deal with any attack that may occur. By making self-defense a science, you have not only become a more competent fighter, but also a better martial artist.

GROUND FIGHTING

As can be witnessed by watching any skirmish that takes place on the street, the confrontation often times ends up in a grappling match on the ground. The first thing that the practitioner of taekwondo comes to understand, in regards to self-defense, is to not end up on the ground. There are many reasons to not end up fighting on the ground. Not the least of which is that the techniques that can be used in your defense are substantially limited.

Sometimes, however, when an attacking opponent charges at you, there is no alternative but to end up in a ground-fighting encounter. For this reason, the advanced practitioner of taekwondo makes ground fighting a science, thus increasing his odds of emerging victorious from any ground-level encounter.

Ground Fighting Basics

The most important thing to remember if you find yourself on the bottom of a ground-fighting skirmish is to not attempt to recklessly wiggle out from under your opponent. This type of ground-fighting tactic will only leave you exhausted and with limited results. Any defensive action that is taken must be done in a very competent manner not only to substantially limit the length of the fight but also to save yourself from unnecessary injury.

The appropriate time to launch into any ground defense is the moment you find yourself on the floor. As each moment passes, your opponent possesses the ability to get you in a hold that you cannot break free from or strike you to a vital point from which you cannot successfully recover.

Protect Your Head

The first step the advanced taekwondo practitioner must take when located on the bottom of a ground fight is to protect his or her head and neck from assault. Most trained and untrained fighters, alike, will attempt to either kick you in the head if they are still standing or punch at your face, if they are in the superior upper position. As anyone who has ever been engaged in a fierce street altercation will attest, it only takes a few well-delivered strikes to the head, and your ability to competently defend yourself is greatly diminished. Therefore, not allowing this type of attack to occur is paramount.

Ground Fighting: The Three Types of Attacks

To see the best approach to ground-level defensive strategy, we can look at the three predominate types of attacks an opponent will launch at you in a ground fight: the kicking attack, the punching attack, and the chokehold.

The Kicking Attack

There are three forms of defense that the advanced practitioner of taekwondo utilizes when he finds himself on the ground, encountering an attacker who is

Protecting your head and neck from ground-level combat does not mean that you should only "cover up" and do nothing further to protect yourself. Doing nothing results in your opponent maintaining the fighting advantage. What this does mean, however, is that you must first halt any type of forceful attack that your opponent may be launching at your head and then immediately follow up with a competent counterattack. The most efficient way to accomplish this is to encounter your opponent's attack in a way that will not only stop his assault on you but will also give you defensive position from which you can remove him from his superior position and continue forward with additional self-defense.

GROUND FIGHTING KICK

attempting to kick him. The first is to put taekwondo's extensive arsenal of kicks to work and deliver a low roundhouse or side kick to the opponent's knee or mid-section (see Ground Fighting Kick). This is the preferred method of self-defense from a ground-level position because it allows you to rapidly take control over the altercation.

Simply kicking your opponent from the ground and taking control of the confrontation may not always be possible if you find yourself on the ground. The next form of self-defense you would employ if you are the first one to find yourself on the ground and your opponent is still standing would be to remove your opponent from his feet. Because the advanced taekwondo practitioner has developed a mastery of his or her legs, this is most efficiently accomplished by performing a scissor kick to your opponent's legs. With one of your legs striking low, and the other high, you can take him off of his feet (see Ground Fighting 1-1 through 1-4). At this point, you must immediately launch into an appropriate counterdefense, to keep him from coming back at you with a second offense. You may find that the best counterassault is a powerful axe kick to his head (see Ground Fighting 1-5).

Because each ground-fighting situation is dominated by its own set of criteria, the techniques in the previous two examples may not effectively protect you from a kicking opponent. The next method you, as an advanced taekwondo practitioner, should employ to defeat a kicking opponent from a ground-level position is to block any oncoming kick before it has the ability to strike you. To achieve this, you would simply perform a cross-arm block, at shin level, to the kicking leg of your opponent (see Ground Fighting 2-1 and 2-2). The moment his kick is blocked, you then take hold of the back of his heel on his kicking leg with your free hand. Then, you lift up on his heel, while you push back at his shin, and your opponent will be sent to the ground where other self-defense techniques can be unleashed (see Ground Fighting 2-3 and 2-4).

The Punching Attack

In the case of the ground-level punching attack, there are two elements of your opponent's body that you must initially recognize in order to best deal with the assault: they are the holding arm and the striking arm. By initially identifying these two elements and their location in relation to you, you can begin to effectively deal with the onslaught of the attack.

The most effective element to attack is your opponent's base arm. This is the one that will most commonly be holding you down as he is attempting to punch at you. The most effective method of self-defense is to encounter the base arm

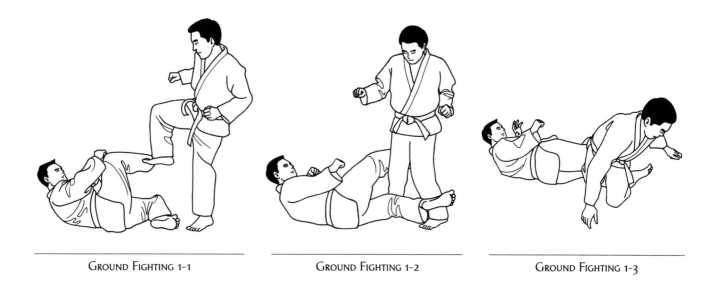

GROUND FIGHTING 1-1   GROUND FIGHTING 1-2   GROUND FIGHTING 1-3

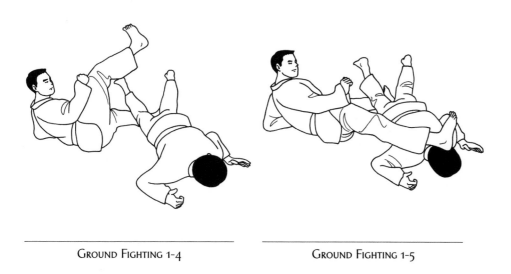

GROUND FIGHTING 1-4   GROUND FIGHTING 1-5

before he begins to strike at you. This can be effectively accomplished at the moment he attempts to position his base arm to hold you. Once his arm is in place, you can deliver a powerful knife hand strike to the interior region of his elbow. This will cause his elbow to bend, and your opponent will collapse onto you. At this exact moment is the time to flip him off of your body, because he will be most vulnerable. From this, you can gain superior positioning and move forward with your self-defense.

The other very suitable option when you are about to be struck from above is to strike at your opponent's base arm elbow from the outside before he has a chance to punch at you. This is most effectively accomplished by first grabbing onto the upper portion of the hand of his base arm, where it touches your body. This will effectively lock it in place. Then, with your other arm, powerfully palm strike to the outer area of your opponent's elbow. By maintaining control over his hand and by delivering continued force and pressure on his outer elbow after the strike, you will force him, face first, to travel downward toward the ground. With this, you can gain the superior position.

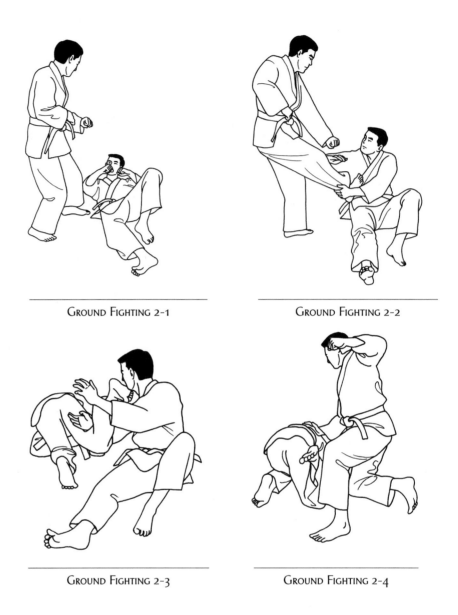

GROUND FIGHTING 2-1

GROUND FIGHTING 2-2

GROUND FIGHTING 2-3

GROUND FIGHTING 2-4

The Striking Arm

If you are being held down and struck from above, your attacker's punches need only travel in a downward path. Thus, they possess additional gravitational force and momentum. Therefore, this type of punching attack must be halted immediately, or you can very easily be knocked out or severely injured.

Instead of simply covering your face, if you find yourself in this unsuitable position, you should immediately launch into an effective form of self-defense that will get you out from under your opponent. One of the most effective ways to begin to achieve this is to encounter the outside of your adversary's punching elbow as it is traveling toward you. This can be best accomplished by intercepting it with an out-to-in cross block, directed at the outside of your opponent's elbow. Once this block has made contact, it will deflect the oncoming punch from striking your face, and your opponent's own downward punching momentum will force him to continue forward with the gravitational power of this punch. This deflecting action will cause one of two things to occur. First, his punch will travel on and make forceable contact with the ground. This is obviously the most desirable option because it may injure him and give you the momentary option to quickly escape from his grasp. The second probability is that because he is in a superior position, he will catch the punch before it travels too far and attempt to retract it in order to strike again. If this occurs, you must take control of his arm. This is most successfully accomplished by maintaining your blocking hand's position on his outer elbow and then shoving his arm tightly into his body. With this, you will have interrupted the fight long enough that you can strike him to a vital point with your free hand and then use appropriate methods to dislodge him from the top of your body.

The Chokehold

The ground-level chokehold is another common type of grappling attack. When an attacker has you in this grasp, he is directing the majority of his energy at holding both of his hands tightly around your neck. Attempting to wrestle them loose may eventually be effective, but in doing so you will waste much of the energy—which may later be needed if a secondary attack is launched against you by your opponent. Therefore, to most effectively defend against a ground-level choking attack, you must first take control of the confrontation. You can most effectively accomplish this by powerfully striking your opponent in a debilitating location. This will lossen his hold on your neck.

The most effective type of counterstrike to launch at an opponent from the lower position is one that will hit one of his easily accessible vital points. The most exposed of these are his temples, his neck, his nose, and to a lesser degree, the side of his ribs. The force of the chokehold your opponent has you in can only

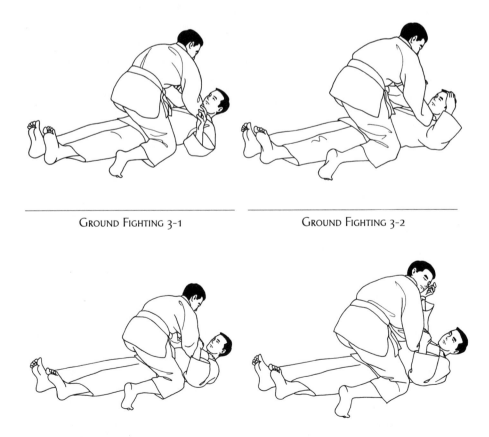

GROUND FIGHTING 3-1

GROUND FIGHTING 3-2

GROUND FIGHTING 3-3

GROUND FIGHTING 3-4

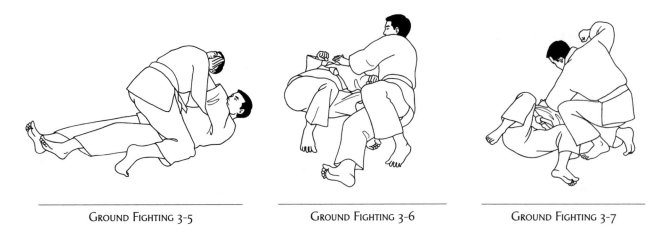

GROUND FIGHTING 3-5   GROUND FIGHTING 3-6   GROUND FIGHTING 3-7

define the type of actual strike you will use and the distance your attacker is above you. For example, if his face is close to yours, a knife hand strike to his temples may be the most effective type of initial counterstrike. If he is back a bit farther off your body with his arms more extended, then a straight punch to his trachea or a palm strike to his nose will be most effective.

In extreme cases, if you find yourself being held in a ground-level chokehold and your attacker has extremely long arms, you may need to bring him closer to you. To successfully accomplish this, you can bring both of your arms up over the top of his arms and deliver simultaneous knife hand strikes to his inner elbows (See Ground Fighting 3-1 through 3-3). This will cause him to bend naturally inward, and he will be forced to move closer to you. From this position you will then possess the ability to effectively strike him (see Ground Fighting 3-4).

Once you have made this initial counterstrike, it is imperative that you immediately continue forward and remove him from on top of your body, because this is the time when he will be most vulnerable. To achieve this most effectively, you should not interrupt your fighting momentum by changing to a completely different strategy and attempting to recklessly wrestle him off of your body. Instead, you should move forward, progressing in a similar fashion to your initial strike. For example, if you have used a palm strike to his nose, you can continue on by leaving your striking hand in place (See Ground Fighting 3-5). Do this as you reach your other arm behind his neck and by pulling downward toward you, by his hair, as you push upward, away from you with his jaw level, you will have powerfully arched his neck into an unnatural angle, thus, locking it. Once you have achieved this hold, directing him off of your body can be accomplished with ease, by simply applying additional pressure to this technique. Immediately upon removing your attacker from your body, you should strike him to a debilitating location so that he will not possess the ability to continue the grappling match any further (see Ground Fighting 3-6 and 3-7).

Each ground fight is very different. Thus, there are no universal rules for how the advanced taekwondo practitioner defends himself or herself in each individualized confrontation. There are, however, a few rules of thumb that need to be remembered. First of all, never allow a ground fight to become a muscle-to-muscle confrontation. That type of combat is to no one's advantage. Instead, always remember to deliver an initial strike to vital points on your opponent when possible, and then use your opponent's own body elements to remove him from his upward position. As discussed, this is most effectively accomplished by taking control of his arms or by grabbing his head with both of your hands and power-fully arching his neck to one side.

It is very important that you, as an advancing taekwondo stylist, include ground-fighting practice in your training regimen. That way, if you ever end up in a grappling fight on the ground, it will not be an alien experience to you. Instead, you will possess the knowledge from your practice sessions to understand how to successfully deal with each type of ground-level attack.

EFFECTIVE DEFENSE AGAINST STREET WEAPONS

With the growing proliferation of violent crime in our streets, and the use of the weapons that are often directly linked to these crimes, the advanced taekwondo stylist must learn to effectively defend himself or herself against a weapon-based attack. The advanced practitioner of taekwondo understands that the key element of self-defense against a weapon is to discard any technique that is too elaborate to be truly effective on the streets.

> In taekwondo dojangs and in taekwondo demonstrations, weapon defense techniques are, often, visually beautiful to watch but possess little effectiveness when actually attempting to defend against a weapon-wielding opponent on the street. With this understanding, the advanced taekwondo practitioner leaves behind those techniques that are too elaborate to be truly effective on the street and focuses his or her training on those techniques that have been proven to be effective in self-defense against weapons.

Guns

The issue of guns is often the first question brought up in self-defense. Guns are no doubt the most dangerous of all weapons now commonly found on the street. If your attacker possesses a gun, and it is at any distance from you, the best thing you can do is run. For the speed a bullet travels and the likelihood of it having the ability to fatally injure you is too great a risk to ever take a chance against an adversary who is truly willing to use his gun.

When the opponent possesses a gun and is in close proximity to your body, however, and you are sure that your life is truly threatened, there are certain basic self-defense techniques that can be used to protect yourself. Remember, the squeezing of a trigger is so fast and so deadly, you must be sure that your life is ultimately in danger and the assailant is not simply after your money or jewelry, which is replaceable, before you put any self-defense into action.

The quickest and simplest way to defend against a gun from a frontal attack in very close proximity to your body is to simply rapidly deflect it with an in-to-out forearm block and then quickly strike the opponent with a devastating blow such as a palm strike under his nose. By defending against the gun in this fashion, even if the trigger is pulled, your deflection will hopefully have been rapid enough to have the bullet fly off, hurting no one.

This type of simple gun defense and immediately following through with a powerful counterstrike is effective if the assailant is close in front of you or if he holds a gun directly to your back, from the rear. In each case you know the exact location of the weapon, and thus, this defense can be effective.

The Knife

The knife, as a common weapon on the streets, has long been documented. Every martial art style has devised its own individual methods to deal with the knife's oncoming blade. The various styles of martial arts, including taekwondo, have devised elaborate methods for you to move in rapidly and catch the arm of your opponent before he launches an attack at you. Attempting to intercept a knife, however, is not an effective method of self-defense for three reasons. First of all, the arm of an opponent generally moves too fast for you to be sure that in any instant you will have the ability to reach in and catch it with the hope of then performing some elaborate self-defense technique and ultimately disarming him. Second, do not believe that the avid street fighter does not have the ability to see your hands moving in toward him in order to catch his arm. In fact, if you do attempt to grab his arm, all he has to do is move slightly. With this, your grab will have missed, and you will have left yourself open to being attacked with the knife. The third problem with attempting to catch your opponent's knife-holding arm is, even if you can accomplish this feat, he will not remain in one position allowing you to control him and perform whatever type of self-defense technique you have planned. Inevitability, he will simply shift the knife in his hand and cut you. Though this cut may inflict less damage than the straight-ahead assault of his knife, nonetheless, getting cut is not to your advantage.

It is also not a good idea to rapidly move in toward your armed opponent with the hope of defeating him with a powerful punch or kick. Many taekwondo stylists can kick a hanging bag with extreme power. They believe this power is all they need on the street. They are wrong. To an opponent who possesses a knife, any movement that you may make, as stylized as it may be, allows him the ability to stab you as you move in toward him.

Knowing what not to do, the advanced practitioner of taekwondo then learns what style of techniques are actually beneficial in defense against the knife. This is where the true weapon self-defense training begins.

The Forward Attack

If you should encounter a forward stabbing knife attack head-on, your primary form of self-defense should be avoidance. No matter what form of counterattack you choose to launch once the oncoming blade has been moved away from its path to your body; it must be avoided first before any further maneuvering can successfully be accomplished.

CONSCIOUS AVOIDANCE

At the heart of taekwondo's advanced level of weapons self-defense is conscious avoidance. Taekwondo's theory of conscious avoidance means that you move in a pattern that does not allow an attacking opponent to gain or maintain control over the conflict. This is to say that advanced practitioners never allow themselves to be dominated by the aggressive movements of their adversary. Instead, the moment an altercation has begun, the advanced practitioner immediately begins to take control over the confrontation by subtly controlling the attacking motion of the aggressor by taking no defensive action at all. If the attacker advances in an aggressive forward posture, simply step back. If he lunges in toward you, simply sidestep the attack. With this form of initial self-defense, no forceful block is necessary and the weapon-wielding opponent will expend all of his energy. When his attack has missed is the moment when the advanced practitioner then launches into a powerful counterattack.

The assailant who possesses a knife inevitably will attempt to stab you with it. Whether or not he moves it around in an effort to confuse you, as is often the case in street combat, is irrelevant, for sooner or later the blade will be launched at you.

The primary advanced taekwondo knife avoidance technique used for a stabbing assault is to rapidly sidestep the forward thrust of the knife and then immediately counterattack with a powerful offensive technique such as a palm strike to the nose or a front kick to the knee. This counterattack must be made immediately, or your opponent will have the time necessary to deliver a secondary attack with his knife.

The Slashing Attack

The second form of attack that a knife-wielding opponent commonly utilizes is the side-to-side slashing attack. For this style of knife attack, avoidance is also a useful tool.

An effective knife deflection technique against a side-to-side slashing attack is to step slightly back, allowing the slashing knife to pass by you. At this point, you must immediately take control of your opponent's knife-holding arm. To do this, you must rapidly close in on him and shove his arm tightly into his body by taking control over his outer elbow. Then, you must immediately launch a powerful yet simple counterstrike, such as a circle hand to his throat.

In all knife avoidance techniques it is important that you never grab your opponent's hand or arm in such a manner that it will allow your opponent to come back and easily cut you. This is generally accomplished by never locking yourself into a deflection technique so tightly that you cannot quickly and effectively move out from it and onto another.

Encountering the Knife

At times, there is no alternative but to take control over the knife-wielding arm of your opponent. If this is the situation, the moment you block any oncoming attack, you must immediately powerfully counterstrike your opponent to a debilitating location. This must be done to stun your opponent to the degree that he is knocked out or thrown to the ground. For example, suppose that your opponent attacks you with an outside knife slash (see Knife Defense 1). You would intercept his arm in midswing and then, immediately, deliver a palm hand strike to his nose (see Knife Defense 2 and 3). This strike may completely debilitate him. Or, you

KNIFE DEFENSE 1   KNIFE DEFENSE 2

KNIFE DEFENSE 3

KNIFE DEFENSE 4

KNIFE DEFENSE 5

can force him to the ground by taking control over his knife-holding arm, forcing it behind him, as you throw him to the ground (see Knife Defense 4 and 5).

Taekwondo Knife-Fighting Rules

Each knife-fighting attack is defined by its own set of circumstances. For this reason, no one can tell you exactly what to do. You must utilize judgment to decide which defense is best in any given knife assault situation. There are, however, three rules for knife self-defense:

1. Avoiding a knife is always preferable to directly encountering a knife.
2. Once a knife attack has been avoided, your opponent's knife-wielding arm must be held in check so that it cannot immediately launch a secondary attack on you.
3. Any avoidance and arm check technique must be rapidly followed by a strong and debilitating counterattack to protect you from your assailant launching further assaults on you.

The Club

The third style of weapon that is commonly used on the street is a pipe, chain, club, or other similar elongated striking objects that are used to hit your body. Though these weapons differ slightly in their makeup, you use similar techniques to defend against them.

There are two primary methods of dealing with the club-type weapon. The first is to deflect its onslaught as described with that of the knife. The second is to directly block its oncoming strike and then follow through with the appropriate technique to end your assailant's further advances.

Avoidance

Avoidance of the club-type weapon is very effective. In the case of the club or the chain, it is even more effective than with a knife, because the motion of this type of weapon cannot easily be altered and its construction does not allow its user to simply shift its impact point and cut you.

| CLUB BLOCK 1-1 | CLUB BLOCK 1-2 | CLUB BLOCK 1-3 |

Because these weapons are generally swung, simple avoidance is accomplished by simply stepping out of the way and then powerfully counterattacking. No doubt one of the most effective avoidance techniques against the club or chain, once it is launched in a side-to-side assault, is simply to step back, allowing the force created by the weapon's swing to carry your opponent's arm by (see Club Block 1-1 and 1-2). Then, instantly, you counterstrike with a powerful kick, such as a hook kick to your opponent's head (see Club Block 1-3).

Blocking

At times, it may be necessary to directly block the oncoming strike of a club. This is quite easily accomplished simply by intercepting your opponent in midstrike position. The most appropriate time to block his club strike is as close to its beginning point as possible. By impacting it early in its swing, not only has his striking arm not had the time to develop much velocity, but also your arm will not be easily injured in the block.

The taekwondo block against the pipe and other club-type weapons should be focused at your opponent's midforearm. Not only is your opponent most susceptible to an effective block at this focus point, but also by blocking with a cross-arm block, this allows you to have more range of movement and the ability to compensate if your assailant moves his weapon slightly.

To attempt to simply catch your opponent's strike with your hand is generally a mistake. First of all, your hand is much smaller than your forearm. If you

| CLUB BLOCK 2-1 | CLUB BLOCK 2-2 | CLUB BLOCK 2-3 |

miss that initial catch, the club will strike you. Second, if you do, in fact, catch the attack of the oncoming club, what do you do then? Catching and then holding your opponent's arm or wrist gives him several advantages in the confrontation. He can effectively strike you with his other hand or kick you with his knees or legs, while you struggle with his weapon-holding arm, attempting to keep him from hitting you with the club.

By blocking the pipe attack with a cross-arm block (see Club Block 2-1 and 2-2), you can easily launch into an appropriate counterstriking technique, such as a front kick to his groin (see Club Block 2-3).

Because there can be no hard-and-fast rules for to what defensive technique will work best for you against an attempted strike with a club, pipe, stick, or chain, the only way any advanced taekwondo practitioner can develop the appropriate hand-eye coordination necessary to be effective in the defense against weapons is to practice with partners in a controlled environment. The key element to making this type of partner training effective is to not allow any block to work, unless it truly blocks the attack. As a result, you, as an advanced practitioner of taekwondo, will raise your self-defense skills to new levels of excellence.

SELF-DEFENSE TECHNIQUES

Taekwondo is best known for its advanced arsenal of kicking techniques and its status as an Olympic sport. At the heart of this system, however, is a scientific system of self-defense. In fact, all of the techniques used in modern taekwondo, both

| SELF-DEFENSE 1-1 | SELF-DEFENSE 1-2 |

| SELF-DEFENSE 1-3 | SELF-DEFENSE 1-4 |

the studio-oriented and competitive, evolved from an ever-developing understanding of self-defense.

The essence of self-defense is based upon an individual's ability to successfully defend him- or herself once engulfed in the realms of hand-to-hand combat. To this end, taekwondo possesses an exacting system of hand-to-hand combat designed to educate the practitioner in the most effective way to encounter each style of grabbing and strike attack.

Taekwondo Self-Defense One

An adversary has grabbed you by the shoulder (see Self-Defense 1-1). With your arm closest to him, you guide your arm up, over, and under his grabbing arm (see Self-Defense 1-2 and 1-3). You powerfully lift up at his elbow region (see Self-Defense 1-4). This will lock his arm in place and possibly break his elbow, depending on how much force you exert.

SELF-DEFENSE 2-1

SELF-DEFENSE 2-2

SELF-DEFENSE 2-3

SELF-DEFENSE 2-4

Taekwondo Self-Defense Two

An opponent takes a hold of your wrist (see Self-Defense 2-1). By pivoting your hand down and under your opponent's grabbing hand, you dislodge his hold on your wrist, as you grab hold of his arm (see Self-Defense 2-2 and 2-3). As you pivot your body around behind him, you deliver a powerful knife hand strike to his elbow (see Self-Defense 2-4). This strike has the potential to break your opponent's elbow.

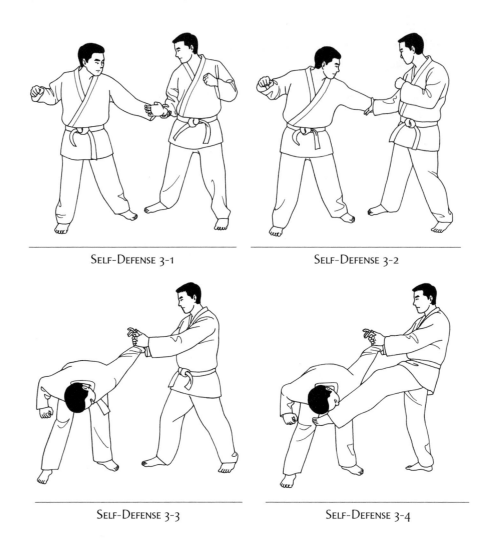

SELF-DEFENSE 3-1   SELF-DEFENSE 3-2

SELF-DEFENSE 3-3   SELF-DEFENSE 3-4

Taekwondo Self-Defense Three

An attacker grabs you by the wrist as he prepares to punch you. Before he can unleash his strike, you make a circle hand and drive it back into his grabbing wrist (See Self-Defense 3-1). As you push his arm to his back, you shift your hand's position and take control over his hand (see Self-Defense 3-2). You bend his hand back, locking his wrist as he is driven toward the ground as a result of the pressure on his wrist (see Self-Defense 3-3). You deliver a front kick to his face (see Self-Defense 3-4).

SELF-DEFENSE 4-1   SELF-DEFENSE 4-2

SELF-DEFENSE 4-3

SELF-DEFENSE 4-4

Taekwondo Self-Defense Four

An attacking opponent grabs your wrist (see Self-Defense 4-1). You powerfully drive your grabbed arm forward. As you do, you use your free hand to dislodge his grasp by placing your fingers inside the palm of his hand (see Self-Defense 4-2). The moment his grasp is dislodged, you maintain control over the confrontation by holding on to his hand. You immediately deliver a knife hand strike to his throat, sending him back onto the ground see Self-Defense 4-3 and 4-4).

SELF-DEFENSE 5-1

SELF-DEFENSE 5-2

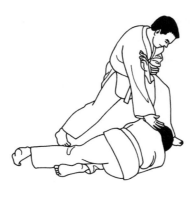

SELF-DEFENSE 5-3

SELF-DEFENSE 5-4

Taekwondo Self-Defense Five

Your shoulder has been grabbed (see Self-Defense 5-1). You immediately strike your attacker with a knife hand to his throat (see Self-Defense 5-2). Once he has been disabled and his grasp has loosened, you maintain your control over the altercation by initially holding his grabbing hand in place (see Self-Defense 5-3). You then reach behind him and shove powerfully to the rear of his shoulder, sending him to the ground face first (see Self-Defense 5-4).

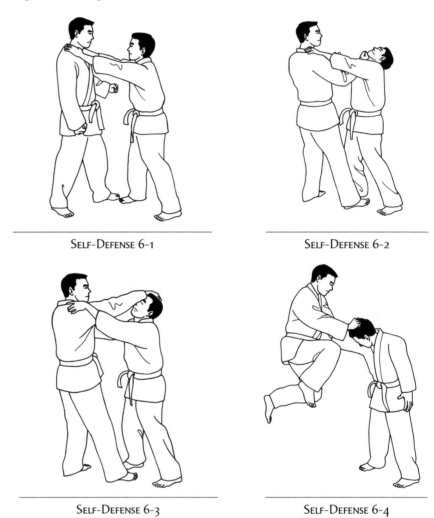

SELF-DEFENSE 6-1   SELF-DEFENSE 6-2

SELF-DEFENSE 6-3   SELF-DEFENSE 6-4

Taekwondo Self-Defense Six

You are grabbed in a frontal chokehold (see Self-Defense 6-1). You immediately deliver an uppercut punch to your attacker (see Self-Defense 6-2). The moment he is dazed and releases his grasp, you grab the back of his head and deliver a jumping knee strike to his head (see Self-Defense 6-3 and 6-4).

SELF-DEFENSE 7-1

SELF-DEFENSE 7-2

SELF-DEFENSE 7-3

SELF-DEFENSE 7-4

Taekwondo Self-Defense Seven

You are grabbed in a frontal chokehold (see Self-Defense 7-1). You reach up and over your opponent's grabbing arms and drive downward at a 45-degree angle as you pivot your body forward (see Self-Defense 7-2 and 7-3). The moment your opponent's grasp is released, you deliver a powerful reverse elbow strike to his head (see Self-Defense 7-4).

STRAIGHT PUNCH BLOCK 1-1

STRAIGHT PUNCH BLOCK 1-2

STRAIGHT PUNCH BLOCK 1-3

STRAIGHT PUNCH BLOCK 1-4

Taekwondo Self-Defense Eight—Straight Punch One

An opponent attempts to strike you with a straight punch (see Straight Punch Block 1-1). You step inside the oncoming punch and block it with an in-to-out knife hand block (see Straight Punch Block 1-2). You continue forward with your movement and continue to pivot on your lead leg. You deliver a reverse elbow strike to his head (see Straight Punch Block 1-3 and 1-4).

STRAIGHT PUNCH BLOCK 2-1

STRAIGHT PUNCH BLOCK 2-2

STRAIGHT PUNCH BLOCK 2-3

Taekwondo Self-Defense Eight—Straight Punch Two

An attacker launches a straight punch toward you. You block it with an in-to-out forearm block. You immediately deliver a circle hand strike to your opponent's throat (see Straight Punch Block 2-1 through 2-3).

STRAIGHT PUNCH BLOCK 3-1

STRAIGHT PUNCH BLOCK 3-2

STRAIGHT PUNCH BLOCK 3-3

STRAIGHT PUNCH BLOCK 3-4

Taekwondo Self-Defense Nine—Straight Punch Three

Your adversary launches a straight punch at you. You step in and block it with an in-to-out forearm block. You continue through with you circular motion and deliver a jumping spinning axe kick to your opponent (see Straight Punch Block 3-1 through 3-4).

ROUNDHOUSE PUNCH BLOCK 1-1

ROUNDHOUSE PUNCH BLOCK 1-2

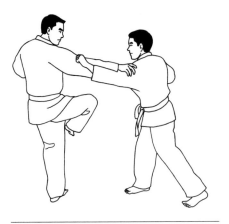

ROUNDHOUSE PUNCH BLOCK 1-3

ROUNDHOUSE PUNCH BLOCK 1-4

Taekwondo Self-Defense Ten—Roundhouse Punch One

A roundhouse punch is launched at your head. You block it with an in-to-out knife hand block. You then take a hold of your opponent's arm to hold him in place as you deliver an inside front kick to his face (see Roundhouse Punch 1-1 through 1-4).

ROUNDHOUSE PUNCH BLOCK 2-1

ROUNDHOUSE PUNCH BLOCK 2-2

ROUNDHOUSE PUNCH BLOCK 2-3

ROUNDHOUSE PUNCH BLOCK 2-4

Taekwondo Self-Defense Eleven—Roundhouse Punch Two

An attacker attempts to hit you with a roundhouse punch. You block it with an in-to-out knife hand block. You immediately follow through by delivering a spinning heel kick to his head (see Roundhouse Punch Block 2-1 through 2-4).

DOUBLE PUNCH DEFENSE 1

DOUBLE PUNCH DEFENSE 2

DOUBLE PUNCH DEFENSE 3

DOUBLE PUNCH DEFENSE 4

DOUBLE PUNCH DEFENSE 5

Taekwondo Self-Defense Twelve—The Double Punch

An opponent attempts to strike you with a roundhouse punch. You intercept this strike with an in-to-out block (see Double Punch Defense 1 and 2). Immediately, your attacker launches a secondary punching attack at you with his other arm. You also intercept this punch with an in-to-out block (see Double Punch Defense 3). To maintain control over you opponent's punching arms, you reach around and grab both of his upper arms. You immediately deliver a knee strike to your opponent, thereby ending the confrontation (see Double Punch Defense 4 and 5).

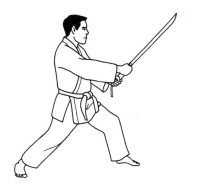

Chapter 11
Weapons Training in Taekwondo

Taekwondo has gone through a long period of downsizing over the past thirty years. As the numerous kwans merged under the umbrella of the World Taekwondo Federation, many aspects of traditional taekwondo began to be lost as the focus of this system shifted to sport-orientated competition.

> During the early evolution of taekwondo, weapons training was part of the curriculum of most kwans on the Korean peninsula. Today, this is no longer the case. There are, however, numerous practitioners of the original system of taekwondo who still hold fast to training their advanced students in the use of martial art weaponry.

The Foundations of Weapons Training on the Korean Peninsula

Weapons training has been an essential part of martial arts developed on the Korean peninsula since the beginning of recorded history. The Japanese forces, which occupied the Korean peninsula from 1909 until 1945, destroyed virtually all records of the actual techniques of the ancient Korean martial arts, however. Many modern masters of the Korean martial arts falsely claim they can trace the origins of their systems back to the dawn of Korean civilization. Unfortunately, this is historically not the case. There are only two remaining documents: the *Mu Yea Jee Bo* and the *Mu Yea Do Bok Tong Gi*, which give us insight into Korea's martial history. These are the only two sources through which the history of Korean martial arts can be traced.

The conflicts between Japan and Korea are not unique to the twentieth century. They have been ongoing for centuries. Between 1592 and 1598 an attempted Japanese invasion of Korea took place. The Japanese invaders were defeated. Near the end of this conflict, a Chinese military text titled *Ki Hyu Shin Zu* written by the Chinese military strategist and martial artist Chuk, Kye Kwang was discovered. The text had been acquired from a slain Japanese General. This manuscript was presented to Korean King Sun Jo (1567–1608). Within its pages was a system of Chinese weapon and hand-to-hand combat. King Sun Jo was so impressed by the methods presented in this text that he invited Chinese Generals and Chinese martial art masters who employed this system to visit his capital. From this contact, he ordered one of his Generals, Han Kyo, to take what he had learned from both of the texts and the demonstrations and design a new system of battlefield combat. This system was eventually written in six chapters and published as *Mu Yea Jee Bo, The Illustrations of the Martial Arts.*

This text became the basis for formalized warfare for the Korean military. Within the pages of the text, the techniques are outlined for the *sang soo do*, or long sword; *jang chang*, or spear; *dang pa*, or triple-end spear; *kon bong*, or long staff; and *dung pa*, or shield defense.

Korean King Yong Jo (1724–1776) had the text revised during his reign. Twelve additional approaches to fighting were added. The manual was renamed *Mu Yea Shin Bo, The New Illustrations of the Martial Arts.*

The fighting techniques added to the pages employed the *bon kuk kum*, or Korean straight sword; *wae kum*, or Japanese sword; *jee dook kum*, or admiral's sword; *yee do*, or short sword; *sang kum*, or twin swords; *wae kum*, or crescent sword; *juk jang*, or long bamboo spear; *hyup do*, or spear with a blade; *kee jang*, or flag spear; *pyun kon*, or long staff with end like a nunchaka; *kyo jun*, or combat engagement strategy; and *kwon bop*, or literally, karate.

In 1790, at the direction of the next King of Korea, King Jung Jo (1776–1800), the Korean military strategists Yi, Duk Moo and Park, Je Ga again revised the text. He added six additional chapters to the manuscript: *ma sang*, or combat horsemanship; *ki chang*, or spear fighting from horseback; *ma sang wol do*, or sword fighting from horseback; *ma sang sang kum*, or twin sword fighting from horseback; *ma sang pyun kon*, or long staff with shorter end like nunchaka, fighting from horseback; and *kyuk koo*, or gaming on horseback.

The text was retitled *Mu Yea Do Bok Tong Gi, The Comprehensive Illustrated Manual of the Martial Arts.* This text is the primary remaining document that modern Korean martial art practitioners turn to to search out their foundational history.

Many people who hear of this book believe that it will hold all of the answers to all of their questions on combat. Unfortunately, this is not the case. The techniques presented in this manuscript are extremely limited, and the drawings, which depict the maneuvers, are not exact, because they were created several hundred years ago.

As a source point for understanding the evolution of Korean history, *Mu Yea Do Bok Tong Gi* is a great text. It was written for a different age, however. Thus, it is not the holy grail of martial art manuscripts, as some people believe it to be. What you take away from it will be based on your own understanding of the martial arts.

THE KOREAN LONG STAFF

In ancient Korean martial art texts, such as *Mu Yea Do Bok Tong Gi*, the staff is described as being one of the primary weapons that an individual must master in order to become proficient in physical warfare. During the middle ages, the Korean staff was designed with a sharp-edged stabbing or cutting instrument at one end. As time has moved on, the modern staff, which is known as bong in Korean, no longer possesses this cutting instrument, because the need to deliver a devastating blow each time this weapon is unleashed has decreased. Today, the

THE KOREAN LONG STAFF

staff is still understood to be a weapon used for gaining advanced mastery over your physical movements. Thus, integrating this weapon into your martial art practices not only allows you to expand your knowledge of ancient warrior techniques but also will give you advanced understanding of body dynamics.

Understanding the Staff

For the modern taekwondo practitioner to begin to master the use of the staff he or she must first and foremost understand the proper grasping techniques. Positioning of the hands is elemental in maintaining control over the staff and utilizing it with the most proficiency.

To begin to understand how to properly hold a staff, pick it up with one hand—approximately at midshaft, and hold it a few feet away from your torso. Experience its weight. If you are not holding it exactly in its center, it will be off-balance and its weight will cause one side to travel toward the ground. This simple experiment will allow you to understand how important proper grasping of the staff is and how, if you do not maintain proper control over its center of gravity, it can easily set your entire body off-balance with any physical movement you attempt to perform with it.

> With the dawn of the modern era and the advent of superior self-defense weaponry, the focus on traditional martial art weapons has changed sharply. No longer are weapons such as the sword, the bow, and the staff thought of as primary tools in an individual's self-defense arsenal. Instead, these weapons have evolved into becoming implements for practitioners to refine their physical and mental coordination, while mastering age-old techniques in warfare.

Grasping the Staff

To properly grasp a staff, you should hold it with both of your hands—separated by approximately 18 to 24 inches. This hold will allow you to maintain maximum balance and control over the staff in all offensive and defensive applications. If your hands are closer than this, balancing the staff becomes difficult. Additionally, by holding your hands substantially farther apart, you lose the exaggerated striking distance the staff provides.

As you progress in your staff mastery, you will come to understand that there are some techniques where a single-handed grasp is applicable. The single-handed grasp is only used in advanced applications, however, and should not be attempted until you have come to fully understand the dynamics of staff balance and movement.

Whenever you use the staff, your grasp should not be so tight that you cannot easily slide and reposition your hands to a new location on the staff in order to perform striking or blocking techniques. You should also leave your wrists loose and fluid in order to allow them to naturally compensate for the momentum and power that any movement of the staff produces.

The Offensive Staff

Once you have come to understand how to correctly hold the staff, you will want to move forward to the first level of staff training and develop the ability to offensively strike out with this weapon. Due to its length, staff strikes allow you to extend your range of offense and effectively penetrate your opponent's defenses. There are five basic striking techniques that can be used with the staff—each possesses its own advantages and application. The five basic strikes are:

1. The side strike.
2. The reverse side strike.
3. The overhead strike.
4. The upward strike.
5. The forward thrust.

In each of these basic offensive movements, it is best to maintain control over the staff by holding onto it with both of your hands throughout the application; thus, maintaining maximum control.

The Side Strike

The side strike witnesses your holding the staff with both hands. As your offense begins, you rapidly step in with your lead leg as your lead arm simultaneously guides the end of your staff in a circular motion toward its target. Impacting your target with the lead-in side of the staff actualizes the strike. Ideal striking locations, for the side strike, are your opponent's head and his outer knee.

The Reverse Side Strike

The reverse side strike witnesses you rapidly stepping in with your lead leg, as with the side strike. The staff is simultaneously brought inside of your body with a circular motion, and target impact is made by quickly pulling back on the forward end of the staff and snapping its forward side back, into your opponent's head or knee.

The Overhead Strike

The overhead staff strike has you rapidly move in on your target with the staff. You then, with a circular motion, lift it up and over your target and powerfully bring the lead side down—ideally onto the top of your opponent's head.

The Upward Strike

The upward staff strike is ideally targeted at your opponent's groin. This striking technique is accomplished by rapidly moving in on your adversary as you simultaneously bring the lead end of the staff into position. Your lead arm then powerfully guides the staff up, making contact with its target.

The Forward Thrust

The forward thrust witnesses you driving the end of this weapon deeply into your opponent. This is accomplished by bringing the staff to a horizontal position. Your staff is quickly retracted by your arms and then, instantly, powerfully driven into its target, in a very linear fashion. This strike is ideally targeted at your opponent's solar plexus and his face.

The Defensive Staff

The staff is an ideal weapon to block the various styles of attacks that an opponent may direct toward you. Certainly, one of the best methods of utilizing the defensive staff is to strike out at your attacker with an effective offensive technique, such as the forward thrust. With this style of defensive maneuvering, you can halt your adversary's attack before it can be fully realized. In certain defensive situations, you will have no choice but to formally block an attack with your staff. In these cases, there are two primary blocks that are most effective: the horizontal cross block and the vertical block.

The Horizontal Cross Block

The horizontal cross block witnesses you bringing the staff into a horizontal position, held with both of your hands. This blocking technique can be used in a low- or high-blocking format.

To use this technique in low-block format, to defend against such techniques as a front kick, the staff is brought to a horizontal position. The front kick is launched at you, you step back slightly and bring your staff down powerfully, impacting your opponent to the shin region of his kicking leg. It is important that the staff between your two hands intercept his kick. In this way, you will maintain maximum control over the staff, and its force will be magnified.

The overhead horizontal cross block is ideally used when you halt the overhead strike of a club or a knife. To counter this type of attack, the staff is again brought into horizontal position and rapidly brought up into the attacking forearm of your opponent. With this, the attack is immediately halted and further staff self-defense may be unleashed.

The Vertical Block

The vertical block witnesses your bringing the staff to a straight up and down position. The side of the staff is then driven into the attacking element of your opponent's body. This block is ideally used against such techniques as the roundhouse kick.

As with the case of the previous horizontal cross block, the staff should encounter your attacker midway between your hands. That way you will maintain control and possess the ability to quickly change your positioning and deliver a powerful counterattack.

Combination Techniques

When using a staff as an offensive or defensive weapon, a single technique is rarely enough to ensure your victory in a confrontation. Therefore, once you master the basic strikes and blocks with the staff, you should move forward and develop the ability to immediately follow one technique with the next.

The Korean word *kyung* describes a prescribed pattern of blocks and strikes organized into a precise group of movements in order that the student may come to better understand the usage of the staff. It is not necessary, however, for practice purposes that you follow the prescribed movements exactly. Simply by coming to understand, through practice, the various blocks and strikes the staff can effectively unleash, you can formulate your own pattern and, thereby, come to realize which techniques, be they offensive or defensive, most appropriately follow one another.

Staff Meditation

The use of the staff in solo training exercises not only allows you to become intimately aware of how your body moves in association with the staff but also allows you to become consciously aware of how your mind experiences movement in association with this external object. This body and mind unification is the basis for entry into a state of movement meditation. Whereas the average individual never takes the time to truly come into harmony with his or her physical movements, the refined martial artist comes to this naturally through training and, thus, a meditative mindset is born.

Partner Practice

Partner practice is a very effective method for you to come to truly understand the self-defense dynamics of the staff. The staff can be very dangerous, however, when not used with proper respect. Therefore, before you begin any partner practice, you and your training partner must have mastered the basics of the staff and not simply enter into a free-for-all of smacking each other with this weapon.

To begin proper partner practice, it is essential that you wear protective gear. This is especially the case with head and hand protection. It is very common in the early stages of partner practice that you will inadvertently strike your opponent's hand while unleashing an attack. A misdirected staff strike can easily break the bones of your hands and fingers. Thus, you must wear protective hand gear. Protective gloves are readily available, even boxing gloves work well in this application.

At the point you begin partner practice, you should begin very slowly by discussing what technique you will unleash on your partner and how he or she will block it. Your partner can then perform the same technique at you, and you block. You should very slowly build up from this, practicing one technique at a time. As you gain more mastery with the staff, you will be able to choreograph several striking and blocking techniques in one segment. It is only at the point when you and your training partner have truly come to understand the various applicable techniques of the staff that you should begin very controlled free sparring.

Training with the staff is not defined by how fast you unleash a technique. What is important is how precisely and properly you deliver each movement. To this end, it is far better to maintain your meditative association with the staff and move through each technique slowly than to randomly unleash wild maneuvers that allow your body and mind to be overpowered by the momentum and velocity of the staff, thus throwing your being out of balance.

THE KOREAN MIDDLE STAFF

Escrima, kali, and arnis are not the only styles of martial arts to have developed a defensive system using short lengths of wood as weapons. Korean warriors from the ancient period also devised a system of self-defense using the baton. In Korean, the weapon is called the *jung bong*.

Jung Bong Basics

To begin our understanding of the use of the Korean baton, we must first let go of all previous visions of the escrima sticks in action. For though escrima sticks appear similar in appearance, they were developed as a weapon of martial arts in a completely different time period than that of the Korean jung bong, and the foundation of their use is based in a separate set of parameters and defensive understandings.

THE KOREAN MIDDLE STAFF

The Korean middle staffs are not simply objects that you pick up and swing at an opponent. They are a highly developed and practical tool that, when put into proper application, are a very viable weapon of self-defense.

One Korean middle staff can be used as a single defensive weapon, but they are also commonly used in pairs. It is understood that their defensive applications are more exact when a pair of jung bong is utilized.

The middle staffs are properly grasped by holding them approximately 5 inches from the end. From here, they are allowed to naturally extend outward.

The common opening stance with the Korean middle staff is to have your arms extended approximately 1 foot away from your body. Have your elbows slightly bent. The staffs themselves are crossed in front of you, a few inches away from each other. In this way, they both equally have free movement and can either go up or down to block your opponent's advances or strike at him offensively.

The middle staff is never swung randomly. Whenever a strike, be it offensive or defensive, is launched, it always has an intended target in mind. The middle staffs are also not swung widely, for if you swing them up or out too far in order to gain momentum, you then open yourself up for counterattack. To this end, they are kept in tight to your body, thus protecting you from attack.

The Offensive Jung Bong

To properly strike with the middle staff and achieve concise opponent hits, you place your body into a natural stance. You should never tighten up or lock yourself into a rigid stance while using the batons, because this will hinder your freedom of movement.

When it is time to strike, you rapidly move into attack range of your opponent. The middle staffs are moved in toward your target with your upper arms and then snapped out, making impact, from your elbow.

The power and impact of the baton's strike comes from this snapping out of the elbow, not from momentum caused by swinging your arms up or out from the shoulder and then forcefully bringing them down.

When a strike with the middle staff is performed, the striking arm is never fully extended. The elbows always remain slightly bent. This aids in any confrontational situation you may find yourself in for two reasons. First of all, it keeps your elbow joint from being damaged from hyperextension. Second, this allows you to keep the batons in tight enough to your body to not allow the momentum the baton may develop to open up your stance to such a degree that your opponent may penetrate it and counterstrike.

Your wrists are allowed to pivot freely when you perform techniques with the middle staff. If you tighten your wrist muscles, the impact force of the attack or the momentum of the middle staff technique itself could cause you to inadvertently injure your wrists.

All strikes or blocks with the middle staff are made in a linear fashion. It is a straight-to-the-target weapon. Though circular applications are used, there is nothing ornamented about any technique performed with the Korean batons.

Any hit is directed at its objective. No flamboyant twirling of the baton is ever used—because this is an unnecessary use of energy, and it gives the trained opponent the ability to counterstrike while this type of meaningless activity is taking place.

Certain striking techniques are delivered most effectively by driving the full power of the baton's strike into your opponent, while other ones are much more effective when finesse is used. The only way to learn the appropriate applied power of each technique is through practice, thereby coming to a deeper understanding of the jung bong.

How to Practice

The quickest way to gain understanding of the middle staff is to get two pieces of wood approximately 1 feet in length and hold them in the manner previously described. Then, begin to block and strike at an imaginary opponent with them.

It is important that you never allow these blocks and strikes to be just randomly executed techniques. All techniques used in the practice of the jung bong have a purpose and are performed as extensions of your arm.

Range Effectiveness

The two key mistakes many practitioners of the middle staff initially make is first, to overextend their body while encountering an adversary. You should never reach to strike or block your opponent. By reaching, you leave your body open for counterattack. Second, the middle staffs are somewhat large pieces of wood. Thus, you should not place yourself into such tight proximity to your opponent that they cannot be effectively used.

To keep these negative occurrences from happening, a consciousness of effective range should always be maintained when the middle staffs are employed.

Effective range, in terms of the Korean middle staff, refers to the distance that you may effortlessly strike at your opponent, while leaving him the least amount of ability to block, counterstrike, or perhaps even take the weapons away from you.

To define your own effective range with the Korean baton is a twofold process:

1. Ask yourself, "By moving toward your opponent, who is given the advantage of your new location?" If your opponent is, then do not close the distance. Instead, allow him or her to come to you, where you can define the next level of attack or counterattack. If it is you who will take the superior position, however, then move forward.
2. Ask yourself, "How far can you effortlessly strike at your opponent without extending your arm past the slightly bent elbow point?"

Once these two questions have been answered, your defense or attack can take place with your chances of being injured minimized and your opportunities for victory being heightened.

Because there is virtually no difference between the striking techniques used in attacking or blocking, your actual motion is not affected by whichever application you are engaged in.

Offensive Applications

In offensive applications with the middle staff, there are precise points that you should strike for on your opponent. The common strike points may come to mind: the head, the solar plexus, and so on. These targets can be used, but there is a vast array of other points on your opponent's body that are equally vulnerable. These strike points include, but are not limited to, the elbow joints, the wrists, the shins, and the ankles.

Often you will not want to extensively injure your opponent. When you strike at a person's joints with a middle staff, the impact of the wood on bone is a quite successful way of debilitating your opponent, without causing permanent injury. For this reason, it is important to develop the focus to strike at these regions.

The ability to consciously attack these strike points comes from steady practice and the development of hand-eye coordination with the use of the middle staff. This can be acquired through the practice of hanging a small tennis ball from a string and consciously striking at it—especially while it is moving.

Defensive Applications

Though it is common that an individual views the jung bong and immediately sees them as primarily an offensive weapon, the Korean batons are equally useful as a defensive tool. The use of the middle staff as a defensive instrument does, however, take additional practice and a deeper understanding of the weapon.

The simplest defensive application of the jung bong is to simply do with them what you would do with your hands or arms when an opponent punches or kicks at you. By blocking with the jung bong, not only have you saved your body from possible damage incurred from impacting your opponent's strike, but you have possibly injured him in the process—depending on where the blow of wood to skin occurred on his body.

Blocking techniques are easily experimented with. In a practice situation, allow your opponent to straight punch at you. By sidestepping slightly and impacting the outside of his arm with an out-to-in block, you have deflected the punch and the assault has been diverted.

When you use the Korean middle staff, as with any martial art weapon, all defensive applications should instantly be followed by an offensive move. This not only ensures your victory in the confrontation but also prevents you from incurring further attacks from your opponent. Thus, the moment the aforementioned block has been completed, a follow-up strike should be initiated.

The best counterstrikes are always ones that easily follow the blocking technique just performed. This is to say, your strike should not be a clumsy and awkward attempt to get one of your jung bong's to a location that perhaps you desire to reach but that is not easily reachable.

At times, these initial counterstrikes may not be fully debilitating hits to your opponent. Nonetheless, they will set the stage for the next technique, which will be launched much more easily because your opponent has been stunned by the first strike.

Because every confrontation is different, there is no simple answer that can inform you of which strike should follow what block. Through practice, however, it becomes obvious which technique easily follows the last.

In terms of the previously described straight-punch blocking technique, it is quite easy to simply strike your opponent in the ribs with the other baton immediately upon completing the previously described out-to-in block. It is this type of continuous motion sequence that will ensure your victory in any altercation.

Joint-Locking Techniques

Joint-locking and -trapping techniques have long been a part of the Korean martial arts. These were first developed by the Hwa Rang warriors and later emphasized by hapkido and, to a lesser degree, advanced practitioners of taekwondo.

Joint-locking techniques are integrated into the art of the Korean middle staff. These joint-locking maneuvers, in association with the use of the middle staff, have been highly developed in Korea. This is one of the great differences between the Korean understanding of the baton and the Filipino martial arts.

As the middle staffs are wooden extensions to the hands, the joint-locking techniques themselves are not as precise as with the hand-to-hand techniques originated in Korea. Yet, they are equally effective.

While joint locking with the middle staff, the emphasis is placed more on the major bone junctures, such as the elbows, the knees, and under the neck, rather than where the more intricate hand-to-hand joint-locking techniques are emphasized on the wrists, finger joints, and so on.

The purpose of any joint lock is to place your opponent at a disadvantage in order to end the confrontation more quickly. With the jung bong, this is aided by the fact that you may integrate very effective strikes either just before or just after any joint-locking application.

For example, assume that your opponent performs the same straight punch as described earlier. You now sidestep it while you block the punch with an out-to-in deflection with one middle staff as you did before. Now, while leaving the blocking middle staff in place to control your opponent's ability to hit you, continue through with a strike to his ribs with your other middle staff. Because his punch has been deflected and his ribs struck, he will be vulnerable. Now, bring the striking baton down into his elbow joint as you force his punching arm back onto itself with your blocking baton. You can now easily throw him back onto the ground, where further counterattacking actions can be launched.

The jung bong is a highly stylized weapon of both offense and defense. With practice, any practitioner can easily and effectively add it to his martial arts arsenal, making himself a more complete warrior, while practicing a time-honored tradition of Korea.

KUMDO: THE KOREAN ART OF THE SWORD

The Korean martial art of *kumdo* literally means sword way. At the end of World War II, with Japanese annexation lifted from the Korean peninsula, Korea entered into a period of cultural reestablishment. Indigenous martial arts, which had been banned by the occupying forces, began to be rediscovered and new martial art systems were formed. Due to the long period of Japanese occupation, the Japanese understanding of martial arts influenced many of these new martial arts. Kumdo was no exception.

The parallels between modern kumdo and the Japanese sword arts are significant. A kumdo student practices with a bamboo sword called a *juk do*, which is identical to Japanese kendo's *shinai*. Korean students also use the *mok kum*, wooden sword, which is the same as the Japanese *bokken*. During demonstrations and cutting drills, kumdo students wield a long, straight steel sword known as a *jung kum*, while their Japanese counterparts use a *katana*—commonly known as a samurai sword.

The modern Korean long sword, as popularized by the Korean martial arts of kuk sool won and hwa rang do, is straight-bladed. The illustrations in *Mu Yea Do Bok Tong Gi* illustrate that the traditional Korean long swords were arched, similar to those of the samurai. Many modern kumdo practitioners opt to use the Japanese katana because the Korean long sword is fairly expensive and difficult to find.

Understanding the Modern Korean Sword Arts

As the modern era dawned, the sword was no longer the predominant offensive or defensive weapon in combat. The sword arts of Korea and Japan survived by being transformed into a method for achieving unity of mind, body, and spirit.

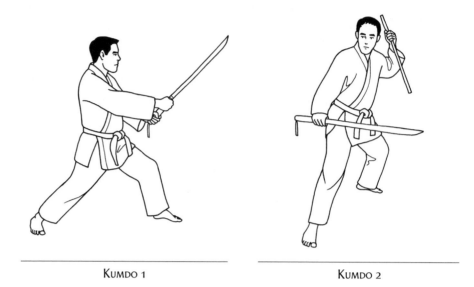

KUMDO 1   KUMDO 2

The act of unsheathing a sword and delivering a focused strike to an imaginary target can work wonders on an undisciplined student.

To achieve that goal, kumdo students progress through three levels of understanding:

1. Physical mastery
2. Mental mastery
3. Spiritual alignment

At the first level, years of practice make students proficient in all physical aspects of the art, including etiquette, stances, and drawing and moving techniques. At the second level, they begin to rise above the objective techniques of the sword and no longer concern themselves with technical details because their movements have become like reflexes. At the third level, they transcend the limitations of their body and develop their meditative consciousness. Their mind is silenced through refined focus, and their sword becomes a tool to link their body and mind with the infinite.

Evolving Kumdo

Kumdo is similar to Japanese iaido in that it has fragmented into different schools that teach slightly different techniques. Nevertheless, certain fundamental elements are embraced by all. These include respect for the sword, development of proper stance, use of breath in association with the execution of each technique, and the weapon's interaction with the martial artist's ki.

The Stance

When one begins the practice of kumdo, the primary focus is placed upon *iwa sae*, or proper stance. It is understood that without a proper stance, no sword technique can be performed efficiently. Therefore, extensive emphasis is placed on this element of kumdo training.

An essential part of learning how to stand is knowing where to locate the center of gravity, or *tan jun*. Kumdo teaches that all sword techniques should be launched with the consciousness focused on the center point—or the student may be set off-balance by his sword.

Because ki is directly linked to breath, kumdo practitioners inhale and mentally direct their internal energy to their tan jun at the outset of each sword movement. When they strike, their ki-laden breath is expelled with a ki hap, signaling that energy is being released as the sword slices into its target.

Holding the Sword

In kumdo, the sword is held with your lead hand placed just under the sword guard. In some designs, the jung kum possesses no sword guard. In these cases, your lead is placed in the same location, at the upper region of the sword's handle. Your rear hand is located at the bottom of the sword's handle. With this grasp, maximum control is maintained over the sword.

In certain kumdo techniques, the sword is wielded with one hand. In this case, the hand holding the sword remains close under the sword guard, thus maintaining maximum balance and control over the sword.

When the jung kum is held, your elbows should remain slightly bent. This is true in all kumdo drawing, ready position, and striking techniques. With this approach, you allow your arms to remain loose, thus maintaining the ability to readily direct or redirect your sword technique with speed and accuracy.

Drawing the Sword

In kumdo, the primary focusing technique witnesses the practitioner precisely drawing the sword and unleashing a highly defined striking technique. In kumdo, once the sword has been unsheathed, these defined strikes include the use of the sheath as a blocking tool. This use of the sheath as a defensive weapon is one of the factors that separates kumdo from most schools of iaido.

Sword Strikes

In kumdo, the strike of the sword is never overextended. The practitioner must always control the blade as opposed to being controlled by its weight and

---

All techniques used in kumdo are based in eight primary strikes:

1. Overhead strike, straight
2. Overhead slash, left side
3. Overhead slash, right side
4. Side Slash, from the left
5. Side Slash, from the right
6. Under Slash, from the left
7. Under Slash, from the right
8. Under body strike

Variations are added to these techniques as the kumdo practitioner becomes more advanced with his use of the sword.

momentum. This is accomplished by never randomly striking at the imaginary targets. All strikes are performed consciously with precise impact points in mind.

Forms

Another defining difference between kumdo and the Japanese sword arts is the *bon guk kum beop*, or indigenous Korean sword forms. Purportedly recreated from the sequence of techniques recorded in *Mu Yea Do Bo Tong Gi*, these forms contain movements that are assembled in a way that is unlike anything seen in iaido. This is the only uniquely Korean part of kumdo.

There are ten sword forms that define kumdo. In most schools of taekwondo, the techniques of kumdo and the forms associated with this are only taught to advanced practitioners. It is believed that one must first learn the basics of body mechanics associated with the physical techniques of taekwondo before one possesses enough understanding of bodily movement to move on and master the techniques of the sword.

The Kick in Kumdo

As the modern Korean martial arts have continued to evolve, the kick has become one of the primary components of all of the systems of self-defense founded on the Korean peninsula. This too is the case with kumdo.

Hand in hand with sword strikes, the kumdo practitioner unleashes advanced kicking techniques. This is particularly the case with those practitioners of kumdo who have come from a taekwondo tradition.

Many of the forms of kumdo exhibit these advanced kicking techniques. And, in individual practice, it is not unusual to see a kumdo practitioner release a powerful sword strike followed by a spinning heel kick.

The Short Swords

In Korean sword training, the twin short swords, known in Korean as *tan sang kum*, are also used. These are straight short swords with an approximate 12-inch blade. As is the case with the Korean long sword, these swords are hard to come by and tend to be very expensive. Thus, the short Japanese swords are often used as replacements for them for kumdo training.

The tan sang kum are used in much the same way as the Korean long sword. Because they are smaller, they tend to be unleashed in a much more rapid and direct fashion. From this, the kumdo trainee comes to understand how to use weapons in association with body dynamics and how to master a new weapon in the ongoing evolution of his or her martial development.

The Wardrobe

Japanese kendo has also influenced kumdo by defining its wardrobe. Most schools that teach solely kumdo in Korea wear clothing similar to their Japanese counterpart. The kumdo practitioner wears the *hakama*, the large pleated pants. The Japanese practitioners commonly wear a black or dark blue hakama, whereas the Korean practitioners commonly wear the color gray. Kendo armor, known as *hoogo* in Korean, is also commonly worn during competitions.

Hoogo is made up of the *ho myun*, a head and face protector; *gap*, which protects the chest; *ho wam*, which protects the hands; and *gap sang*, the apron that protects the waist and groin.

There is, however, a big difference between the taekwondo practitioner who comes to master the Korean sword arts and those who solely study kumdo. The

SHORT SWORD

taekwondo practitioner of kumdo leaves behind much of this traditional wardrobe and practices solely in the taekwondo dobok.

At the root of taekwondo training is the essential alliance to self-defense. As a result, much of the formality of kumdo is left behind, and the advanced taekwondo practitioner who comes to master the Korean sword arts does so to gain new insight into the physical and meditative aspects of the martial arts.

Appendix A
Taekwondo Timeline

1931   Chosun Yun Moo Kwan founded by Lee, Kyung Suk.

1944   Chung Do Kwan founded by Lee, Won Kuk.

1944   Song Moo Kwan Ro founded by Byung Jick.

1944   Song Moo Kwan closes.

1945   Korean Independence from Japanese occupation.

1945   Chosun Yun Moo Kwan begins teaching Kwon Bop (Japanese Karate). Program name, Chosun Yun Moo Kwan Kwon Bup Bu.

1945   The foundations of Moo Duk Kwan begin founded by Hwang, Kee.

1945   Chung Do Kwan closed.

1946   Chung Do Kwan reopens.

1946   Song Moo Kwan reopens.

1946   Hwang Kee titles his martial art organization Kyo Tong Bu Woo Hae and teaches Tang Soo Do Bu.

1946   Chang Moo Kwan founded by Yoon, Byung In.

1950–1953 The Korean War. Most kwans close.

1953   Oh Do Kwan was founded by General Choi, Hong Hi and Major Nam, Tae Hi.

1953   Hwang Kee retitles his system Moo Duk Kwan.

1953   The Korea Kong Soo Do Association is formed.

1955   General Choi, Hong Hi formally coins the name Taekwondo.

1955   Moo Duk Kwan Central Gymnasium opens.

1956   Kang Duk Won is founded by Hong, Jung Pyo and Park, Chul Hee.

1956   Yoon, Kwe Byung renames Chang Moo Kwan, Ji Do Kwan.

1959   The Korea Taekwondo Association is formed.

1961   The Korea Taekwondo Association collapsed.

1961   The Korea Tae Soo Do Association is formed.

1962   Hwang Kee's Korea Soo Bahk Do Association is granted governmental recognition.

1965   The Korea Taekwondo Association is formed.

1965   Moo Duk Kwan splits into two separate organizations: Taekwondo and Tang Soo Do Moo Duk Kwan.

1966   The International Taekwondo Federation is formed.

1971   Construction of Kukkiwon begins.

1972   Construction of Kukkiwon is completed.

1972   The International Taekwondo Federation moves to Toronto, Canada.

1972   Taekwondo became the National Sport of Korea.
1973   The World Taekwondo Federation is formed.
1973   The first World Taekwondo Championships.
1974   The first Asian Taekwondo Championships.
1980   International Olympic Committee recognizes the World Taekwondo Federation.
1981   Taekwondo participates in the first World Games.
1982   Taekwondo is adopted as a demonstration sport in the Olympic Games.
1983   Taekwondo participates in the Pan American Games.
1988   Taekwondo is a demonstration sport in the Olympic Games.
1992   Taekwondo is a demonstration sport in the Olympic Games.
1994   Taekwondo is selected as a full Olympic sport for the 2000 Olympic Games.
1996   Taekwondo is a demonstration sport in the Olympic Games.
2000   Taekwondo becomes an official sport of the Olympic Games.
2004   Taekwondo participates as an official sport of the Olympic Games.

Appendix B
Poomse Performed at Belt Levels

TAEKWONDO LOWER BELT FORMS

Belt Level	Poomse Performed
9 Gup	Basic Forms
8 Gup	Taeguek 1
7 Gup	Taeguek 2
6 Gup	Taeguek 3
5 Gup	Taeguek 4
4 Gup	Taeguek 5
3 Gup	Taeguek 6
2 Gup	Taeguek 7
1 Gup	Taeguek 8

TAEKWONDO BLACK BELT FORMS

Belt Level	Poomse Performed	Time in Rank
1st Dan	Koryo	
2nd Dan	Keum Gang	2 years of continued training after receiving 1st dan
3rd Dan	Tae Baek	3 years of continued training after receiving 2nd dan
4th Dan (Instructor)	Pyong Won	4 years of continued training after receiving 3rd dan
5th Dan (Master)	Sip Jin	5 years of continued training after receiving 4th dan
6th Dan	Ji Tae	6 years of continued training after receiving 5th dan
7th Dan (Grand Master)	Chon Kwon	7 years of continued training after receiving 6th dan. The individual must also have made a substantial contribution to the art.
8th Dan	Hansu	8 years of continued training after receiving 7th dan
9th Dan	Il Yeo	9 years of continued training after receiving 8th dan

Appendix C
Pressure Point Locations

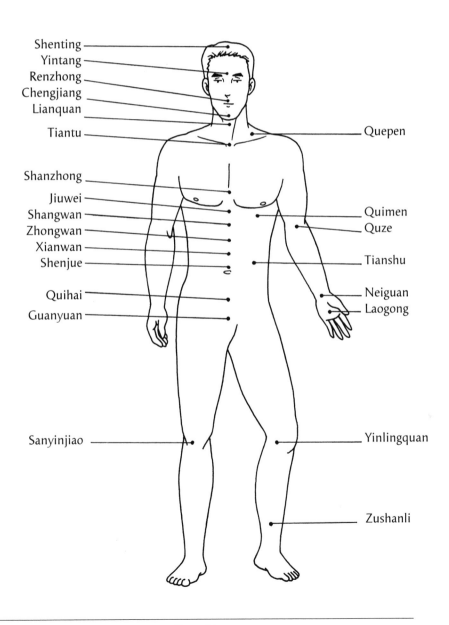

Shenting
Yintang
Renzhong
Chengjiang
Lianquan
Tiantu

Quepen

Shanzhong
Jiuwei
Shangwan
Zhongwan
Xianwan
Shenjue

Quimen
Quze

Tianshu

Quihai
Guanyuan

Neiguan
Laogong

Sanyinjiao

Yinlingquan

Zushanli

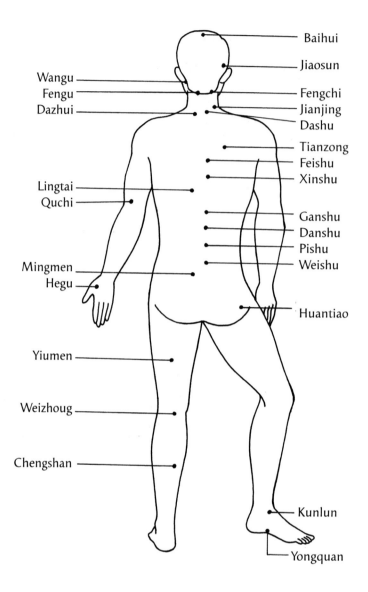

Baihui
Jiaosun
Wangu
Fengu
Dazhui
Fengchi
Jianjing
Dashu
Tianzong
Feishu
Xinshu
Lingtai
Quchi
Ganshu
Danshu
Pishu
Weishu
Mingmen
Hegu
Huantiao
Yiumen
Weizhoug
Chengshan
Kunlun
Yongquan

REAR VIEW

Appendix D
Rear and Frontal Attack Locations

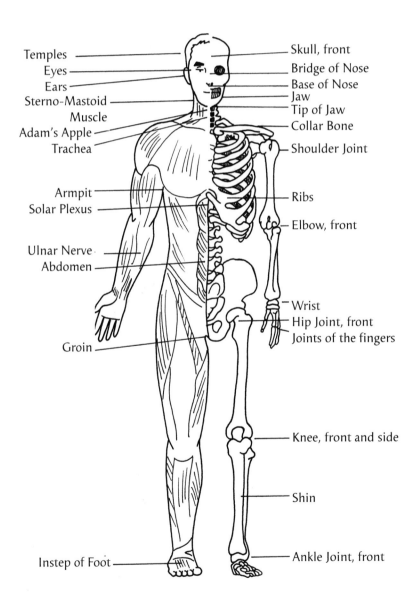

Temples — Skull, front

Eyes — Bridge of Nose

Ears — Base of Nose

Sterno-Mastoid — Jaw

Muscle — Tip of Jaw

Adam's Apple — Collar Bone

Trachea — Shoulder Joint

Armpit — Ribs

Solar Plexus — Elbow, front

Ulnar Nerve —

Abdomen — Wrist

— Hip Joint, front

Groin — Joints of the fingers

Knee, front and side

Shin

Instep of Foot — Ankle Joint, front

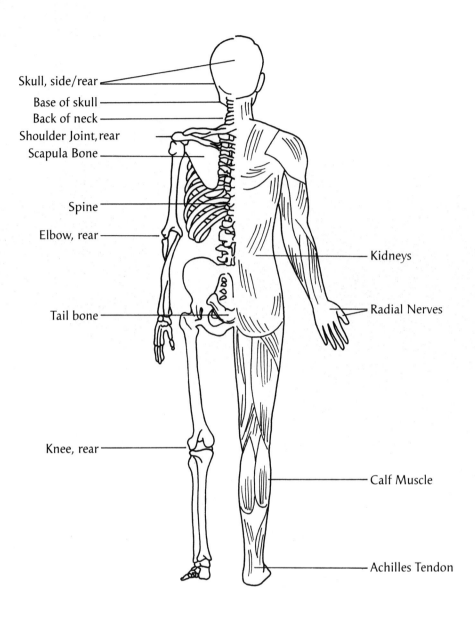

Skull, side/rear

Base of skull

Back of neck

Shoulder Joint, rear

Scapula Bone

Spine

Elbow, rear

Tail bone

Knee, rear

Kidneys

Radial Nerves

Calf Muscle

Achilles Tendon

REAR VIEW

Appendix E
Meridian Pathways

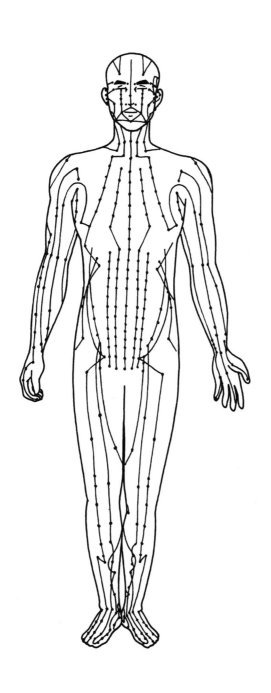

Recommended Reading

Cho, Hee Il. *The Complete Master's Jumping Kick*. Los Angeles: Cho's Taekwondo Publishing House, 1988.

———. *The Complete Master's Kick*. Burbank, California: Unique Publications, 1999.

———. *The Complete One Step & Three Sparring*. Los Angeles: Cho's Taekwondo Publishing House, 1988.

———. *The Complete Tae Geuk and Black Belt Hyung: W.T.F.* Burbank, California: Unique Publications, 1990.

———. *The Complete Tae Kwon Do Black Belt Hyung: W.T.F.* Burbank, California: Unique Publications, 1990.

———. *The Complete Tae Kwon Do Hyung*. Burbank, California: Unique Publications, 1984.

Cho, Sihak Henry. *Tae Kwon Do: Secrets of Korean Karate*. Rutland, Vermont: Charles E. Tuttle, 1992.

Choi, Hong Hi. *Encyclopedia of Taekwondo, 15 volumes*. Geneva: International Taekwondo Federation, 2000.

———. *Taekwondo*. Ontario: International Taekwondo Federation, 1972.

Chun, Richard. *Advancing in Tae Kwon Do*. New York: HarperCollins, 1983.

———. *Moo Duk Kwan Tae Kwon Do: Korean Art of Self Defense*. Valencia, California: Ohara Publications, 1975.

———. *Moo Duk Kwan Tae Kwon Do: Korean Art of Self Defense, Volume 2*. Valencia, California: Ohara Publications, 1976.

———. *Taekwondo: Spirit and Practice Beyond Self Defense*. Jamaica Plain, Massachusetts: YMAA Publications, 2002.

———. *Tae Kwon Do: The Korean Martial Art*. New York: HarperCollins, 1976.

Eden, Karen and Yates, Keith D. *The Complete Idiot's Guide to Tae Kwon Do*. Indianapolis, Indiana: Alpha Books, 1998.

Gwon, Pu Gill. *Taegeuk: The New Forms of Tae Kwon Do*. Valencia, California: Ohara Publications, 1980.

Kim, Sang H. *Taekwondo Kyorugi: Olympic Style Sparring*. Wethersfield, Connecticut: Turtle Press, 1999.

Lee, Haeng Ung. *The Way of Traditional Taekwondo*. Memphis, Tennessee: American Taekwondo Association, 1993.

Lee, Kyong Myong. *Dynamic Taekwondo: A Martial Art and Olympic Sport.*

Trumbull, Connecticut: Hollym International, 1997.

Lee, Kyong Myong. *Dynamic Taekwondo: Kyorug*. Trumbull, Connecticut: Hollym International, 1996.

———. *Taekwondo: Philosophy and Culture*. Trumbull, Connecticut: Hollym International, 2001.

Lee, Soon Man. *Modern Taekwondo: The Official Training Manual*. London: Sterling Publications, 1999.

Little, John R. and Curtis F. Wong, Eds. *Ultimate Guide to Tae Kwon Do*. Chicago: McGraw Hill/Contemporary Books, 1999.

Park, Yeon Hee. *Tae Kwon Do: The Ultimate Reference Guide to the World's Most Popular Martial Art*. New York: Checkmark Books, 1999.

Park, Yeon Hwan and Thomas D. Seabourne. *Taekwondo Techniques and Tactics: Skills for Sparring and Self Defense*. Champaign, Illinois: Human Kinetics, 1997.

Rhee, Jhoon. *Chon-Ji of Tae Kwon Do-Hyung*. Valencia, California: Ohara Publications, 1975.

———. *Chung-Gun and Toi Gye of Tae Kwon Do Hyung*. Valencia, California: Ohara Publications, 1975.

———. *Hwa-Rang and Chung-Mu of Tae Kwon Do Hyung*. Valencia, California: Ohara Publications, 1975.

———. *Tan-Gun and To-San of Tae Kwon Do Hyung*. Valencia, California: Ohara Publications, 1975.

Rhee, Jhoon. *Won-Hyo and Yul-Kok of Tae Kwon Do Hyung*. Valencia, California: Ohara Publications, 1975.

Shaw, Scott. *Taekwondo Basics*. Boston: Tuttle Publishing, 2003.

INDEX

Acknowledgments

Special thanks to Paul Crispell, John Ill Soo Kim, Kenneth H. Kim, Vincent L. Spezze, and Hae Won Shin.

About the Author

Scott Shaw is one of the world's most prolific proponents of the Korean martial arts. He began studying hapkido and taekwondo as a young boy and today holds advanced black belts and master instructor certifications in both of the arts. He is a frequently published contributor to martial art journals and is the author of a number of books including *Hapkido: Korean Art of Self-Defense* and *Taekwondo Basics* from Tuttle Publishing.